Rhetoric and Composition

Wikibooks.org

March 14, 2013

Contents

0.1 The Authors and Editors of this Wiki Book

Please consider adding to the prestige of this text by adding your name to the list below.

Barrett, John. Professor of English at Richland College in Dallas, Texas.

Barton, Matthew D.[1] An assistant professor of English at Saint Cloud State University in Saint Cloud, Minnesota.

Cadle, Lanette[2] An assistant professor of English at Missouri State University in Springfield, Missouri.

Christenson, Jeremy W. Junior Undergraduate student at Saint Cloud State University.

Denman, Traci. Junior Undergraduate student at Saint Cloud State University. Double majoring in Rhetorical and Applied Writing and Psychology, doubling minoring in English and Intercultural Communications.

Doberstein, Ben. Graduate Student at St. Cloud State University studying Modernist American Literature.

Grayson, Martin[3] The University of Sheffield, (retired).

Groth, Kelly M., Junior. Undergraduate student at Saint Cloud State University. Majoring in Information Media.

Heimermann, Mark. Graduate student at St. Cloud State University.

Kath, Sarah. Graduate student at St. Cloud State University studying English and Philosophy.

Kaye, Deborah. Instructor of English, Director of Professional Development, Los Angeles Valley College.

Kirchoff, Jeffrey. Graduate student studying English and researching Graphic Novels at St. Cloud State University.

---

1   http://mattbarton.net
2   http://techsophist.net
3   http://martin-grayson.staff.shef.ac.uk/

Klint, Karl Russell. Graduate Student at St. Cloud State University in the English Rhet/Comp program. Focus towards hyper-text writing and the effect on rhetorical theory. BFA in Creative and Professional Writing from Bemidji State University (MN).

Koval, Jamie M. Senior at St. Cloud State University majoring in Public Relations and minoring in Rhetorical and Applied Writing.

Murphy, Emily E. BFA, Printmaking, Minor English, St. Cloud State University, 1998. Currently pursuing a BA in English, Applied and Rhetorical Writing Emphasis, and a BFA in Graphic Design at St. Cloud State University, St. Cloud, MN.

Nicholson, Adam M. M.A. English, University of Illinois at Springfield. Adjunct instructor of English, Lincoln Land Community College.

Pickens, Alex[4] - PhD student studying Rhetoric and Composition at Purdue University.

Rasmussen, Stacy. Graduate Student at St. Cloud State University studying to gain a M.A. in English with an emphasis in College Teaching.

Reimer, Cody J.. Graduate Student at St. Cloud State University

Rosalez, Mary. Graduate student at Michigan State University, East Lansing MI, studying Digital Rhetorics.

Schaaf, Luke. Graduate Student at St. Cloud State University.

Schauble, Bruce. English Department Chair at Punahou School, Honolulu, HI

Speich, Brittany Junior at Saint Cloud State University, Double Majoring in Mass Communications and Political Science, Double Minoring in Rhetorical and Applied Writing, and Public Administration

Springer, Jodi. Fifth year student at St. Cloud State University double majoring in Rhetorical and Applied Writing and Theatre with a minor in Music.

Tham, Jason[5]. Graduate student at St. Cloud State University studying MA Rhetoric & Composition, and MS Mass Communication.

Timp-Pilon, Michele L. - Graduate student studying Rhetoric and Composition at Saint Cloud State University in Saint Cloud, Minnesota.

Wolf, Stephanie M. Senior Undergraduate at St. Cloud State University, majoring in Rhetorical and Applied Writing

Worth, Benjamin. Professor, English, Bluegrass Community and Technical College. Assistant Dean, Distance Learning.

Category:Rhetoric and Composition[6]

---

4   http://en.wikibooks.org/wiki/User%3AApickens

5   http://jasontham.blog.com

6   http://en.wikibooks.org/wiki/Category%3ARhetoric%20and%20Composition

1 The Stages of the Writing Process

2 Overview: The Writing Process

2.1 Overview

Writing is a complicated and often mysterious process. Although we may think of it as little more than arranging letters and words on a page, a few moments' reflection reveals that it is much more than that. On the one hand, writing is an art--we don't say Shakespeare's language is "correct" but rather that it is beautiful. On the other hand, writing is a science-- we want the instructions that came with our Blu-Ray player to be accurate, precise, and easy to understand.

Then there is the matter of what makes writing "good writing." Although we might say that both an instruction manual and a play are "well written," we appreciate them for different reasons. A play written in the clear, unambiguous language of an instruction manual would not be a hit on Broadway. In other words, writing must be judged according to its context--what is its purpose and audience? Finally, even readers with a great deal in common may not agree about the quality of any particular text, just as people's opinions differ about which bands are really great. We really don't know why people have such preferences and can't make accurate predictions about what they will like or dislike. Simply put, writing isn't simple.

If writing is so complicated and mysterious, can it be taught? Since Aristotle, great teachers have taught complex processes to their students by breaking them into smaller, more understandable processes. Aristotle thought that effective communication skills, like good math skills, can be learned and taught. Math teachers don't teach trigonometry to their elementary students; instead, they begin with addition and subtraction. Everything else builds on those simple processes. No one is born a mathematician. Similarly, while luck certainly plays a role in any successful writer's career, successful writers (or speakers) are not just born into the role--and everyone else is not just fated to flunk English. You can learn to write with substance and style. It takes work, but it is within your power. You have already taken the first step.

Most of what we know about writing is also true of speaking. Aristotle wrote a famous treatise on the subject of effective communication called "The Rhetoric." This book is meant for speakers; however, teachers and students also have long used it to polish their writing. "The Rhetoric" is still widely read and applied today by people desiring to learn how to speak and write more convincingly to an audience. Your first-year composition course may even have the word "rhetoric" or "rhetorical" as part of its title. Aristotle taught us that rhetoric isn't just about winning arguments. Instead, rhetoric is the ability to determine all the available means of persuasion at our disposal. Ultimately, it's up to you to guess the best course of action, but rhetoric helps you make this a more educated guess.

Compared to speaking, writing is a much more recent phenomenon, and for many centuries it was assumed that the best way to learn to write well was either to pray, entreat the muses, or carefully imitate writings that were already considered great. Eventually, as more people wanted to write, teachers created rules to help them write "correctly." Unfortunately, this heavy emphasis on correctness and writing with a narrow set of rules did little to improve student writing. Simply knowing how to write grammatically correct prose is important, but it is not enough, by itself, to make writing effective or persuasive. Indeed, too much attention to correctness can result in unintentionally rigid or even comical writing. Legend has it that Winston Churchill grew so irritated at pedants telling him not to end his sentences with prepositions that he said to one of them, "Madame, that is a rule up with which I shall not put."

Since the 1970s, writing instructors have been teaching writing not as the following of fixed rules but rather as a dynamic process: a series of steps that writers follow to produce texts. At first in the '70s, these steps were taught as a somewhat rigid sequence. Now, however, writing teachers emphasize "recursivity"--moving forward through some steps and then circling back to redo previous steps--as the more natural way that many successful writers work. In other words, while we still think of writing as a process taking place in a series of steps, we now understand that good writers tend to switch frequently among the different steps as they work. An insight gained while editing one chapter might convince the writer that an additional chapter is needed; as a result, she might start another drafting phase--or even decide to divide one chapter into two or three, and begin reorganizing and developing new drafts. Likewise, failure to satisfy a publisher--whether it is your boss looking at a pamphlet you've written or a book publisher deciding whether to print and sell your book--might lead the author all the way back to the idea-development or organizing stages. In short, while it is very useful to think of writing as a process, the process is not a clear, always-the-same series of steps. Instead, it is a sometimes messy, forward-and-backward process in which you strive for simplicity but try to appeal to your audience, create but also organize, enjoy yourself if possible but also follow some rules, and eventually create a product that works.

If this sounds difficult, it's not--at least, not if you learn a few lessons this book can teach you--and you practice, practice, practice. The more real writing you do, the more of a real writer you will become. If you are reading this book, then your first goal likely is to do well in a college (or upper-level high school) "composition" or "rhetoric" class. In short, you want to learn how to write a good academic paper. There are a large number of tips and methods this book can show you. They will work best if, like the writing process itself, you go back and forth between reading this book and doing some actual writing: try some of these lessons out by writing; then return to new lessons or review some of the lessons you've already read to discover what you next can do with what you've written--or with a new writing. Your next goal after learning to write a good general academic paper (or several types, perhaps--some of the most common being a summary, an analysis, an argument or "thesis," an evaluation, and a research paper) is to write in your specific discipline or major. Each discipline or major has its own writing style, organizational method, and purpose or goal. Your major or discipline teachers can help you quite a bit as you learn to apply your academic writing skills to their discipline. And eventually, your goal is to write for your work--for your future profession.

With each of these types of writing--general academic, specific discipline/major, and future profession--you'll eventually become increasingly successful. As you learn the types better, you will find--like the experienced journalist on a quick deadline for a story--that often your writing will come more quickly and easily. However, whenever you have a major challenge in your future as a writer, you will know how to return to the circular or "recursive" steps of the process to develop difficult ideas, explain difficult concepts to your audience, and create pleasure and knowledge in both yourself and your audience because of your writing skills.

2.2 Five Evaluation Criteria

There are five criteria we can use to evaluate any piece of writing. These criteria are Focus, Development, Organization, Style, and Conventions.

Focus. What are you writing about? What claim or thesis are you defending? This criterion is the broadest, concerned with the context, purpose, and coherence of a piece of writing. Is your topic appropriate for an assignment? Do you stay on that topic or drift off on unhelpful tangents? Have you focused too minutely or too widely? For instance, an essay about the American Civil War in general is probably too broad for most college essays. You might be better off writing about a particular battle, general, or incident.

Development. Development is concerned with details and evidence. Do you provide enough supporting material to satisfy the expectations of your readers? A proper research paper, for instance, usually includes many references and quotations to many other relevant works of scholarship. A description of a painting would probably include details about its appearance, composition, and maybe even biographical information about the artist who painted it. Deciding what details to include depends on the intended audience of a piece. An article about cancer intended for young children would look quite different than one written for senior citizens.

Organization. Organization, often called "arrangement," concerns the order and layout of a paper. Traditionally, a paper is divided into an introduction, body, and conclusion. Paragraphs are focused on a single main idea or topic (unity), and transitions between sentences and paragraphs are smooth and logical. A poorly organized paper rambles, drifting among unrelated topics in a haphazard and confusing fashion.

Style. Style is traditionally concerned with clarity, elegance, and precision. An effective stylist is not only able to write clearly for an audience, but can also please them with evocative language, metaphors, rhythm, or figures of speech. Effective stylists take pains not just to make a point, but to make it well.

Conventions. This criterion covers grammar, mechanics, punctuation, formatting, and other issues that are dictated by convention or rules. Although many students struggle with conventions, the knowledge of where to place a comma in a sentence is usually not as important as whether that sentence was worth writing in the first place. Nevertheless, excessive errors can make even a brilliant writer seem careless or ignorant, qualities that will seldom impress one's readers.

2.3 Stages of the Writing Process

Although we've mentioned that writers often work recursively--that is, frequently switching between drafting, editing, proofreading, and so on--it is useful to break the writing process into different functions or activities. To that end, we have divided it into eight smaller processes: Planning and Prewriting, Collaborating, Researching, Drafting, Editing, Reviewing, Revising, and Publishing.

2.3.1 Planning and Prewriting

Writers generally plan their documents in advance. This stage, often called "prewriting," includes everything from making a tentative outline, brainstorming, or chatting with friends or colleagues about the topic. For some writers, the prewriting stage is mostly mental--they think about their projects, but do not write until they are ready to start the actual document. Others plan extensively and map out exactly how they want their document to look when it's finished.

This chapter[1] describes common planning and prewriting strategies and should help you "hit the ground running" when starting out your writing projects.

2.3.2 Collaborating

While there is a long history of thinking of writing as a wholly individual act, most workplace compositions (and composing in many disciplines) involve collaboration. If you're working on a collaborative text, this chapter will help you develop a collaboration plan, establish strengths and weaknesses in the group, assign roles, and do what ever else will help in producing a co-authored text.

This chapter[2] offers some helpful tips and strategies for collaborating on documents.

2.3.3 Researching

Writers frequently require reliable information to support their documents. A writer's personal opinions and experience are sufficient evidence for many types of documents, but audiences will often demand more. Seeking out the information required to support your writing is called "research," and it comes in many forms.

One form of research is the interview, in which you call up or meet with someone who has information on the topic you are pursuing. Another type, "field research," involves travel to places where the topic can be studied first-hand. You might also circulate a survey. These three examples are all part of what is called "primary research" -- research you conduct yourself.

---

1   Chapter 3 on page 11
2   Chapter 9 on page 25

While many writing teachers assign primary research to their students in the process of writing a "research paper," much of the research that writing at the college level asks you to do is "secondary research" -- exploring other people's writing in the form of books, scholarly journals, newspapers, magazines, websites, and government documents.

This chapter[3] describes different research strategies and provides you with the tools you'll need to properly back up the claims you make in your writing.

2.3.4 Drafting

Drafting means writing or adding to a piece of writing--composing it. It may seem like a straightforward process, but can often be made difficult by writer's block or other anxieties.

This chapter[4] describes drafting strategies and how to avoid common pitfalls like perfectionism and writer's block.

2.3.5 Editing

You can't edit what hasn't been written. That's why editing comes after drafting. For our purposes, it's important to distinguish between deciding what needs to be improved and actually making the changes. We'll call the decision-making process "editing" and making the changes the "revising" process.

Unlike publishers, who hire professional editors to work with their writers, student writers do most of their own editing, with occasional help from peer reviewers.

This chapter[5] describes macro editing (editing at the level of content and arrangement) and micro editing (editing at the sentence level), and provides strategies for improving your text.

2.3.6 Reviewing

Having other people review your writing is essential to producing the best piece you possibly can. We often don't make the best readers of our own work because we are so close to it. Reviewers, on the other hand, bring valuable perspective we can't get any other way. A reviewer is anyone who is willing to look at your work and provide feedback. You're a reviewer, too -- for others' texts.

This chapter[6] explains how to successfully review a document as well as how to make the most of the feedback you receive from other reviewers.

---

3   Chapter 10 on page 33
4   Chapter 11 on page 43
5   Chapter 12 on page 53
6   Chapter 13 on page 63

2.3.7 Revising

Revising is making the changes you or your editors determined were necessary during the editing process. Revising is hard work, but it's probably some of the most valuable work you can do to become a better writer. Dive into the task with the willingness to wrestle with your writing and bring out the best in it, and you will learn why revising is often considered the "meat" of the writing process.

This chapter[7] examines the revision process and identifies some strategies that will help you improve your documents and reduce the likelihood of creating even bigger problems. This chapter will also cover proofreading, or carefully scanning a document for typos and other simple errors.

2.3.8 Publishing

What's the point of writing if no one will ever read it? Though some of us are content to write diaries or notes to ourselves, most writers desire for others to read and hopefully enjoy or benefit from their documents. This is where publishers come in: They help connect writers to readers. The Internet has introduced countless new ways for writers to publish their own documents electronically, but print publishing is still the preferred avenue for most professional writers. Of course, getting your documents accepted for publication can be a long and frustrating ordeal. We've all heard the stories of now-famous novelists who were rejected time and time again by unimaginative or overly-cautious publishers.

This chapter[8] describes the print and electronic publishing industry, then identifies strategies that will help you distribute your documents to their intended audience. We will also discuss why so many authors fail to ever secure a publisher for their work.

---

7   Chapter 14 on page 73
8   Chapter 15 on page 83

3 Planning and Prewriting

4 Overview

> "The role of a writer is not to say what we all can say, but what we are unable to say."
> --Anaïs Nin

This chapter begins with some prewriting strategies to help you generate ideas and pick a topic. In addition to learning ways to overcome writing anxiety (writers' block), you will also learn how to craft an outline to keep your ideas on course, organize your draft, and tailor it to your audience.

Before you actually begin writing, ask yourself the following questions: Who? What? When? Where? Why? How? Which?

For instance, you might ask yourself:

1. Why am I writing?
2. What is my subject?
3. Which subject has the most potential to attract readers?
4. Who is my audience?
5. Where does my background information come from?
6. How can I persuade my readers?

Keeping these questions in mind before, and during, the writing process will help you identify and develop ideas. If you experience difficulties, seek your instructor's advice to steer you back on course.

5 How do I pick a topic?

Have you ever been stressed out because you can't think of a good topic for an important writing assignment? You're not alone. As a student, you'd probably prefer it if professors would just assign topics rather than leave you to find one on your own. However, professors aren't vague because they want to punish you; they usually just don't want to constrain your creativity or discourage you from writing about topics that truly interest you. Professors also want to be surprised by their students' ingenuity, and very few teachers want to read a big stack of essays all on the same stale topic. Unfortunately, just being told to "be creative" is unlikely to calm you down when you've got a major paper due next week and still haven't found a topic to write about!

Imagine that you are in an introductory literature course. The professor has assigned a 3-5 page essay on a Shakespearean play that requires multiple sources. You try asking the professor to be more specific, or offer some suggestions. The professor responds, "No, it's up to you. Surprise me." What do you do?

One smart option is to go to the library and look for scholarly journals that cover Shakespearean studies. You might also try scholarly books about Shakespeare and his plays. Browsing these sources should give you some ideas about the aspects of Shakespeare and his plays, that scholars have found worth writing about. You might find that an idea that you thought was "totally original" has already been done. However, you shouldn't let this worry you. If every essay or book had to be 100% original, we'd have precious few to read!

If you keep reading and skimming articles and books, you'll find many different discussions and possibilities for writing topics. Scholars frequently engage in complex and long-lasting arguments that span across different journal articles and books. Professor X's article on climate change will be mentioned, discussed, or challenged by Professor Y in a book and Professor Z in another article. None of them are worried about saying things that have never been said before; the key is just to say them differently and perhaps better.

You will always have one advantage over any other scholar you read--their articles and books cannot take advantage of all the relevant scholarship that appeared after their publication date. Don't be afraid to freshen up an old article with new supporting evidence--or challenge one whose conclusions are called into question by subsequent research.

You should also look for an issue that you can reasonably cover given the time and space (page count) you have available. After that it's a simple matter of supporting your argument by bringing in relevant quotations from those who agree with you. You should also identify the counter-arguments and provide pertinent background information.

This technique also works well for writing theses and dissertations. Instead of writing about "things never written about before," try to make a new contribution to one of the many ongoing conversations in the field. This approach is especially handy if you hope to publish your work, since some publishers tend to favor works that fit with their existing line of publications. Readers also expect you to be familiar with, and probably refer to, works of other scholars who have written on your topic. Think of your work as either extending existing work or taking it in a new direction.

If you intend to publish fiction, it's a good idea to first familiarize yourself with the work of successful fiction writers and consider what it is about their work that appeals to publishers. There is no shame in following the same roads that led to their success. This isn't the same as "copying" or "ripping off" an author; there is a difference between duplicating techniques and duplicating content.

In essence, the easiest way to find a topic to write about is to see what other writers are writing about and join their "conversation." The conversation metaphor is a very useful way to understand what scholarship is all about. Rather than thinking of essays or books as isolated units of scholarship, try envisioning them as the fruits of a massive network of scholars who converse with each other via scholarly documents, conference presentations, e-mail, phone calls, and other forms of communication. Research *what* is available and *where* you can make the most valuable contribution.

6 What are Some Other Ways to Get Ideas?

"The best time for planning a book is while you're doing the dishes."
--Agatha Christie

Still stuck even after pouring over all those books and journals? Don't worry. There are plenty of other ways to stimulate your brain.

In general, though, remember that good ideas may arise anytime and anywhere. You might be struck by a brilliant insight as you're running on the treadmill or even while dreaming. Always be prepared to record new ideas. Carry a small notepad with you or use your mobile phone to record a voice memo. You might even try writing the idea on a napkin and taking a picture of it. The important thing is to get it down quickly, because you're all too likely to forget all about it by the time you're ready to write.

Another good way to generate ideas is to read and listen actively. Your texts and professors will discuss relevant issues in the field, and they might make comparisons to related ideas and other thinkers. A professor might say, "There is still work to be done in this area," or "there is great controversy over this issue." Be alert to these sources for good ideas. The biggest mistake a novice writer can make is to rely solely on "inspiration." As a scholar, you are never alone--don't be afraid to listen and respond to the work of others instead of always trying to be original or profound.

Even chatting with your classmates might help you think of a good topic. You can also check with your college or university's writing center. Many of them have tutors who can help you find and hone a great topic for your paper.

Let's look now at three other techniques for getting those brain juices flowing: brainstorming, clustering, and freewriting.

6.1 What is a Brainstorm?

Brainstorming allows you to quickly generate a large number of ideas. You can brainstorm with others or you can brainstorm by yourself, which sometimes turns into freewriting. To effectively brainstorm, write down whatever ideas come to mind. Sometimes it works better to write down each idea on a separate piece of paper. It also helps to ask yourself some questions:

1. What do I care about or what am I interested in?
2. What do I know that I could teach others?

3. What irritates me?

In order to capture more of your thoughts, you may want to brainstorm a few times until you have enough ideas to start writing.

Examples

Imagine you are in a class. Your instructor says you will have to write a paper on your favorite free-time activity, and that you must also persuade your reader to try it.

First ask yourself, *What do I care about?* or *What am I interested in?*

It is easiest to write about a topic that you are interested in. This could be anything from gardening to ice skating, or from writing poetry to playing the piano. Your list, in this example, would then read:

1. gardening
2. ice skating
3. writing poetry
4. playing the piano

At this stage, every idea is good since you are trying to come up with as many ideas as possible.

Second, ask yourself, *What do I know that I could teach others?*

You may be able to teach someone else something that you really enjoy. Good for you! If you cannot, don't worry; you are still just brainstorming. Perhaps you teach swimming lessons or t-ball, or maybe you bake really well and are able to offer some of your insights. Your list, in this example, would then read:

1. swimming lessons
2. t-ball
3. baking

Anything is fine. You are still brainstorming.

Let's think of another example. How about the common situation in which the instructor wants you to write about "something you care about" or an "issue you have"?

Again start by asking yourself a question. Ask yourself, *What irritates me?*

Everyone has things that irritates them, some small and others larger. An example of something small that's irritating could be people in your dorm who leave trails of toothpaste by the sink and never clean up after themselves. A personal example can be useful as a bridge to a larger issue that will be your topic -- in this case it could be community living and personal responsibility.

In academic writing with a less personal slant, the source of irritation is often another writer/theorist with whom you disagree. Your "irritation" then would lead to an effective piece about why you have a better conception of what's really going on. A less direct version of this would be a writer/theorist who makes some good points but lacks something in his/her argument that you can add to the "conversation."

A majority of academic writing begins with brainstorming. Go ahead! Try one or many of the ideas for brainstorming either by yourself or in a group. Working together to come up with ideas means that there are more ideas coming from many different minds.

6.2 What is Clustering?

Clustering is a process in which you take your main subject idea and draw a circle around it. You then draw lines out from the circle that connect topics that relate to the main subject in the circle. Clustering helps ensure that all aspects of the main topic are covered.

Example

After using the brainstorm example, let's say you decided on gardening as your topic. Your main idea of gardening would be in the center of your page circled. Anything else that you want to say about gardening you would connect to the circle with lines. You can also add more lines to extend the ideas that relate to thoughts around the circle. When finished, your clustering might look like the following:

Figure 1

6.3 What is Freewriting?

Freewriting helps generate ideas and set them in motion. To begin, start writing without worrying about spelling or grammatical errors. You should write your ideas naturally and spontaneously so that you can record many ideas quickly. Do not look back at what you wrote until you are satisfied that you have written enough. An easy way to freewrite is to set a time limit and then begin writing. You can write anything at all, and in the end, you will often find some quality ideas scattered throughout your writing.

Example

1. I set my kitchen timer for a specific amount of time. Let's say 5 minutes.
2. I just begin writing without worrying about what I am putting onto the page.

Things I like to do. Watching TV is a great way to unwind after a long day. Playing video games is too. I like talking to my friend Steph on the phone, but I get annoyed when she doesn't call me back. I like shopping. My favorite store is JC Penney. They have everything that you need there. I can buy clothing, luggage, things I need for my kitchen, wall coverings. I love that store. I like going to the theater. Last year, I saw *The West Side Story*. It was amazing. For some reason, I always look forward to fall and spring yard work. I don't know if it is the sense of accomplishment I feel when the yard is ready for the season or what, but I really do enjoy it. There are so many things that need to be done each year too. In the spring, you need to be sure to fertilize before

---

A sample freewrite.

---

3. The timer went off, so I stop writing.

4. At this point, I review what I have written and decide which point(s) to elaborate on.

With these simple writing tips, you should be able to find a topic and begin the process of writing the assigned paper. Established authors use brainstorming, clustering, and freewriting, so you're in good company when you use these techniques to help you overcome writer's block or writing anxiety. If none of these work for you, try to come up with your own strategy. What works for someone else may not work for you. After all, these prewriting strategies are just ways to put your ideas on the paper so you can develop them at a later time. Try to enjoy the process of writing instead of seeing writing only as the chore of finishing an assignment your instructor has given you. Done this way, writing might become a pleasure that can also improve your critical thinking ability.

7 How Do I make an Outline?

Developing an outline, such as the examples below, can be helpful because you can keep an overview of what you want to say, check whether you have covered everything, and find what is out of scope and should be excluded. The outline can grow during the writing process as new points come to mind.

Outline example I

I. Introduction and Thesis Brief description of issues that arise when reading "Hamlet" II. Issues of feminism uncovered through reading "Hamlet" a. What other scholars have discovered about feminism in "Hamlet" b. Which of these discoveries was most evident to me and how c. Ideas of feminism that I uncovered on my own III. How uncovering ideas of feminism in "Hamlet" has led me to better understand what Shakespeare thought of the role women played in society IV. Conclusion
A sample outline.

Outline example II

I. Mixed marriages States this issue briefly, why I am interested in exploring this, and whether this issue exists in my culture II. Issues of mixed marriage within your culture a. Is it acceptable to get married to a person who is a different religion? b. Is it acceptable to get married to a person who is a different race? c. What are the advantages or disadvantages of mixed marriages? III. Personal experiences a. An example from my own life or my family. b. An example from the news. IV. Conclusion
A sample outline.

8 External Links

- Finding a Topic[1]
- Additional Advice on Preparation[2]
- Prewriting Strategies[3]

---

1   http://library.webster.edu/wbt/t-w1-00.html
2   http://www.mica.edu/writing/starting/planning/
3   http://www.writing.ku.edu/students/docs/prewriting.shtml

9 Collaborating

9.1 What is Collaboration?

During your educational career, and later in your professional career, you will sometimes have to write with other people. Unfortunately, few students learn how to collaborate effectively since most school writing assignments are not collaborative. Outside the classroom, however, people often compose documents collaboratively (even though only a single author may receive credit for the piece). Newspaper reporters, novelists, and magazine writers collaborate extensively with their editors. Scholars collaborate with other scholars to review and add insight to each other's work. Business writers work closely with colleagues, administrators, and consultants to ensure that their work meets the relevant standards. Even poets meet to discuss their ideas and techniques. In short, all kinds of writers collaborate.

This chapter offers some strategies for successful collaboration. It also discusses some of the common pitfalls that can wreck an otherwise promising collaborative opportunity.

9.2 Advantages to Collaboration

Figure 2   alt=An image of two shaking hands of different races.

Collaborating writers often produce strong documents because they have a greater pool of knowledge from which to draw. No two people have the exact same backgrounds, skills, knowledge bases, or thought processes. When collaborating with your team members, you can compare notes, ask each other questions, and discover how each member can best contribute. For example, perhaps one of your team members has extensive computer skills, while another is especially artistic. While these skills might seem to have little in common, they may actually end up complementing each other, which should allow your team to create a better project than any one person could do alone.

9.3 Disadvantages to Collaboration

Not everyone loves the idea of group work. Collaboration can take more time than individual writing, since the team will often need to meet to discuss changes or additions. Sometimes the document can become disjointed, especially if the authors have not tried to match their style and tone. Team members can also get pigeonholed into certain roles when they could be helpful in multiple parts of the project. A more common problem is that some team members do more work than others; you may end up picking up the slack for less responsible or motivated classmates or colleagues. More than one collaboration has ended with one or more team members quitting in disgust.

9.3.1 Overcoming these Disadvantages

- Meet early on in your project to decide its direction.
- Devise a way to **evenly** split up the work between members.
- Create a time line for when the various sections are due.
- Set up meetings where members can gather and share progress or obstacles.
- Meet near the end of the project to make revisions.

9.4 Conducting Meetings

Figure 3   alt=A meeting.

9.4.1 In order to have a successful meeting

- Create an outline for the meeting.
- Review the outline with members before the actual meeting begins.
- When critiquing a team member's work be diplomatic.

- Smaller meetings with partial attendance can work well when warranted.

9.4.2 Setting an Agenda

One group member is usually responsible for organizing the agenda. It is important to note that the agenda describes the purpose of the meeting. Without it, members may become frustrated or question why they are at the meeting in the first place. The agenda organizer should give all members a copy of the agenda well before the actual meeting takes place. He or she may need to communicate with the other members to gather ideas for the agenda, which can be done via email before the meeting. Each group member might want to look over the assignment sheet and discuss possible items to add to the agenda. They will want to consider all the stages that need to be accomplished in order to complete the assignment. The person organizing the agenda will record the suggestions and create an agenda (or outline) which can be distributed to the members and used to guide the subsequent meetings. Including a time line can also help keep the group on task.

Sample Agenda

Meeting Date:
Attending:
I. Introduction (10 Minutes)
  a. Introduction of agenda and discussion of any assignment related questions
  b. Review agenda, including timeline II. Discuss work completed toward the project (20 Minutes)
  a. Briefly present your work to the group
  b. Respond to members' work III. Brainstorm future steps toward completion of the project (10 minutes)
  a. Provide suggestions for each group member
  b. Consider time frame and due date of project IV. Discuss upcoming individual projects (5 minutes)
  a. Get people to brainstorm what they will be working on
  b. Describe the steps that will be taken by each member before the next meeting V. Complete unfinished work as a group(10 minutes)
  a. Do any work that needs completing as a group VI. Wrap up (5 minutes)
  a. Questions and answers
  b. Decide on time and place of next meeting

A sample agenda.

9.4.3 Taking Minutes

It is important to keep a brief and accurate record of group meetings, with infromation such as:

- Dates
- Attendees
- Discussion Points

At each group meeting, elect one member to record the discussion, or take the meeting minutes. The minutes should be a brief summary of the main points discussed, and will roughly follow the agenda format. A copy of the minutes should be distributed to each member within a day of the meeting. A record of decisions made and tasks assigned can prevent conflicts by keeping team members from playing "the blame game."

9.5 Communicating Away from Meetings

| "The single biggest problem in communication is the illusion that it has taken place." |
| --George Bernard Shaw |

Figure 4   A videoconferencing room.

There are other ways to communicate with team members when face-to-face meetings are impossible. E-mail allows you to quickly deliver the same message to multiple people, and the recipients can respond at their convenience. The telephone works great if you only have to call a small number of people and deliver a short message. Memos are a lot like e-mail, but will take more effort to send. A fax will also work to communicate information to other group members. All you need to do is decide which form of communication will work best for the respective message.

9.6 Strategies for Effective Collaboration

The two most important aspects of effective collaboration are discussion and planning.

If group members participate in active, open discussion, the group will be more likely to share a clear understanding of the assignment. The assignment may be divided up among the group members or all aspects of the assignment may be worked on collaboratively. Open discussion can also help an individual overcome obstacles. For many students, it is easier to tackle obstacles as a team than it is to do so alone.

It is very important to schedule group meetings when all members are able to attend. Committing to these scheduled times will help the group meet the required deadline in a timely manner. Although it is most useful to meet with the group in person, group meetings can also take place online when meeting in person is impossible.

- Be honest about your abilities. If you know you aren't good at something specific, let your group members know. They'll respect you for your honesty.
- If you're unhappy with the way a project is going, say so. This is your grade and you have a right to let your instructor know when things aren't going the way you think they should.
- Respect your group members. Everyone has something unique to contribute to the project. You may not agree on everything, but being kind is sometimes the most important ingredient in getting things accomplished.
- Have fun. Although it's homework, this is an opportunity to get to know new people.
- Be responsible for your part. Do the work that's expected but don't be afraid to ask for help if you need it.

9.7 An Example of Collaborative Work/Group Conferencing

Figure 5   Acrobats at Cirque du Soleils Nouvelle Experience Finale 1994.

Many students struggle with group/peer editing, and when they are put in small groups and told to help each other with their papers, they have no idea how to do so effectively, usually resulting in a lot of patting one another on the back, fixing a few commas, and then having a long conversation about last night's game. Little constructive work comes from these meetings. Many have created worksheets for students to follow, but these worksheets often invite brief and unhelpful comments. Students, however, can be taught how to do this well by having "group conferences." A group conference consists of three steps: One, students are put into groups of three, four, or five (four is ideal) and give drafts of their papers to one another, so that each student has a copy of every other student's paper in the group. Two, students read each others' papers and fill out a "group conferencing worksheet," which is very much like a peer editing worksheet; be sure to only ask open-ended questions. Three, students get together as a group with an experienced writing instructor or tutor who leads them through the worksheet, asking them the questions on the worksheet but making sure that they answer them thoroughly. The key to this is that the instructor or tutor has not read the papers. Because they don't know what the papers are about, how they are organized, how they support their arguments, or even what the purpose of the paper is, they can ask all kinds of probing questions that help the students to not only think critically about the papers they are working on, but also learn what kinds of questions make peer review effective.

If students go through this process with some guidance a couple times, their self-directed peer sessions should be more productive afterward. Students will learn to think critically about the writing of others as well as their own. Additionally, it is more productive and interesting for students because, unlike a regular one-on-one conference with an instructor, they get the input of several readers.

10 Researching

10.1 Introduction to Research

Research can be an intimidating but rewarding process. It allows you to gain additional knowledge on a topic, assemble outside support, and provide credibility for your assertions.

Creating a research paper can be divided into three main steps: finding sources, evaluating sources, and integrating sources. This section will provide instruction on each of these steps, along with additional links and information to guide you through the research process.

10.2 Determine the Role of Research in Your Writing

Depending upon the purpose of the assignment, research can be used to accomplish many things.

Whether you are writing to inform, persuade, or critique, research should be used in conjunction with your own ideas to support your thesis and your purpose. Do not let the research speak for itself. You, the writer of the document, are the most important voice. You are using outside sources to support your thesis. Therefore, let your comments, connections, objections, etc. play the strongest role in your paper. When you quote or paraphrase an outside source, always bring the paper back to your thoughts.

It is essential to use outside sources that are going to back up your argument. In many cases, researching will reveal evidence that might relate to the topic but does not support your side of the argument. Many assignments will ask you to acknowledge the other side of the argument, so be sure to research your topic thoroughly and from many angles.

For some assignments, outside research may not be necessary. Thus, in determining the necessary amount of research needed, first evaluate the topic of the assignment. For example, a paper that is based solely on one's opinion will likely require much less research than one that covers a highly scientific subject. To be sure, always ask your instructor for specific instructions.

10.3 Finding Scholarly Sources

Before you begin your search, it is important to know that sources are divided into two categories: primary and secondary sources. Primary sources include original documents created by an author or group of authors such as historical documents, literary works, or lab reports. They also include any field research you conduct on your own such as interviews, experiments, or surveys. Secondary sources are sources written about primary sources and include scholarly books and articles, reviews, biographies, and textbooks.

Most often in academic writing, you will want to consult scholarly secondary sources along with any primary sources available. A scholarly source would be one that has been written by a professional in the field; the person may hold a doctoral degree or have a great amount of expertise in the field you are studying. Oftentimes, an author's credentials will be listed as a footnote within the source, but if not, an Internet search may reveal whether the writer can be determined to be a scholarly author or one that has done a vast amount of research on the topic. The author of the source will always be an important consideration, as your view of the quality of the article may change depending upon the author's credibility. In addition, you must ask yourself whether your source is scholarly.

In many fields, there will be a number of academic journals or publications that deal with publishing scholarly articles related to the subject. By discovering and accessing these journals, you can be sure that the piece from which you are quoting is a scholarly source. Many universities pay fees in order to provide their students with access to these journals in their electronic form, and an even greater number of university libraries will shelve current and back issues of these journals.

Furthermore, conducting an Internet search of these journals and articles may prove fruitful. Search engines such as Google offer the option of searching "Google Scholar" in order to access only these scholarly articles. Finding these sources online, depending on the journal and the site, may require that you pay a fee to view the article. This is where university libraries come in handy, as they offer free access to the same materials. If you cannot access a university library, some clever hunting of the Internet may still yield what you are looking for at no cost.

Popular scholarly databases include:

- Academic Search Premier[1]
- Project MUSE[2]
- JSTOR[3]
- Entrez-PubMed[4]
- The MLA International Bibliography[5]
- PsychINFO[6]
- ProQuest[7]

...and a large number of other options depending on your field of study.

1   http://library.mtsu.edu/libdata/page.phtml?page_id=32
2   http://muse.jhu.edu/
3   http://www.jstor.org/
4   http://www.ncbi.nlm.nih.gov/pubmed/
5   http://www.mla.org/bibliography
6   http://www.apa.org/psycinfo/
7   http://www.proquest.com/en-US/

10.4 Evaluating Scholarly Sources

Now that you have found your sources, you must evaluate them. Evaluating sources becomes a major component of researching because the materials chosen will reflect upon *your* reputation. Aside from being able to find informative sources, a good researcher is also able to quickly assess the credibility of information. Through practice, this skill will come.

When setting out to write a research paper, there is a vast pool of information available, including books, newspapers, periodicals, reference works, and government documents. Included in this can be your own empirical data, obtained in interviews and surveys, but you will probably not need to use it all. As important as it is to be able to find sources specific to your topic, it is equally vital to be able to correctly assess each source's credibility -- that is, how trustworthy, accurate, and verifiable the sources are. Due to the vast amount of information available on the Internet, it presents an especially interesting challenge in determining the credibility of sources. However, even when evaluating print sources, the same criticism should be maintained.

You must also be aware of the author's possible bias. Even the most credible sources may exhibit forms of bias, as most authors' past experiences will come into play. Bias is most likely to occur in controversial topics such as politics or religion, but is still likely to be present whenever an opinion is voiced. The author's beliefs and experiences can thus affect the objectivity of the text. Another case may be when the author or publisher has ties to a special interest group that may allow him or her to see only one side of the issue. Lastly, make sure to evaluate how fairly the author treats the opposing viewpoints. Complete objectivity is very difficult to attain in writing, but try to find sources that are not incredibly subjective. Nonetheless, the most important thing is simply to be aware of possible biases so that you are not misled.

Here are four approaches to assessing the credibility of the sources you find.

10.4.1 Evaluating Print Sources

The fact that it's in print doesn't automatically make it a reliable source. When evaluating print sources ask yourself these questions:

Book

- *How old is it?* Research projects will have different requirements as to how old your sources can be. For example, when dealing with contemporary issues or a current controversy, using outdated sources will likely provide inaccurate information. For example, a book on euthanasia published in 1978 probably isn't the best choice. While the book may contain useful information for other projects, it does not make sense to use it when there are more current materials available.
- *Who is the publisher?* Books published by a university press undergo significant editing and review to increase their validity and accuracy. When assessing a book published by a commercial publisher, be aware of vanity presses (companies that authors pay to publish their works, rather than vice versa). Also be cautious about using books labeled as "self-published" or books that are published by specific organizations (such as a corporation or a nonprofit group).

- *Is the author objective?* Check biographical information included in the book, as well as other sources, to gather information about the author's background as a way of determining his or her stance on a particular issue. In addition, find out about his or her previous works, past professional experience, affiliations with groups or movements, current employment, and degrees or other credentials.

Periodical

- *Is it a scholarly journal or a magazine?* Scholarly journals are almost always characterized by no advertisements, longer articles, and the requirement that authors cite the sources they use in writing their articles. Articles submitted to scholarly journals undergo substantial scrutiny by other professionals as a way to increase the clarity and accuracy of the information contained in them. Most scholarly journals are not sold on news-stands, but rather are circulated primarily among the academic community. In contrast, magazines are available for purchase; they tend to contain shorter articles, generally don't require writers to cite their sources, and contain advertising. Therefore, while magazines may contain relevant information, the content may not always be entirely accurate.
- *How old is it?* As noted above, dated material can sometimes be inaccurate. Always ask your instructor if you're uncertain about how old is too old.
- *Newspaper article: What do you know about the paper that publishes it?* Some newspapers have a discernible political slant, which can often be found by skimming through the headlines or by seeing how others regard the newspaper. For example, *The Los Angeles Times* is considered a more progressive news source, while its neighbor *The Orange County Register* is considered to have a libertarian slant.

10.4.2 Evaluating Web Sources

For most academic research, teachers will require that students use scholarly sources. For this there are a number of "academic databases" that will always provide credible sources. These sites generally require some form of a subscription in order to access them; however, many colleges provide complimentary access to students. Once logged into the site, users are able to search and sort the articles by criterion such as date, subject, author, and more importantly, whether or not they have been peer reviewed and are scholarly. Examples of these sites include, but are not limited to: EBSCO, JSTOR, and Proquest. Links to these "gated websites" can generally be found on your school's web page. Nevertheless, always ask what databases are available to you as a student.

While the rest of the Internet has a wide range of easily accessible and useful information, discretion must be maintained. Because anyone can put information on the Internet, make it your first priority to know who is behind the sites you find. Individuals? Nonprofit groups? Corporations? Academics? Advocacy groups? Federal, state, or local government? Small businesses or single vendors? Depending on your topic, you may want to avoid dot-com web sites; for many, their primary purpose is commerce, and that can significantly affect what they publish. Of course, other websites can also have agendas. This can lead to false or misleading information. Therefore, it is best to consult a number of sources so that those with agendas will stand out.

Ask yourself:

- **By whom was the website created?** Be cautious if there is no author. Try looking for "about this site" or check the homepage. Does the website discuss the qualifications of the author(s)? Does it give contact information such as an email address or telephone number?

- **By whom is the website sponsored?** Determine whether the website is sponsored by a special interest group. By learning about the affiliated groups, much can be ascertained about the credibility of the author and web site. Also look at the domain name. This will tell you by whom the site is sponsored. For example: educational (.edu), commercial (.com), nonprofit (.org), military (.mil), or network (.net).

- **Is the website relevant?** Decide whether the information is something that can actually be used in the paper or, at the very least, gives a helpful background. If what is found cannot be used, move on to something else.

- **Does the website contain any errors?** Can the definitions, figures, dates, and other facts presented on the website be verified in other sources? Look for grammar, spelling, punctuation, and content errors. If there appears to be more than one or two content errors, move on.

- **Is the website relatively unbiased?** As it is noted above, carefully examining the source behind the website can lead to clues as to what kind of bias and agenda the site may contain. Once the source has been deemed valid, continue to remain alert, especially if the topic is controversial. Look for websites that discuss multiple points of view. Take note of the language used, and avoid sites that seem to exhibit characteristics of bias and/or inaccurate information.

- **Are there advertisements on the Web page?** Do these particular advertisements reflect a possible bias toward the subject matter?

- **What appears to be the website's purpose?** Think about why the site was created. Is its purpose to inform, persuade, or sell a product to the reader? For whom was the site created? Who is the intended audience? If you are not included in the intended audience, carefully consider whether or not the information is relevant to your research.

- **Is the website comprehensive.** A valuable website will cover a topic in-depth and lead to additional sources.

- **Does the website provide references?** Determine whether the references themselves are authoritative.

- **How old is the website?** A website that has remained on the Internet a long time may be better trusted than one that was added a month ago. Make sure that the information is not outdated. When was the site last updated? Credible websites will garner ongoing attention by their creators to make sure that the content is as up-to-date as possible.

- **Has the website received any awards?** Websites that have received awards may have better reputations.

- **Is the website user-friendly?** Does the website download quickly? Can you read all the text? Does any text appear too small, in strange characters, or in a font that is illegible? How easy is it to navigate through the website? Is the content accessible? The information presented should be clear, precise, and easy to understand. Avoid using sites that make use of overly scientific and/or technological terms that are difficult to understand. If it cannot be clearly understood, it may lead to misinterpretation and thus incorrect information in your work.

10.4.3 Consider Your Project

How you evaluate a source will differ depending on the project you're working on. When determining whether a source is credible, biased, or relevant, it is equally important to consider how the source will be used.

For example, Phillip Morris[8] has a web site that touts the company's programs to curb smoking among young people. Obviously, information from a tobacco company and cigarette marketing giant can be considered biased. You must ask yourself whether their program is effective and whether the content of the site can be trusted and in what context.

Should you never use that source? You might want to if you were writing a paper that examined the smoking rates of 10 - 13 year olds. What role might the Phillip Morris site play in your paper? Does the site display information that contradicts the company's advertising campaigns? Would the campaign website be effective in your argument? It all depends on what side of the argument is going to be supported in your research project.

Audience. Purpose. Argument. These intents should be considered since they affect how sources should be evaluated.

10.4.4 Consult ADAM

When faced with assessing a large number of sources in a short period of time, the quickest way to cover the essential points is to remember this acronym:

- **Age.** How old is this source? For almost every topic, search for the most current sources that can be found.
- **Depth.** Does the source go in-depth, or does it just skim over the surface? Does it feature the many details and long discussions that are expected from academic sources, or does it just seem to cover the main ideas? Always use substantive sources.
- **Author.** Who is the author? What is known about his/her qualifications? Is he/she really an expert? Can any bias be seen? What is his/her purpose?
- **Money.** Follow the money. Is the source coming from a place that's trying to "sell" something? Is there advertising where this source appears that might affect what will be printed?

10.5 Integrating Scholarly Sources

To better understand the process of researching, it should be recognized that there are sources of information all around us. We commonly use them in situations ranging from a conversation with a friend to an online discussion. The difference in academic research is that this "casual conversation" turns into a discussion with the readers of your paper. Therefore, it may help to think of doing research and using sources of information as just another way to enhance your conversation with the audience.

---

8   http://www.philipmorrisusa.com/en/policies_practices/ysp.asp

10.5.1 Sources Are Other Voices

Even before you learn the rules of citation, recognize that you already know quite a bit about how to work with sources. It can be helpful here to think of sources as "other voices." Sources are used when you reference an idea that was heard in a conversation. They are used when considering what to buy -- whether the source is an advertisement, a slogan you can't get out of your head, the fact that a friend recommended a product, or that you've looked up price quotes and shopped around. You become knowledgeable about making decisions by piecing together the information from many sources. Sources are part of our lives; they are all around us and are a part of how we breathe life into the words that express what we think.

In research writing, it is similar in the sense that the same act of interacting with other voices is present, and only another layer is added. Because writing is being done, you're also presenting the sources in an organized way, so that your sources are used in a way that supports your point of view. This means that any and all sources that remotely relate to the topic can't be thrown in; instead, pick and choose the best sources for your purposes, and use them strategically for effect.

10.5.2 Purposes of Sources

Sources are capable of playing a variety of roles in your writing. Sometimes sources are used as examples; sometimes they present evidence. Sources can also be used to present a counter-argument. Other times, they are used only to be built upon and refined. Nevertheless, it should be realized that sources can serve multiple purposes in a paper.

This is nothing new. To relate this to an everyday situation, try this: Spend a week paying attention to the conversations and discussions you have. Listen for sources used and try to discern for what reasons they were used. You'll often hear people cite the news or refer to a game when talking about sports. You'll hear friends quote conversations they've had with other friends. You will hear people discussing important issues with the participants in that discussion providing reasons (evidence) -- facts and opinions, but often a mix of the two -- for why they feel the way they do.

In writing, the natural act of conversing with and referring to others is taken one step further. Knowing in advance that you'll be writing for an audience, sources (other voices) will be looked at while exploring an idea and planning how to appeal to those readers, using terms and conventions that they will recognize. However, do not let this part of the research process get in the way of doing what comes naturally. Research is about curiosity and interest. It is about having something to say and finding the evidence to support it. That is the basis of research and working with sources. Thus, the technicalities and rules of research, while important, should not discourage you from doing research and effectively using sources.

10.6 Cite Sources to Avoid Plagiarism

After using other sources to gain information for a report or paper, you might decide to use that information in your paper. If the ideas expressed in your paper are not your original thoughts, you must cite where you obtained that information. If you do not cite where you obtained your information, you are plagiarizing[9]. Plagiarizing is an extreme offense. If you are caught plagiarizing in school you usually will receive a failing grade on the assignment, if not in the entire course. You could also risk being expelled from school. If you are caught plagiarizing in the workplace, it could likely end up costing you your job. If you are a researcher and plagiarize in a scientific paper, your university may lose funding. To avoid the risk of plagiarism, make sure that you cite copied information! The most common forms of citation are direct quotations[10] and summarizing[11] or paraphrasing. After a direct quote or at the end of a summarized or paraphrased thought, you should cite the author and page number of your source. Information on how to cite sources can be found in The Writer's Handbook: Citations[12]. If you are using other sources in your report and are unsure whether or not you need to use citations, it is better to be safe than sorry, so cite the information.

The two most common standards for citing are MLA[13] (Modern Language Association) and APA[14] (American Psychological Association). Each is specific to the field in which the research is done. For example, if you are researching for a psychology class, it is most likely going to be cited in APA format. On the other hand, MLA is used in the liberal arts and humanities fields. Nonetheless, check with the teacher, group, or organization for which the research is being done to find out which method you are expected to use.

Using and correctly citing outside sources is hugely important to the ethical portrayal of you as a writer. It shows that you have done your homework, literally. It also shows that you are a thoughtful writer who takes this work or subject seriously, who respects the hard work of others, and who truly contemplates the intricacies of research and discovering truth in writing.

10.7 External Links

- Learning to Write and Research Using the Web[15]
- Purdue Owl Lab[16] Beginning Your Research
- The Online Books Page[17] Lists over 25,000 free books on the web.
- Bartleby[18] Search dictionaries, thesauri, encyclopedias, familiar quotations, and usage manuals.

---

9   http://en.wikibooks.org/wiki/Rhetoric_and_Composition/Plagiarism
10   http://en.wikibooks.org/wiki/Rhetoric_and_Composition/Quotation_Marks
11   http://en.wikibooks.org/wiki/Rhetoric_and_Composition/Analyzing_assignments#Summary.
     2FResponse_Paper
12   http://en.wikibooks.org/wiki/Rhetoric_and_Composition/Citation
13   http://en.wikipedia.org/wiki/Modern_Language_Association
14   http://en.wikipedia.org/wiki/APA_style
15   http://www.ipl.org/div/aplus/toc.htm
16   http://owl.english.purdue.edu/owl/resource/552/01/
17   http://onlinebooks.library.upenn.edu/
18   http://www.bartleby.com/100/

- Biographical Dictionary[19] Searchable biographical dictionary online.
- Researchpaper.com[20] Relief for Writer's block.

---

19   http://www.s9.com/
20   http://www.researchpaper.com/

11 Drafting

"Close the door. Write with no one looking over your shoulder. Don't try to figure out what other people want to hear from you; figure out what you have to say. It's the one and only thing you have to offer."
--Barbara Kingsolver

11.1 Overview of Drafting

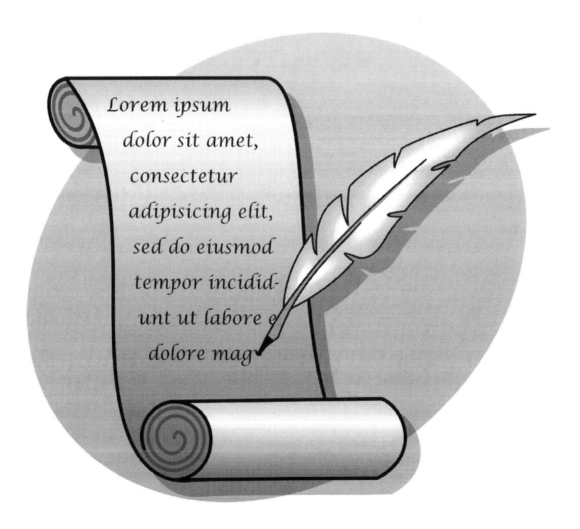

Figure 6   alt=A cartoon centipede reads books and types on a laptop.

Drafting is essential to the organization and flow of your paper. Drafting includes prewriting[1], editing[2], and reviewing[3]. Once your general ideas are down on paper, writing out specific ideas and quotations can make the final writing process much easier. Each step of drafting brings the process a little closer to the final product. Always write down any ideas you have in the drafting process. It is much easier to cut content from your paper than it is to work on adding content. If you collect all your resources, quotations, facts, ideas, and come up with a thesis during the drafting process, your paper will show it. The idea is to provide yourself with as much information as possible in order to create a solid and well thought-out piece. Do less worrying and more writing.

"*Solviture ambulando.* To solve a problem, walk around."
--St. Jerome, who spent 30 years at a desk

11.2 Drafting: The Process

"Fiction is based on reality unless you're a fairy-tale artist. You have to get your knowledge of life from somewhere. You have to know the material you're writing about before you alter it."
--Hunter S. Thompson

The first draft: Prewriting[4] will help you with drafting. Additionally, try writing in full sentences, try to find the best possible quotations, try mindmapping, or try writing out all of the data you have gathered. Weave these things together, and you may end up with a nice framework for your paper. Don't worry about being complete in your drafting. Disorganization and choppiness are fine here; you can smooth that out in later drafts. Drafts are **not** perfect. Drafts may contain grammatical and spelling errors and may lack detail. Rephrasing and expanding ideas may be a part of later drafts.

The second draft: The second draft is about organizing your information logically and effectively. If you created a thorough first draft, this should be easy. Organize the main points that you plan to make, find supporting evidence for each point, and spend a few sentences explaining what conclusions you are able to draw from the information. Don't be afraid to show off. Professors like it when students are able to draw conclusions on their own. Sometimes it weakens your argument to use softeners like "might" "I think" and "maybe," so keep an eye out for these.

You will want to come up with an overall organizational strategy and stick to it. Parallelism is very attractive in a paper. However, there is also no quick and easy format that works for every topic. You may want to organize things chronologically, with fact and then opinion, or by order of importance.

---

1   http://en.wikibooks.org/wiki/Rhetoric_and_Composition/Planning_and_Prewriting

2   http://en.wikibooks.org/wiki/Rhetoric_and_Composition/Editing

3   http://en.wikibooks.org/wiki/Rhetoric_and_Composition/Reviewing

4   http://en.wikibooks.org/wiki/Rhetoric_and_Composition/Planning_and_Prewriting

The third draft and more: The third and any subsequent drafts are really about finesse. These are the drafts that will hook your reader and earn you an "A." Try to write an attention-grabbing introduction, as well as a conclusion that leaves the reader thinking about your paper. If you are still struggling with the overall flow of your paper, go back to you first draft and start rewriting. Often your main point will change by the time you get to this draft, and that is fine. However, you may need to go back to your first draft when this happens.

The elusive "show, don't tell" line comes into play in this draft. Professors want to be entertained, and they want more than just facts. You need to show the professor that you can think for yourself, that you know what you're talking about, and that you can write in an engaging style. If you are bored reading the paper, chances are your professor will be, too. Add action verbs, remove passive ones, and use examples. Pretty soon you'll be ready for a final draft.

Be sure to follow a timeline. Make sure that you start early to have enough time to go through many drafts. If you wait until the day before, you will have time for only one draft!

11.3 During the Drafting Process

Many writers often narrow -- or expand -- the topic as they write. Overly broad topics can be difficult to manage and can lead to summarization rather than descriptive explanation. Narrowing your topic will provide you with a more workable idea to focus on. Asking questions about what you want to know regarding your topic and what you want your readers to know will help focus your writing. If you choose to narrow your topic, first try to picture a larger context into which your thesis fits. Make a claim which forecasts the main point(s) of your thesis, then deliver the source which supports the argument. During this stage, scan for grammatically weak areas and unsupported claims. You may always add background information, term definitions, literature review, reasons for your assumptions, and counter-arguments to strengthen your own argument.

"My starting point [in writing] is always a feeling of partisanship, a sense of injustice . . . I write because there is some lie that I want to expose, some fact to which I wish to draw attention, and my initial concern is to get a hearing."
--George Orwell

Sometimes you will find that it is easier to write the introduction after you have written the body of your paper. Consider waiting to write the introduction until you have a definite sense of what direction you want your paper to take. Many times, if you write an introduction first, it can limit the information or collaboration of ideas for the bulk of the paper. If you do decide to save the introduction for later, go over what you have written and identify the main point, or points, of your paper. Next, craft an introduction with a thesis statement that forecasts what will follow. Be aware that you need to rework some of the body after you do the introduction. No matter what you choose to write first, it is important to stay on track. Emphasize several points that are related to your thesis by adding more information and going deeper into detail. It is important to gather sufficient information to support your thesis. You may be required to provide a reference or in-text citation, or you may find that you do not yet know enough about your topic, and more research is required. Research may be necessary for multiple reasons: to learn more about the topic, to provide examples for your thesis, or to use as support for your thoughts, opinions, and the overall direction of your paper.

11.3.1 Let It Flow

As you draft, do not stop to edit or look up small pieces of information; there will be time for precision later. Luke Sullivan, author of "Hey Whipple, Squeeze This," suggests that you must "write hot and edit cold." In other words, write off the top of your head and allow your thoughts to be spontaneous. You never want to leave a good idea out. However, when it comes to polishing the final product, become critical by taking out unnecessary words or ideas that stray from the main message. Do not keep text that distracts or causes misunderstandings. If you have a question, place it in brackets or make a note of it and refer back to it later. First, just get your ideas out without worrying about punctuation or spelling. Similarly, if you notice a big gap which requires more research, skip it and work on other sections. The important thing is to let your ideas keep coming and make progress on the page. No matter how irrelevant your words may appear, keep writing. If you have to stop, be sure to end in a place where it will be easy to pick up from later. Don't get distracted when your initial drafts aren't "A" quality work. That's the reason they are drafts. The important thing is to get your ideas down on paper. You can spend time evaluating them later on.

"Write 1,000 words a day. That's only about four pages, but force yourself to do it. Put your finger down your throat and throw up. That's what writing's all about."
--Ray Bradbury

11.3.2 Dealing with Writer's Block

Writer's block can occur at any point during the writing process. You may find yourself sitting down to write when you suddenly realize that you can't think of a single thing to say. Don't panic! It's a common problem with a variety of solutions.

Figure 7   alt=A none *Using Wikibooks*[a].

a   http://en.wikibooks.org/wiki/Using%20Wikibooks

Here are a few...

- Staring at a blank screen can be intimidating. Try writing out your dilemma in the form of a question: "What is it I'm trying to say?" "What are my goals?" Then brainstorm[5] to answer these questions.
- Take a break. Ten minutes away from your work will usually recharge your creativity.
- Review the literature on your topic to see what other people are saying. Even opposing views can be inspiring.

---

5   http://en.wikibooks.org/wiki/Rhetoric_and_Composition/Planning_and_Prewriting#What_
     is_a_Brainstorm.3F

- Bounce ideas off someone else. Speaking about your writer's block with friends, family, and fellow students may help untangle ideas or generate new ones.

11.3.3 Experiment

How do you start your draft? While the occasional flash of inspiration can lead you to scribble out great work on the back of an envelope with a stubby pencil, paying brief attention not only to 'what you write', but 'how you write' can inspire you to write differently or even more effectively. If you start drafting from the conclusion, for example, it could be like having a "Guiding Star" for your paper. Or you could leave the introduction and conclusion blank until the end. With that said, you can make up your own approach to create your own way of writing. All the technological tools you have access to make it possible for you to write virtually anytime, anywhere, and however you want. Take advantage of it. Type on your computer, do research on it, record your own voice if the pen is slowing down your thinking. Many people find it helpful to brainstorm; start writing for an extended period of time without stopping, and see what you can come up with. Charting can be a good way to come up with ideas and see connections you may not otherwise notice; when you chart, you write down a topic in the center of the paper. Then write other words or ideas that fit in with the topic. Draw lines that connect the related ideas. Experiment with your approach to writing.

Figure 8

11.3.4 Meeting the Minimum Word Count

If you are having trouble meeting the minimum page length, look over your paper again and see if you can find spots that could use additional detail. Also, look at your assignment sheet again to see if you met the assignment's requirements. It is okay to add more detail to certain sections; for instance, is "a blue car" sufficient, or would "a 2007 Vista Blue Ford Mustang" work better? But be careful not to make your paper too wordy. Remember that quality is more important than quantity. Just adding needless words to add to the word count keeps you from actually developing your ideas and strengthening the content of the paper.

Also see Generating Ideas[6] in the Drafting section of this book.

11.3.5 Title of Your Essay

Coming up with a good title for your essay might seem difficult, but there are several techniques that can help. Although some writers start with a good title and write a paper to fit it, others (and probably most) worry about coming up with a good title after they're finished with the draft. The advantage of waiting until the end to work on the title is that you know exactly what you've written.

Many academic writers prefer a two-part title structure separated by a colon. The "catchy" bit goes before the colon, whereas the latter part is a straightforward description of the paper. For example, "Cutting out the Cut and Paste: Why Schools Should Use Plagiarism Detection Software."

Here are some tips for coming up with good titles:

- Get inspiration from best-selling books or well-known essays, particularly those closely related to your topic (e.g., "Men are from Mars, Women are from Snickers: Candy Bars and the Obesity Epidemic.")
- Look through your paper and see if you can identify some "key words" or special phrases that might serve as part of a title (i.e., "Edit this Page: How Wikis Enable Collaborative Writing" or "The Blue Screen of Death: How to Respond to Technical Difficulties During a Presentation.")
- Consider poetic devices, such as repeating consonant sounds (e.g., "The Cost of Caring").
- Get inspiration from famous quotations or song lyrics (e.g., "I Shaved My Legs for This?: A Feminist Perspective on Country Music.")

If you can't come up with a good title right away, shut down your word processor and think about other things for a while. If you just can't come up with anything clever, just remember that a clear and precise title is much better than none at all. A title like "The Use of Skull Imagery in Hamlet" may not sound profound, but at least the reader will know what the paper is about.

"When you get an idea, go and write. Don't waste it in conversation."
--Kenneth Koch

11.4 Final Thoughts on Drafting

Here's a quick summary of the key guidelines in drafting:

---

6   Chapter 6.1 on page 17

- Don't worry about your audience before you draft. Your audience may dictate the style and tone of your writing, but it is more important to get a good start before adding potential complications to the mix.
- You may need to narrow or expand your topic as you develop your paper.
- If you are stumped about how to start the introduction, it might be helpful to simply skip it and come back to it later. The bigger picture might become clearer as you approach completion.
- While drafting, keep all of your research close at hand. This will prevent the need to stop writing to look something up, which could break your concentration.
- Writing in 30-minute stretches, or longer, will establish momentum, making your job as a writer much easier.
- If you come across a small detail that you are unsure about, simply write yourself a note and come back to it later.
- The first draft will not be perfect. Your priority should be getting your thoughts out on paper (or on-screen). Leave the fine-tuning for later.
- If you must stop writing, be sure to end in a place where you have a good idea of what comes next. You will be able to pick it up again more easily.

11.5 External Links

- Writing the First Draft[7]
- First Drafts Made Easy[8]
- Going Beyond the Five-Paragraph Essay[9]
- Transitions[10]
- Introductions and Conclusions[11]

---

[7] http://pratt.edu/~wtc/firstdraft.html
[8] http://riverbendlaw.com/firstdrafts.htm
[9] http://www.calstatela.edu/centers/write_cn/fivepara.htm
[10] http://www.asu.edu/duas/wcenter/transitions.html
[11] http://www.asu.edu/duas/wcenter/introconc.html

12 Editing

12.1 Editing and Revising: One and the Same?

"Substitute "damn" every time you're inclined to write "very"; your editor will delete it and the writing will be just as it should be."
--Mark Twain

Figure 9   Samuel L Clemens, 1909.

Although many writers and even some instructors use the terms interchangeably, you may find it helpful to see editing and revising as two different activities. For our purposes, editing means going through a piece of writing and making comments and suggestions about how it could be better--or even whether it's appropriate at all. Revising, on the other hand, occurs when a writer attempts to make the changes suggested during the editing process.

For example, an editor might suggest that you tweak your introduction to make it better fit the rest of the paper. The actual process of changing the introduction is called revising and comes with own set of difficulties. We talk more about that process in the Revising[1] chapter.

You may be called upon to edit other students' writing. This process is often called Peer Reviewing and is given a separate chapter[2] in this book. If you're concerned about how to diplomatically edit someone's work without being offensive, be sure to read it carefully.

You can (and should) also edit your own work. This simply means going back over what you've written and finding ways to improve it. Most writers frequently switch between drafting new sentences and paragraphs and editing ones they've already written.

In this chapter, we go over some basic editing strategies and some specific things to look for during the editing process.

As previously mentioned, revision concerns large sections of text, while editing concerns individual sentences. Below is a list of potential errors to consider while editing.

- Fragments
- Run-on sentences
- Dangling or misplaced modifiers
- Adjective and adverb use
- Verb usage and tense
- Subject/verb agreement
- Pronoun/antecedent agreement
- Sentence balance
- Comma Use
- Spelling
- Word choice (connotation vs. denotation)
- Format/presentation

12.2 Sentence Structure

"In my sentences I go where no man has gone before."
--George W. Bush.

---

1   Chapter 14 on page 73
2   Chapter 13 on page 63

Figure 10   Official photograph portrait of former U.S. President George W. Bush. .

Use active verbs.

Be-verbs (is, am, are, was, were, be, has/have been) indicate condition and often require an extra sentence or clause to be sound. *Active verbs* allow you to compose sharply without numbing the rhythm of your writing. Read your writing with an objective eye and think: "How can I make every sentence and paragraph straightforward and simple?" Below are examples in italics of wordy and confusing verbiage. Below the italics are the same sentences that have been simplified.

'The sharp rise in fuel prices is a serious challenge to trucking firms. It makes it hard for them to provide timely service to customers and to meet payroll expenses.

Sharply rising fuel prices **challenge** trucking firms by causing delays in customer service and payroll.

Primary causes of the rise in fuel prices ***are*** *an issue of confusion for many citizens. They don't know how to fight the rise because they don't know its cause.*

Primary causes of rising fuel prices **elude** many citizens, making them unaware of how to fight the increase.

Name the people. Directly state *who or what group* is acting in your sentences. Note the contrast in power and clarity among the sentences below

Without people: *A citywide ban on indoor smoking in Duluth originally caused a marked drop in bar patronage.*

With people: *When the Duluth City Council passed a citywide ban on indoor smoking, many people stopped going to bars.*

Eliminate wordy phrases. Certain stock phrases are weak and wordy. They can make you sound stuffy or as though you're just trying to fill up space. Use these replacements

Because, Since, Why: *the reason for, for the reason that, owing/due to the fact that, in light of the fact that, considering the fact that, on the grounds that, this is why*

When: *on the occasion of, in a situation in which, under circumstances in which*

About, Regarding: *as regards, in reference to, with regard to, concerning the matter of, where ABC is concerned*

Must, Should: *it is crucial that, it is necessary that, there is a need/necessity for, it is important that, it cannot be avoided that*

Can: *is able to, has the opportunity to, has the capacity for, has the ability to*

May, Might, Could: *it is possible that, there is a chance that, it could happen that, the possibility exists for*

Luckily, Internet users can find numerous web sites about how to eliminate wordiness.

Use Parallelism in sentences. Parallelism sounds difficult but is easy to write or edit. Parallelism uses the same pattern in words and structure to show equal importance or provide balance in sentences

John likes reading, **his studies,** and talking.

Corrected: John likes reading, studying, and talking.

We were asked to calculate scores, record them, and **putting them** on the bulletin board.

Corrected: We were asked to calculate scores, record them, and post them on the bulletin board.

The science class had to dissect frogs or **were experimenting** with gases.

Corrected: The science class had to dissect frogs or experiment with gases.

To check for parallelism, first circle or highlight every **and** or **or** to check for balance in the sentence. List the phrases from your sentence on a separate piece of paper. Example: **reading, his studies, and talking.** Make corrections to your list to create balance: **reading, studying, and talking.**

Once you fix a few sentences, problems with parallelism become easier to recognize and to correct!

12.3 Editing Tips

"Bad spellers of the world, untie!"
--Graffito

Figure 11   alt=A pair of glasses sitting on a computer keyboard.

Editing is like going over your writing with a fine-toothed comb, scanning the surface and the depths for errors, misstatements, and a lack of clarity. First, **keep resources close.** Gather your writing handbook, dictionary, thesaurus, handouts, and any other editing resources and *keep them close*. This way, you will not be tempted to guess at the correct way to do something. Instead, use your resources when you need them. Spelling errors can be avoided if you have a dictionary nearby. Don't rely on spell check. It will only correct the spelling, not the proper usage of a word. For example, the word **their** means someone's possession of something. When used in a sentence, "We sat in *their* chairs." On the other hand, **there** is used to express an area or place. When used in a sentence, "We sat over *there*." Looking up these words in a dictionary will prevent unnecessary errors from occurring.

Secondly, **know your errors**. Keep a list of the errors you tend to make next to a corresponding list of corrections. No writer makes unique mistakes all the time; instead, our mistakes are habitual. Know what yours are by looking at your instructor's comments on past papers or by working with a writing tutor. That way, you can enhance your editing strategies by watching specifically for these types of errors. If there are grammar rules you find yourself looking up more frequently than others, write them down for future reference.

Thirdly, **break it down**. Edit one thing at a time. Instead of reading your paper through from start to finish once or twice and trying to catch everything, try searching for one thing at a time. For example, you might go through your paper once to tighten up wordiness. Then, read through a second time, while looking for one type of error which you frequently make, such as comma splices. Then, try reading a third time looking for words that may have been misspelled when you ran a spell check. Read a fourth time for another characteristic error, such as subject-verb agreement.

Next, **reduce visual clutter**. Use two pieces of blank paper to cover up everything but one sentence at a time. This forces you to pay closer attention to the words because they are the only thing you see. Normally, our eyes move all over a text as we are reading; this trick will prevent that tendency. Lastly, **work backwards**. Read from the end of your paper to the beginning, one sentence at a time. When we read in the conventional manner--top to bottom or left to right--we tend to read quickly and are constantly leaping ahead without really focusing on the words. We tend to see what isn't there, because we know what it is supposed to say. Reading backwards forces us to slow down, thereby allowing us to catch more errors within individual sentences.

When reviewing your work, it is also important to ensure that the tense you choose remains consistent. **Tense** refers to the relation of details in the past, present, and future. For example, one writer may tell a story about going to the mall in the present tense by saying, "I **am** walking around the mall and I **see** my third grade teacher." Another writer may choose to relate this story in the past tense by saying, "I **was** walking around the mall when I **saw** my third grade teacher." Although it is important to select the tense that best suits the particular context a writer is using, it is equally important to remain consistent with whatever tense is chosen. Inconsistency within tense is extremely confusing for readers. It is important to review your use of tense to ensure that your language is clear. For example, if you were to say "I was walking around the mall and I see my third grade teacher" your audience would be very confused, wondering if you were seeing your teacher in the present or last week. By keeping your tense consistent your reader will always know when you experienced what you're writing about.

12.4 Perspectives on Style

> "Style is knowing who you are, what you want to say, and not giving a damn."
> --Gore Vidal, American writer

Figure 12   Gore Vidal at the Los Angeles Times Festival of Books, April 27, 2008.

Prescription and description litter these pages and others. Some writers tell you how to write: how your writing should look, sound, and feel. These writers prescribe rules (writer's handbooks are their bibles). Should you follow them? Prescription can be limiting. In some instances, it may be profitable or necessary to follow a formula (when writing a legal document or a theme for your fifth grade teacher, for example). It is necessary to learn the rules, if only to break them. Rules are not static, however. They evolve. Rules are added, changed, omitted. Current fashion is the only certainty.

Other writers describe how text is actually written. They analyze past and present text, highlighting similarities, differences, and respective efficiency. They define goals and purpose. It may be purposeful to apply rules, yet at other times it may not. But do not allow yourself to become limited by prescription.

Examine your goal and determine the best approach to reach it.

Why discuss style in a section on editing? As you write, you make choices. As you edit, you examine the effectiveness of those choices. Some choices are more effective than others and may reinforce your message. It all depends on your goal, your purpose, and your audience. Are you writing a birthday greeting or a dissertation? An instant message or a public address? Your choices determine your text's effectiveness; they help relate meaning.

As you can imagine, there are as many perspectives on style as there are available topics for writing. The following is an attempt to present some of those perspectives.

12.4.1 Richard Lanham on Prose Styles

"You can always count on a murderer for a fancy prose style."
--Vladimir Nabokov

A book written by Richard Lanham titled *Analyzing Prose* is a great tool for writers looking to pick up ideas for new styles. Through this work, one can can gain techniques covering the following styles:

- Opaque and Transparent
- Noun and Verb
- Paratactic and Hypotactic
- Periodic and Running

Learning how to properly incorporate these styles into your own writing can transform your work from everyday textbook style writing into colorful, creative, individualistic styles.

12.5 External Links

- English Writing Style[3]
- Style Guide[4]
- Rhetoricainc[5]
- Our Own Online Rhetoric and Style Manual[6]
- The Elements of Style[7]
- Check-Sheet for Papers[8]

---

3   http://en.wikipedia.org/wiki/English%20writing%20style
4   http://en.wikipedia.org/wiki/Style%20guide
5   http://www.rhetoricainc.com
6   http://cla.calpoly.edu/~smarx/courses/134/onlinerhetoricstyle.html
7   http://www.bartleby.com/141/
8   http://www.andrews.edu/WC/checker.html

- 12 Common Errors: An Editing Checklist[9]
- Revising vs. Editing[10]

Category:Rhetoric and Composition[11]

---

9   http://www.wisc.edu/writing/Handbook/CommonErrors.html
10   http://jerz.setonhill.edu/writing/style/rev-edit.htm
11   http://en.wikibooks.org/wiki/Category%3ARhetoric%20and%20Composition

13 Reviewing

13.1 Overview of Reviewing

"No passion in the world is equal to the passion to alter someone else's draft."
-- H.G. Wells

Sooner or later, someone is going to hand you a piece of writing and ask for your opinion. You may be asked to review another student's essay as part of your class work. Perhaps a friend or a younger brother or sister has come to you for help. If you develop a reputation for being a good writer, then the chances are good that even your boss might ask you to look over letters or policy statements and offer your professional opinion. In any case, if you really want to do a good job in these situations, you're going to need reviewing skills. You're going to need to be able to identify problems, suggest alternatives, and, more importantly, support everything you say with reasonable claims. Furthermore, you must do all this in a convincing way that makes the writer want to make the changes you suggest. You must know what's wrong with a document, why it's wrong, and how to fix it.

You've probably heard the saying, "A writer is his own worst critic." Whoever said this undoubtedly suffered from poor self-reviewing skills. After all, it's easier to spot problems in other people's writing because our own ego (or pride) doesn't get in the way. Another problem is that sometimes we get so caught up in what we want to get across in our writing that we don't pay enough attention to how we're expressing it -- a sentence that makes perfect sense to us might be total gibberish to someone else. Thankfully, these are all problems that can be overcome. You can learn to fairly and accurately review your own work. One way you can get better at self-reviewing is to spend time reviewing other people's work. Eventually, you'll develop a knack for spotting errors that will serve you well as you edit and revise your own work.

Writers, particularly new writers, often find that letting other writers review their work is tremendously helpful. Most universities have writing centers, where students can have their essays reviewed for free by experienced student writers or tutors. These tutors can work with you one-on-one to help you improve your writing and earn better grades.

You should realize that reviewing your work, like planning, drafting, or revising, is a recursive process. It is not something a writer does just at the end of his work. For instance, you may want to write an introduction to an essay and have it reviewed by a teacher or classmate before trudging forward. If you're on the wrong track, you'd be better off knowing about it sooner rather than later -- especially if a deadline or due date is looming.

In the academic world, journal articles and books are nearly always "peer reviewed" before they are accepted for publication. Sometimes these reviews are "blind," meaning that neither the writer nor the reviewers know each others' identities. This process is meant to make the process fair and ensure that every scholar gets a chance to get her work published. Academic reviewers must evaluate a work, recommend that it be published or rejected, and (hopefully) offer the writer substantial advice about how his work can be improved.

In this chapter, we'll talk about how to develop the skills you'll need to become a star reviewer. We'll start by discussing "criteria," or the standards you'll stick to when writing reviews. We'll talk about what to look for in a document and how to provide the very best advice to the writer. Finally, we'll talk about how to handle criticism from reviewers who evaluate your work.

> "You write to communicate to the hearts and minds of others what's burning inside you. And we edit to let the fire show through the smoke."
>
> -- Arthur Plotnik

13.2 Establishing Criteria

Let's suppose that you just gave your paper to your roommate and asked her to look it over. You explain that you've been working on the paper for three days and that you really want to earn an A. "I want your honest opinion," you say. "Don't worry about hurting my feelings. What do you think?"

You watch your roommate's face as she reads your paper. She grimaces. Laughs. Yawns. Finally, she hands you the paper back and says, "This sucks."

This may be the type of "review" you are accustomed to receiving -- overly critical and not very helpful. Perhaps you agree that your paper is in trouble and needs help, but without a better understanding of what's wrong, you aren't likely to be able to do much about it. Furthermore, how can you trust your roommate's judgment of your paper? What if it just so happens that your roommate is neurotic about starting sentences with "But," and, seeing such sentences in your paper, decided right there that the paper was terrible?

Ultimately, what makes an evaluation worthwhile is the soundness of its criteria. As a writer, you want to know not just whether someone likes your paper, but also what factors they are taking into consideration when they review your paper. Both the reviewer and the person being reviewed need to be as clear as possible about the criteria that will be used to evaluate the work. Are your reviewers only looking at your grammar, or are they also determining the rationality of your arguments? Does a comma splice make a bigger difference than a rough transition between paragraphs?

All of these matters should be spelled out clearly beforehand, either by the writer or the reviewer. As a writer, what are you personally working on? It's not a bad idea to think about your strengths and challenges as a writer before handing over your paper to a reviewer, or to use work that has been returned to you in the past with feedback. For example, if you're writing a paper for a professor you've had before, and who has made comments on your past work, use those comments to provide your reviewer with a focus. If you are the reviewer in this situation, ask to see the assignment and rubric, if possible. You can also ask the writer for specific guidelines, areas of greatest need, or even anything s/he might know about the grader. Is the person giving the grade unconcerned with punctuation conventions but a martinet about tense shifting? The point is, the more focused the reviewer and writer are, the more effective the reviews are.

13.3 Writing Helpful Comments

"There are two kinds of editors, those who correct your copy and those who say it's wonderful."
-- Theodore H. White

In the example above, you were not able to gain any insights or knowledge from your roommate letting you know that your paper "sucks." What you wanted was some kind of feedback that would help you improve your paper, so you could get a good grade. You don't know if your paper "sucks" because it lacked a strong thesis, if it sucks because your writing strayed from the assignment, or if it sucks because of grammatical errors. You can be a better self- and peer-reviewer than your roommate was. Given the previous example, how hard can it be? When you're reviewing your own paper or the paper of a friend or classmate, ask yourself a few questions:

ORGANIZATION

1. What are your initial thoughts? What strengths and weaknesses does the paper have? What parts confused you, or might be confusing to other readers? What's the most important thing that the writer is trying to say?
2. How is the paper you're reviewing organized? Again, does it start with the broad and move to specifics? Do all sentences support the paragraph's topic sentence, and do all paragraphs support the thesis? Is there an Introduction that draws in the reader, or does it restate the assignment and become redundant? Is the paper organized in a way that will make sense to readers? Does the writer employ transitions effectively? Does the paper flow from beginning to end?

FOCUS

1. Is the paper focused on the assignment? Does it follow the same thought throughout the paper, or does it jump from subject to subject? Do I feel like I'm still learning about/thinking about the same subject at the end of the paper that I was at the beginning of the paper?

2. Try to paraphrase the thesis of the paper as a promise: *In this paper, the writer will...* Does the writer fulfill his/her obligation stated in the thesis?
3. What's the writer's position on the issue? What words does the writer use to indicate his/her position?

STYLE

1. In what style is the paper written? Does it work for the subject matter and assignment? Will the paper appeal to its intended audience? Is the writing at an appropriate level for the target audience?

DEVELOPMENT

1. Does the title indicate what the paper is about? Does it catch your interest? Does the opening paragraph draw you in? If not, can you suggest a different approach to catch the readers' attention?

2. How is the development of the paper carried out? Does it start with a broad subject and then move to something more specific?

3. Does the concluding sentence draw the argument of the paper to a close by bringing together the main points provided in the paper, or does it just end? Does the writer conclude in a memorable way, or does he/she simply trail off? If the ending is too abrupt or too vague, can you suggest some other way to conclude the paper? Does the ending introduce any new topics?

CONVENTIONS

1. Are common or appropriate writing conventions followed? Are grammar, spelling, punctuation and other mechanics observed?

While reviewing the paper, make notes in the margins of any problems you find. If you believe that developing a paragraph a little bit more would be helpful to the argument, write <more>. If you are unclear of something, write <? not sure>. If you notice a missing comma, insert it in the correct spot, but be sure to set it off somehow so that you or your friend will notice the correction. If another word might work better, write <WC> to indicate inappropriate word choice.

Please note: It is important not to overwhelm your writer with comments. As much as possible, try to avoid repeating similar comments (e.g. don't correct every single comma error you find). Also, althought it can be tempting to make some of the changes you suggest yourself, you never want to rewrite the work you are reviewing.

13.4 Responding to Criticism

"I am forced to say that I have many fiercer critics than myself."
--Irwin Shaw

Nobody likes to be told that what they are doing isn't right. But what separates good writers from other writers is that good writers are able to take criticism, realizing that nobody is perfect, and use the criticism to help them, either with the assignment at hand, or with writing assignments in the future.

If your roommate tells you that your paper *sucks,* you probably want to ask him or her *why* it sucks. If your roommate says that you are continually writing run-on sentences[1], ask for advice on how to correct them or look in a writing guide to learn how to fix them. By handling criticism constructively, you'll be more aware of your common errors and less likely to repeat them, or at least will know how to find and correct them the next time you write.

---

1   Chapter 60 on page 279

If, while meeting with a tutor, you learn that you need further development of some of your ideas for clarity, revisit your writing and judge for yourself whether or not you do. Ask yourself if you understand since you are the one who did all of the research and *know* what you mean (probably a good indication that the tutor was right), or if you are comfortable that a reader would understand what you are saying without more information.

Remember: as the writer, you're in control of your paper. When people offer criticism, they're usually just trying to help you. Try to keep that in mind. Take the suggestions when you think they make sense, and discard the ones that don't.

13.5 Peer Review Sample

Here is an example of an essay submitted for peer review. The assignment is to write a paper about anything in nature: a plant, an animal, a natural disaster, anything. Practice reviewing with the steps mentioned above. What would you say to the author?

The Jalapeno: an Ode.

In the backyard of my parent's house survives an ambiance of relaxation. An alluring pool has been my oasis that anticipates the hot, yet hardly tormenting summer days (5). As I look on, the pool's surface resembles a trance that sparkles and fades into my squinting eyes. The gleaming blue and white water magnetizes me and nearly forces my body into my bathing suit, tanning lotion in hand. I race for my beach towels, usually the Budweiser one and the other that is striped with green and blue lines. I then carry a reclining chair and head for the poolside, not far from the diving board, where the sun awaits me. With every third or fourth step gracing the searing cement, I must dip my feet in the pool's merciful and cool dampness.

When I arrive to my destination, with the shaded patio still in view, I unfold the towels and lay comfortably on the reclining chair. Beneath the sun and its warm smile, I feel its soft kiss upon my browning skin. I look to my right and see a competitive game of Scrabble in action amongst my family members. Nearby, my dog moseys on over to see if I will give him a gentle pat, knowing all too well that the sun is beckoning. To my left, I gaze upon the intricately planted landscape. A few stubborn, yellow Tulips tend to show themselves from time to time while sitting under a few hanging baskets that support brave pink and purple perennials. Surrounding them are many other bushes and plants hovering over aesthetic night lamps (3).

To my front are the suspicious and rather bitter neighbors just past the determined fence. The day is spent best without catching eyes with them (4). Behind me is the house that has kept watch over me for more than ten years. With its light gray siding and white shudders, it doesn't pose much of a threat but hardly as great of a caress as the yard I lay in. While there are no trees in our backyard, our neighbor's trees lean over the fence gently as if their branches were hands dipping themselves into holy water. Subtly, I glimpse upon a pair of dragonflies making love in midair. I become slightly jealous of their incessant nature. And no sooner is my comfort found that I bounce away from my chair at the sight of bees and their territorial buzz. More often than not, I am unharmed; however, their intimidating presence remains unpleasant in the heat (5). A gentle breeze will bless my begging and perspiring skin, but when it is callous, the pool invites me for a quick dive (3). The surface of the glistening mirage pierces slightly at my skin raising every hair but altogether swathes my entire body. Cast into an oblivion, my hair swells like that of a mermaid's. Although my lips are sealed, the chlorine finds a way to seep into my tongue (2).

As I surge back to the surface, my nose wrinkles blissfully at the scent of the chicken and steak kabobs savored tenderly (5) with orange bell peppers, white onions, and plump, brown mushrooms (1). They cook patiently on the grill (3). Eager for dinner, I paddle myself to the shallow end of the pool and lead myself up the stairs. The steadfast cement is back at my feet. I quickly grab for my towels and head for the patio table that is secured by the rescuing shade. I faintly hear Led Zeppelin singing from the old, makeshift radio. I crack open a mildly cool High Life that has been sitting on the table for some time and let the sour suds have their way. I grab a Marlboro, tuck it between my lips and strike a fast match at it. As the unrefined smoke dances past my fingers, I slowly breathe contently, gazing up at the tranquil sky, fully aware that this place has dependably masked my outside tides (3).

Sample: Backyard Bathing

Sample Comments: Here, the peer reviewer has made matched remarks to specific sentences and passages in the essay and has included a more detailed global comment last.

1. Describe the scent of the location

2. Good descriptions of the essence of the back yard and pool

3. Good use of personification and imagery

4. Include more description of the neighbors

5. Unnecessary descriptive words, particularly adjectives and adverbs

6. You got some weedy adjectives and adverbs going on. EVERYTHING has been gilded and painted up; this is like the prose equivalent of RuPaul[2] (the one on the left). Cut as many adjectives and adverbs out as you can. In fact, I hate to say this, but don't "describe the scent of the location" unless the scent of the location is important/remarkable. Do I care that you ate awesome kabobs? I might, if it's important/remarkable in any way, but so far, no. What this looks like to me is, somebody told you to write a descriptive scene, you thought, "how pointless!", so you wrote a descriptive scene with no point. Is there a reason to describe this backyard pool Eden? Did a murder happen there later on? Is that where you first learned an Important Truth About Life? Are you going to get into a fist fight with the neighbors? Is there, in short, anything interesting at all about it?

13.6 Peer Review Sample 2

Here is another example of an essay submitted for peer review on the same topic as Peer Review Sample 1. Again, practice reviewing with the steps mentioned above.

---

2   http://en.wikipedia.org/wiki/Image:RuPaul.jpg

The Jalapeno: an Ode.

The jalapeno— is it a tasty cooking element, or a national mystery? As a lover of all things spicy, I find myself asking questions about the nation's most elusive pepper: where did it get its name? Where did it originate from? What makes it so spicy? How and where does it grow? And, most importantly, what kinds of food include the jalapeno? These questions are only natural to ask oneself when faced with the utterly fascinating pepper. However, through some difficult research, mental travel to the wild regions of the past, and a little bribery, the answers can and will be found.

But who to ask? If I lived in Texas I would ask Stacey Snow, Ms. Jalapeno 2005. She was crowned Ms. Jalapeno at the 27th annual Jalapeno festival in Laredo Texas. This festival is featured on the travel channel, and is commonly known as the "hottest weekend of the year." This festival has amazingly unique entertainment: the jalapeno egg toss, the blind jalapeno toss, the jalapeno spitting contest, the "some like it hot" cook off, the land raft race, the three-legged sack race, and a good old fashion game of tug-of-war.

The jalapeno is named after Jalapa, capital of Veracruz, Mexico. However, the jalapeno's popularity is not completely foreign. In 1995 New Mexico named the jalapeno the official state pepper, with chili peppers and pinto beans as the state vegetable. The jalapeno is part of the chili pepper family. The family also includes anaheim, cayenne, poblano, and serrano. The jalapeno is not native to Minnesota; in fact, it is not native to the United States. It is thanks to Christopher Columbus that we have the spicy treat. Still today the pepper is a popular favorite, with Texas producing half of the 14 million gallons of jalapenos produced each year in the United States. Jalapeno flavored potato and tortilla chips weigh in at 17 million pounds produced each year.

The spicy bite in jalapenos can send tears down its consumer's face. This burning sensation is no accident; it is due to a chemical called capsaicinoids. There are five varieties, with capsaicin being the hottest and most famous. The capsaicins in jalapenos give them the burning sensation. When the fire in the mouth sensation occurs, the brain releases endorphins into the blood stream. These act as a natural pain reliever.

The jalapeno plant is pod-like, and usually grows from 2 to 3 feet tall. It is single stemmed and grows upright. Though there are literally countless forms of wild peppers, the jalapeno is considered a domestic plant. The pods are cylindrical, which flourish in semi-arid climates with dry air and irrigation. The plant matures between seventy and eighty days generally producing twenty-five to thirty-five pods per plant.

Jalapeno foods come in many shapes, sizes, and flavors. The most recent jalapeno phenomenon to hit the market is jalapeno jelly. Originally from Lake Jackson Texas, jalapeno jelly was first marketed in 1978. This jelly is often lime-green, with a sweet flavor, and the same consistency as normal jelly. It is fitting that this jelly originated from Texas, because the jalapeno is the official Texas state pepper, along with the chiltepin; not so coincidentally, these are the two peppers used in the states official dish: chili. Though there are many types of hot peppers, the jalapeno distinguishes itself in a number of ways. First, the jalapeno is most often green when mature, and is about 2 inches long with cracks in the stem. The hotness is also immediate after a bite. The thing that makes the jalapeno so different from other foods is the cult phenomena surrounding it. Figurines, websites, and even academic papers have been formed on the jalapeno craze.

Most important to the jalapeno are the recipes. Many wild jalapeno recipes do exist, with jalapeno bread, jalapeno sauce, stuffed jalapenos, chicken and cream cheese with jalapenos, coca-cola ham glaze with jalapeno, jalapeno martini, jalapeno hushpuppies, jalapeno soufflé, jalapeno-basil vinaigrette, and tamale pie being just a select few. Dried jalapenos are known as chipotles, another common ingredient in many dishes. In Texas, people even go so far as to drink jalapeno coffee and jalapeno tea! Yuck!

It is safe to say that the jalapeno is both a tasty cooking element and a national mystery. Any time a recipe is made, the jalapeno will be there. Maybe not today, maybe not tomorrow, but

---

Sample Draft

Sample Comments: Here, the peer reviewer has organized her/his comments based on the five criteria and has made specific references to sentences and passages where appropriate.

ORGANIZATION

1. After the introduction paragraph, there is not much narrowing. The topic broadly seems to be jalapenos. Perhaps the writer could try picking one specific question and sticking to that.
2. The organization needs to be improved. Perhaps repeating the questions would help, or as previously stated, sticking to the development of one specific question.

FOCUS

1. The paper seems to fulfill the assignment very well, but it does jump subject somewhat, particularly beween paragraphs 3 and 4. I do like the theme of the jalapeño being presented as a national mystery; perhaps that could become the thesis statement.
2. Unfortunately, he thesis of the paper doesn't seem to exist. The questions in the first paragraph gives the reader an idea of where the paper is headed, but there really is no statement explaining what the writer is trying to prove.
3. Does the author have a position? If he/she does it must be that he/she reveres the jalapeno. There doesn't seem to be much controversy in here for the author to support or oppose.

STYLE

1. The title is clever, but could be a little more specific. It isn't so much an ode, but more of an investigation. However, it does catch interest.
2. The style and tone are spot on. For the topic, which is not very serious, the laid back humorous style seems to fit in very well.

DEVELOPMENT

1. This paper certainly has plenty of personality. The author has a nice balance of humor and information. However, I find myself getting lost in the middle. Perhaps if the author were to repeat a question at the beginning of each paragraph, the reader could be remembered of what the thesis is.
2. The conclusion is funny, but I don't think it really does its job; I find the last sentence especially confusing and unconnected. Perhaps the author could keep what he/she has, but add in some more review of all the information that is covered.

CONVENTIONS

1. The conventions seem to be ok. BUT WHERE ARE THE CITATIONS??? The author needs to develop ethos by sharing where her/his information came from regarding jalapenos.

13.7 External Links

- The Peer Review As Per Wikipedia[3]
- Friendly Advice for Reviews[4]
- Peer Reviews: Responding to a Draft[5]

3   http://en.wikipedia.org/wiki/Peer%20review
4   http://ubinet.engr.uconn.edu/usefullinks/reviewing.html
5   http://www.wisc.edu/writing/Handbook/PeerReviews.html

14 Revising

14.1 Overview of Revising

"Rewriting is when writing really gets to be fun. . . In baseball you only get three swings and you're out. In rewriting, you get almost as many swings as you want and you know, sooner or later, you'll hit the ball."
--Neil Simon

Successful writers understand that revising is an integral part of the writing process. It is so important that most authors spend the majority of their time revising their texts. That revising is a time-consuming and learned skill surprises many beginning writers because they often describe revision as changing particular words in a sentence or scanning a text for misspelled words or grammatical errors. Such changes correspond more appropriately to the term *editing*. To revise, however, is to significantly alter a piece of writing. While editing can be a part of this process, revising generally involves changes that concern bigger issues, such as content and organization. Alternately, while revising, a writer might notice that an idea needs to be developed more thoroughly, another omitted. Or, the writer might decide that rearranging paragraphs will provide clarity and support for his or her argument, strengthening the paper as a whole. Granted, writers will also change grammar and punctuation while revising, but if that is all they are doing then they are really just editing.

This chapter is meant to provide sound advice about the revising process.

14.2 Differences Between Revising, Editing, and Proofreading

It is important to note that revising, editing, and proofreading are very different processes. Despite the differences, however, they often overlap. They are being separated here for ease of explanation.

Revising

- Revising is done throughout the writing process, with special emphasis on the first few drafts.
- Focus = big issues
  - Audience
  - Organization
  - Content

- Support
- Conclusion

Editing

- Editing is done throughout the writing process, with special emphasis on the middle and final drafts.
- Focus = technical issues
  - Usage
  - Word choice
  - Transitions
  - Mechanics

Proofreading

- Proofreading is reserved for the final draft.
- Focus = mechanics and presentation
  - Spelling
  - Punctuation
  - Format
  - Typographical errors
  - Textual inconsistencies

14.3 A Change for the Better

"I write one page of masterpiece to ninety-one pages of sh*t. I try to put the sh*t in the wastebasket."
--Ernest Hemingway

Writing is an intellectually challenging, and draining, activity -- writing well, that is. Putting ideas on paper is a good start, but revising those ideas so that they are persuasive, cogent, and form a solid argument is the real work of writing. As you review what you have written, you will undoubtedly see holes in your logic, sentences that confuse rather than clarify, and sentences and paragraphs out of place. Below are some helpful hints to consider as you analyze and transform your paper.

- Take a break. Looking at your paper later will help you see it from the point of view of the audience. A good rule of thumb is to wait at least a day before revising. Often, writers look at their prose a day later and recognize significant flaws they would not have noticed had they written their paper in one night.
- Be your own critic. You are obviously your own best critic. When writing, most people do not (and should not) turn in their first drafts. So take advantage of your first, second, and third drafts to write your opinions in the margins. Highlight the things you really like, and circle the things you would like to change.
- Read and re-read your paper. In the first read-through consider the overall purpose of the paper and whether it is expressed clearly. In the second read-through analyze organization, logical development, and correctness. Often, reading your text aloud reveals awkward phrasing, missing information, weak points, and illogical reasoning.

- Put yourself in the shoes of your reader. Look at your work through their eyes. Keep in mind that, while you may know something about a topic and write about it with supported research, your audience may be new to the topic. Being specific in your writing helps clarify your message to audiences. Do not assume that your audience already knows what you know.

- Cut unnecessary words. Inexperienced writers should be able to cut 20 percent (or more) of their prose. Look hard at each word, each phrase, and each sentence. Does each and every one help you achieve your purpose? Does each sentence in a paragraph relate to the main idea? If you are like most people, you will find unnecessary repetition rampant in your writing. Pruning the verbiage will result in leaner, tighter, and more forceful writing. Remember E.B. White's mantra: "Omit needless words. Omit needless words. Omit needless words."

- Understand that revising your paper should not be the last thing you do -- revision should be ongoing throughout the creation of a document.

After doing all this by yourself, seek help from others. First, find an individual who knows about the assignment, your intended audience, and the purpose of the essay. Then, share it with someone who fits the description of the audience for whom the document is intended. Ask your readers if everything is clear and easily understood, if phrases are worded correctly, if the document is logically sound, etc. If you have other specific concerns -- Is the second example effective? Does my conclusion resolve the paper nicely? -- ask your readers to direct their attention to those issues.

After your have written your paper, return to the beginning to see how the end relates to the beginning. Have you maintained the same tone and main idea throughout? Does the ending reiterate your main idea without just summarizing what you've already said?

It is also oftentimes helpful to have someone read your paper aloud to you. This will force you to go over the material more slowly and allow you another chance to absorb the content of the paper. When you read your own paper aloud you are more apt to read the paper as you intended it to be read, as opposed to reading what is actually on the page.

After going through the steps above and making changes as necessary, you should feel your paper is nearly complete. The content should be in place, and your text should make your case clearly and forcefully. If you feel this is the case, you are ready to closely edit and proofread your text.

> "Books aren't written; they're rewritten. Including your own. It is one of the hardest things to accept, especially after the seventh rewrite hasn't quite done it."
> --Michael Crichton

14.4 Analyze Each Part of Your Paper

14.4.1 Introductions

When you look over the draft of your paper, the first thing you should focus on is your introduction. Whether it is one paragraph or an entire chapter, the purpose of the introduction is to grab your readers' attention and make them want to know more about your subject. Does it? Make sure you draw your readers in from the beginning and follow with relevant and interesting supportive information. If readers aren't intrigued from the very beginning of the piece, they will quickly become distracted or bored and avoid reading any further. Read your introduction to a friend and judge how compelling it is based on his or her reaction.

What is the difference between a good and a bad introduction? A bad introduction is misleading, rambling, incoherent, boring, or so hopelessly vague that you know less about the topic than you did before you read it. On the other hand, a good introduction gets to the point, gives the reader a reason to keep on reading, and sets the stage for a really exciting performance. An introduction is like a first impression; it is crucial to your image and, once presented, you never get a second opportunity. Your essay's introduction is your reader's first impression of your ability as a writer. Even if you are brilliant and have great ideas, a muddy or boring introduction will turn away many of your readers.

Make sure that you don't beat around the bush in your intro. If you have tedious openers such as "in today's society" or openers that merely relay what the assignment is, change it so that it instead states your argument up front and presents a clear thesis right away, then subtly describe your paper's overall structure. Try summarizing every paragraph into one sentence each, then put them all together to see if your introduction covers each point. Your introduction should state the issue at hand, establish your position regarding it, describe your paper's organization, and identify the scope of your coverage. Let's take each of these in turn.

14.4.2 Thesis Statements

Next, make sure you have a **clear thesis**. Simply put, a thesis is your main point, the line of argument that you are pursuing in your essay. It should answer two simple questions: What issue are you writing about, and what is your position on it? A thesis statement is a single sentence (or sometimes two, which are combined using a semicolon or comma and conjunction) that provides the answers to these questions clearly and concisely. Ask yourself, "What is my paper about, exactly?" to help you develop a precise and directed thesis, not only for your reader, but for you as well.

How can you be sure that your thesis is clear? Will your reader be able to identify it and see that the rest of your paper is supporting your argument? Most American readers expect to see the point of your argument (the thesis statement) within the first few paragraphs. This does not mean that you have to place it there every time. Some writers place it at the very end, slowly building up to it throughout their work, to explain a point after the fact. Others don't bother with one at all, but feel that their thesis is "implied" anyway.

Avoid the "implied thesis" unless you are certain of your audience. Almost every professor will expect to see a clearly discernible thesis sentence in the intro. Remember: The harder it is for you to write your thesis statement, the more likely it is that your entire essay is incoherent and unfocused. If you are having real problems crafting a good thesis statement, you may need to start over, narrow your topic, or dig even more deeply into what you are trying to say and write.

A good basic structure for a thesis statement is "they say, I say." What is the prevailing view, and how does your position differ from it?

Following are some typical thesis statements:

- Although many readers believe *Romeo and Juliet* to be a tale about the ill fate of two star-crossed lovers, it can also be read as an allegory concerning a playwright and his audience.
- The "War on Drugs" has not only failed to reduce the frequency of drug-related crimes in America, but actually enhanced the popular image of dope peddlers by romanticizing them as desperate rebels fighting for a cause.
- The bulk of modern copyright law was conceived in the age of commercial printing, long before the internet made it so easy for the public to compose and distribute its own texts. Therefore, these laws should be reviewed and revised to better accommodate modern readers and writers.
- The usual moral justification for capital punishment is that it deters crime by frightening would-be criminals. However, the statistics tell a different story.
- If students really want to improve their writing, they must read often, practice writing, and receive quality feedback from their peers.
- Plato's dialectical method has much to offer those of us engaged in online writing, which is far more conversational in nature than print.

14.4.3 Position

Make sure that your reader knows *your* position on the issue. This should be properly expressed in your thesis, but check your entire introduction for "wishy washy" sentences. Unless you're only writing a summary, your introduction should make it clear how you feel about the issue at stake.

Avoid sentences or "thesis statements" such as the following:

- Abortion is a very controversial issue in America.
- Capital punishment is both good and bad.
- This paper will present the pros and cons of modern copyright law.

Are these examples stating an issue and taking a position, or merely stating what everyone knows already? Again, your reader should already know that the issue you're writing about is controversial, otherwise there would be little reason to write about it. Unless you've been instructed to merely write a report or summary of an issue, assume that your professor wants you to take a position and defend it with the best evidence you can muster.

14.4.4 Scope

Besides explaining what your paper is about and your argument, an introduction may also state what you will and won't cover. For instance, let's say your paper is about an issue affecting mothers infected with HIV. Your introduction should reflect this focus, rather than present your paper as a general overview of HIV. If your scope isn't clear, then readers will constantly wonder when you'll address the larger topic--or even assume you simply forgot to do it.

Let's say you wanted to write a paper that argued that Ford makes better cars than Chevrolet. However, your introduction didn't mention Chevrolet at all, but instead had the line: "Ford makes better cars than any other car manufacturer." Your reader would quickly begin to wonder why you're not talking about Toyota or Nissan! Try to anticipate what your reader will expect to see covered, and, if necessary, state it explicitly:

- Although my topic is capital punishment, I will focus on one aspect of that larger issue: the execution of convicts who are mentally ill.
- Although we interviewed over two hundred doctors in our study, we will discuss only three of them in detail here.
- In the following essay, I will be discussing only the first edition of *Leaves of Grass,* and my claims may or may not apply to Whitman's later editions.

14.4.5 Body Paragraphs

As you build support for your thesis in the "body" paragraphs, always ask yourself if you are spending your readers' time wisely. Are you writing unnecessarily complex and confusing sentences, or using 50 words when 5 would do? If a sentence is already plain and direct, there's no need to fluff it up. Flowery words and phrases obscure your ideas: when writing, being *concise* is key. For example, why write, "Cats have a tendency toward sleeping most of the day" when you could simply write, "Cats usually sleep most of the day"? How about changing "The 12th day of the month of April" to "April 12th?" Try to pick out such sentences and substitute simpler ones.

But wait--don't you need to inflate your text so you can meet the minimum word count? Wouldn't it be better to use "due to the fact that" for "because" and "in addition to" for "and," since these phrases use far more words? Answer: NO. Any experienced reader will instantly see through such a pitiful scheme and will likely become irritated by the resulting "flabby" prose. If you are having trouble meeting the minimum word count, a far better solution is to add more examples, details, quotations, or perspectives. Go back to the planning and drafting stage and really ask yourself if you've written everything useful about a topic.

Other students worry that their sentences don't sound smart enough. Compare these two sentences:

- Do not ask what your country can do for you; ask what you can do for your country.
- Do not submit a query concerning what assets and benefits your country can bestow upon you and yours, but rather inquire as to what tasks or activities you yourself can perform and carry out that will be useful for the citizens of your own country.

Although the second sentence is longer and harder to grasp, that doesn't make it more intelligent. In fact, it's far more impressive to write a complex thought in simple prose than vice versa.

How about your organization? From sentence-to-sentence, paragraph-to-paragraph, the ideas should flow into each other smoothly and without interruptions or delays. If someone tells you that your paper sounds "choppy" or "jumps around," you probably have a problem with organization and transitions.

Keep in mind that very few writers can write a well-organized paper in one draft. Instead, their first drafts are disorganized and even chaotic. It takes patience to sort through this mess, consolidating related ideas into coherent paragraphs and helping the reader to follow their train of thought without derailing. Compare:

- Proofreading is an important step in the writing process. Read your paper aloud to catch errors. Use spell check on your computer.
- Proofreading is an important step in the writing process. One technique is to read your paper aloud, which will help you catch errors you might overlook when reading silently. Another strategy is to use spell check on your computer.

The second example has better transitions between ideas and is easier to read. Note that the example with better transitions is also longer. Good transitions can improve your style and help you reach the minimum word count!

14.4.6 Conclusions

After all the work you have exerted on your paper, you want to end with a **good conclusion**. The conclusion and the introduction may be similar but may take several forms. Conclusions may be a simple restatement of your thesis to reestablish what the entire paper is about. They may also sum up your main points, reflect on the information presented, ask a thought-provoking question, or present a "call to action," telling your readers what you want them to do with the information you have presented. Often, this choice will be determined by the genre, audience, or purpose of your paper. Nevertheless, your conclusion should accurately reflect the paper's subject and provide the reader with closure.

Be sure not to end a paper with new ideas or a thesis you have not already dealt with in the paper.

14.5 Before and After Revision Examples

14.5.1 Example Before Revision

Household Chore Divisions When We Get Married

My mom does almost everything at our house. She cooks, cleans, does laundry, vacuums, and when my sisters and I were younger, she did most of the child care – not fair! My father, on the other hand, clips the hedges, waters the lawn, and snow-blows the driveway. He makes more money than my mom. My sisters and I take care of mowing the lawn, washing dishes, cleaning the bathrooms, and scrubbing the floors. I was interested to know how Pete and I will split chores once we are married because there (ideally) will not be as large of an earning gap between the two of us as there is between my parents.

Pete and I discussed and debated a lot as we went through the "list of chores". I tried to stand my ground on percentages of time that I should do a chore unless Pete was able to give me a reasonable explanation of why I should do a greater percentage of something than he does; he did the same, and so this assignment was a great communication tool and gave us the opportunity to confer on possible problems which may occur somewhere down the road.

My boyfriend Pete and I talk a lot about getting married. We are now college seniors, so it just seems like the next step in the progression of our relationship. We figure, however, that we will wait until I am done with law school and he has his PhD before we do it. Although that brings us to at least 6 years from now we agree that it will be better if we are financially stable before getting married.

Pete and I have decided to split chores almost evenly. I will be doing 44.43% of the total things that will need to get done. He will be doing 43.24% of them. We decided that our son, who will be named Christian, was old enough to help with some of the chores. Some of the other things, we decided, would be worth paying an outside source to do. Income tax returns, for example, we concluded could be better and more efficiently taken care of by a CPA. We found that I will be doing 50.25% of the housework, while Pete will be doing 43.17%. We also found that I will be doing 10% of the occasional work while Pete will be doing 63.33%. I will do 60% of the child care, and Pete will do 40%. I seem to be doing more daily tasks, and Pete seems to be doing more occasional tasks.

I think that this assignment was a good starting point for a discussion between Pete and myself. I am going to be a lawyer and he is going to be a chemist. Both of our schedules will be tight, and we will have to find a better compromise in real life then we did in our imaginary one. If we do not, neither one of us will be truly satisfied.

From the results of this assignment, I will be doing more of the traditionally "female work", and Pete will be doing more "male work". I think that our assigned careers play a part in this but not as much as I would like. I think that although we have broken many of the stereotypes that control my parents, we are still following some of them. When I look over the results it seems odd that Pete will be doing more of the ironing than I, but he taught me to iron and his job calls for more ironed clothes than mine. We also figured that he will have a little more leeway on time as a manager than I will as a lawyer. Thus, he will be getting the kids ready for school. We broke a couple of stereotypes, but we still have a ways to go before reaching equality.

Sample Essay

14.5.2 Example After Revision

Household Chore Divisions When We Get Married

My boyfriend Pete and I talk a lot about getting married. We are now college seniors, so it just seems like the next logical step in our relationship. We figure, however, that we will wait until I am done with law school and he has his PhD before we do it. Although that brings us to at least six years from now, we agree that it will be better if we are financially stable before getting married.

My mom does almost everything in the home where I was raised. She cooks, cleans, does laundry, vacuums, and when my sisters and I were younger, she did most of the child care – hardly fair or equal! My dad, on the other hand, clips the hedges, waters the lawn, and snow-blows the driveway. My sisters and I take care of mowing the lawn, washing dishes, cleaning the bathrooms, and scrubbing the floors. My dad does make more money than my mom, but it seems to me like she is somehow "making up" for her lack of earning by being a servant. I was interested to know how Pete and I will split chores once we are married because there (ideally) will not be so large an earning gap between the two of us as there is between my parents.

Pete and I discussed and debated a lot as we went through the "list of chores." I tried to stand my ground on percentages of time that I should do a chore unless Pete was able to give me a reasonable explanation of why I should do a greater percentage of something than he does. He did the same, and so this assignment was a great communication tool and gave us the opportunity to confer on possible problems that may occur somewhere down the road. Pete and I have decided to split chores almost evenly. I will be doing 44.43% of the total things that will need to get done. He will be doing 43.24% of them. We decided that when our child was old enough to help with some of the chores, he or she will be. Some of the other things, we decided, would be worth paying an outside source to do. Income tax returns, for example, could be taken care of more efficiently by a CPA. We found that I will be doing 50.25% of the housework, while Pete will be doing 43.17% of the housework. We also found that I will be doing 10% of the occasional work while Pete will be doing 63.33% of the occasional work. I will do 60% of the child care, and Pete will do 40% of the child care. I seem to be doing more daily tasks, and Pete seems to be doing more occasional tasks.

From the results of this assignment, I will be doing more of the traditionally "female work," and Pete will be doing more "male work." I think that our assigned careers play a part in this but not as much as I would like. I think that although we have broken many of the stereotypes to which my parent subscribe, we are still following some of them. When I look over the results, it seems odd, gender-task speaking, that Pete will be doing more of the ironing than I, but he taught me to iron and his job calls for more ironed clothes than mine. We also figured that he will have a little more leeway on time as a manager than I will as a lawyer. Because of this, he will be getting the kids ready for school in the morning. We broke a couple of stereotypes, but we still have a way to go before reaching equality.

I think that this assignment was a good discussion starting point for Pete and me. I am going to be a lawyer and he is going to be a chemist. Both of our schedules will be tight, and we will have to find a better compromise in our real life then we did in our imaginary one. If we do not, neither one of us will be truly satisfied.

Sample Essay

14.5.3 Notes

With only a few changes made, notice how much nicer the Example After Revision reads than the Example Before Revision.

1. The order of a few paragraphs was re-arranged. Notice how the focus changes perspective from the past to the present. It immediately centers and controls what the author wants the reader to "see" and sets the tone for the rest of the essay. Also, notice the way the author repeats the words "Pete and I" to keep the reader on track. Notice that the paragraph that was moved to the beginning provides a more solid introduction. It immediately tells the reader why the rest of the essay is relevant. The writer is considering getting married so it is a good time to talk about household chores. This puts the rest of the essay into context and helps orient the reader to what will be coming and why the author wrote the essay. The concluding paragraph was also rearranged and now offers a more accurate summary of the essay as a whole. The example before the revision had a concluding paragraph that veered off topic to deal with the idea of gender roles, which, although mentioned, is not the main idea.

2. Punctuation was included **inside** of quotation marks rather than **outside** quotation marks. This makes for easier reading and tells your reader/professor that you are conscious of the proper technique when quoting, and keeps the clarity of the speaker consistent.

3. "6" was changed to "six." Be aware of numbers in your writing. Generally, the rule is to spell out numbers one through nine and use numerals for numbers 10 or higher.

4. Some material was added to the Example After Revision for clarity. When you believe something can be added or taken away to provide your reader with a better idea of your meaning or thought process, do so. Clarity is extremely important when writing a paper. If your reader becomes confused, this will damage the paper's effectiveness. Do your best to guide your reader, so there will be little to no *re-reading* and a grade to reflect this.

14.6 External Links

- 18 Revising Tips[1]
- Revision Checklist[2]
- Paradigm Online Writing Assistant[3]
- Revision: From First to Final Draft[4]

---

1   http://www.rpi.edu/dept/llc/writecenter/web/revise.html
2   http://writingcenter.tamu.edu/content/view/27/14/
3   http://www.powa.org/revising/
4   http://www.hamilton.edu/academics/resource/wc/Revision.html

15 Publishing

16 Overview

> "It is now possible for any writer with a book to get it published at nominal cost or free, and to have it on sale at booksellers like Amazon.com."
>
> --Piers Anthony

All authors who publish books and articles have at least one thing in common: they believe their work is interesting, desirable, or useful to other people. Many texts, such as this Rhetoric and Composition wikitext, are published online and are available for free, without any paid authors or editors. Although many authors and readers prefer print publications, it is now entirely possible to earn a good living writing exclusively for the web.

Getting published may seem unlikely or even impossible, but there are readily available resources to help you. If you are interested in freelance writing for magazines, the *Writer's Market* is probably one of the most accessible and helpful sources (see below). If you are interested in publishing scholarly or professional research, you will need to familiarize yourself with the journals and book publishers associated with your field.

It is very important to know a publisher's expectations before sending them a manuscript. Pay close attention to the publisher's policies; some do not accept any unsolicited manuscripts, and many have strict rules about formatting, subject matter, and deadlines. Don't waste time and money sending out manuscripts that are certain to be rejected.

If you want to send an idea for a potential article or book to an editor, you may do this in a query letter. A query letter should be short and to the point. The point is to interest the editor into buying your idea or article or at least requesting a book proposal or entire manuscript. Included in a query letter is a strong opening lead about the article, book, or piece, a description of the development or structure and content, any other information or images you intend to include, why you are qualified to write the piece, and a solid closing requesting to write or submit the piece. It would be wise to include a deadline for reply.

17 Types of Publication

The first thing you should do is figure out what type of publishing venue is appropriate for your needs.

17.1 Do-It-Yourself Print Publishing

Print publication is the oldest and most traditional way to earn a living as a writer and flourish as an academic. Unfortunately, printing books is an expensive process, and you may find it difficult to interest a publisher in your work. Anyone, however, can pay out of pocket to have a book published by a vanity press. The results are often quite good, with a slick and glossy production that is indistinguishable from other books. If you have a manuscript with very limited commercial appeal (such as a history of your family or hometown), or want to control the marketing of the book yourself, a vanity press may be the way to go. Costs vary depending on the size and types of illustrations used in the book.

17.2 Academic Publishing

Academic publishing is how scholars share their research and critically review other works. This type of publishing includes academic journals and books in the sciences and humanities. You are probably most familiar with academic journals in electronic form, since many college libraries offer access to extensive databases of journal articles in electronic form, such as JSTOR and Elsevier's Science Direct. Categories for journals range from physics and geometry to education and art, but all are written for other scholars in a particular field. Authors are rarely paid for publishing articles in academic journals--the reward comes instead in the form of increased prestige or a promotion.

17.3 Commercial Publishing

Commercial publishing means writing for profit and is the way the majority of professional authors earn their living. Commercial publication can include books, articles, journals, magazines, and more. If you want to become a professional author, you should research the publishers who publish in your fields of interest. Familiarize yourself with their titles and consider how your work will complement their existing selections. Visit their websites or call them to learn how they solicit manuscripts. Some will only accept manuscripts delivered to them by agents. In any case, you will need to convince the publisher that your work has commercial value and an adequate audience of potential readers.

Writer's Market is a well-known resource for freelance writers. It offers market information, tips for getting published, advice from agents and editors, and formatting information. These services are available in the *Writer's Market* book and at WritersMarket.com[1]. There is an annual or monthly fee for online access.

17.4 Electronic Publication

Publishing your work online can take many forms, such as blogs, wikis, Adobe PDF files, e-books, and so on. There are plenty of easy ways to make your works available online for free, but earning a profit on them is a different matter. The Amazon Kindle and Apple iPad have opened up new opportunities for writers and publishers interested in selling electronic works. Also, many formerly print-based newspapers and magazines now offer websites, many with original articles published exclusively online. Search the websites for information about submitting a manuscript or query. While the pay is unlikely to match that of print publications, there are still plenty of opportunities to support yourself as a freelance author.

Freelance Writing

Writing, unfortunately, cannot always be done simply for the love of writing. Unless one has a wealthy spouse or a bursting portfolio, spending a significant amount of time writing requires that you treat it like a business. The freelance writer must be part writer, and part business-person. In fact, when considering everything involved in maintaining a living as a freelance writer, the career is similar to that of a small-buisness owner. It involves secure jobs, setting prices, and negotiating skills.

This lifestyle may conjure up images of endless travel and world experience, but the fact is, you never get a paid vacation. Writing for publication results in jobs being canceled, payment delays, and payment shortcomings. One must be very careful in factoring the amount of money he/she will receive each month, as it can sometimes take months to get paid.

---

1   http://www.writersmarket.com/

18 Your Rights

As a writer seeking publication, you should know your rights. Anything you write is automatically protected by copyright--no one else is permitted to publish it without your permission. When you find a publisher, you will likely sign a contract that transfers some or all of your copyright to the publisher. Contracts can be confusing and difficult for authors to understand; it is often worth finding an agent who can negotiate contracts with publishers to better suit your interest. Many terms of a contract can be negotiated, such as how long the publisher retains exclusive rights to publish your work, what media they can use to publish it, or even who controls the movie or television rights.

There are also alternatives to standard copyright, such as Creative Commons[1] licensing. Creative Commons licenses vary in scope and coverage, but the basic idea is that anyone is allowed to copy and distribute your work without getting your permission first.

---

1   http://creativecommons.org/

19 External Links

There are plenty of websites dedicated to supporting aspiring writers of all types. See the links below for more information.

- Academic publishing[1]. Wikipedia's entry on academic publishing has lots of information and links for scholars and researchers.
- WritersMarket.com[2]. Find places to sell your writing, whether you've got a book, manuscript, or article idea.
- Writing Guide Online vs. Print Publishing[3]. Discusses the differences between print and online publishing. Intended for novice publishers.

---

1   http://en.wikipedia.org/wiki/Academic_publishing/
2   http://www.writersmarket.com/
3   http://writing.colostate.edu/guides/processes/onlinepub/

20 Writing Applications

21 Overview of Writing Applications

21.1 Overview

The first part of this book is about the stages of the writing process. Now it's time to shift gears and start thinking about the kinds of assignments you're likely to encounter in college. Each "writing mode" requires a different mode of thinking, and that's why teachers and professors often ask for different kinds of writing (they want you to think about a subject in a variety of ways). But generally, assignments will require you to apply several modes, simultaneously, to accomplish a well-rounded body of writing. Few professors beyond the first-year level of coursework require an assignment that merely focuses on description or narration; other modes are required to generate a well-rounded piece of writing that entertains, informs, and persuades (i.e., narrative, explication, argument).

Most of the time, you'll find yourself switching among all of these modes as you write. You would have a hard time, for instance, reviewing a car without spending any time describing it, and the strength of an argument depends on how well you've evaluated its evidence. What's important is that you recognize the difference between them. Many students lose points each year when they offer their teacher a description instead of the evaluation or argument called for by the assignment. Below, we first give you some hints about analyzing assignments to find out what different types of writing task you need to do. Then, we break down some common writing modes, telling you their characteristics and what makes them unique, then offer examples of informal and formal writing that show them in action.

21.1.1 How to analyze an assignment

Writing successfully for your college classes depends a lot on finding out as much as possible about what you need to do to fulfill the assignment each time you write. While many instructors try hard to clarify their expectations, the final responsibility for making sure you know what it takes to fulfill an assignment is yours. Be your own advocate!

This chapter[1] will give you strategies for interpreting assignments successfully and break down eighteen words commonly used in assignments to help you understand what critical and writing tasks you need to do.

21.1.2 Description

One key difference between a good writer and a bad one is the ability to write vivid, detailed descriptions. What does something look like? Sound like? Feel like? Good descriptions

---

1   Chapter 22 on page 99

make all the difference when you're trying to hook readers and keep them interested. We don't want to read, "The house was scary." We want to read a great description of the house that actually makes us feel that fear for ourselves. This can only be accomplished by observant writers who are willing to "show" as well as "tell" their readers about their subject.

This chapter[2] will introduce you to description and offers some good advice about writing highly descriptive essays.

21.1.3 Narration

"Narrative" is really just a fancy way of saying "story." When you are narrating, you are describing an event, step-by-step, usually in the order that it happened. In other words, a "narration" is a "description" of something taking place in time. As you can probably guess, narration and description are highly related. You can't narrate very well if you lack the ability to describe accurately and vividly what is taking place.

This chapter[3] will introduce you to narration and some strategies for telling good stories.

21.1.4 Exposition

Expository writing is writing that explains or informs. You may encounter expository writing in an assignment that has you describing a process or developing a set of clear instructions. You aren't just describing a "what" ("What is fishing?") but explaining a "how" ("How do you fish?"). Writers with excellent exposition skills are generally good learners, since describing processes well requires a thorough understanding of the process.

This chapter[4] offers tips and suggestions for expository writing and some helpful examples.

21.1.5 Evaluation

Magazines like *Consumer Reports* and movie reviewers like Roger Ebert are famous for the quality of their evaluative writings. They give people the information they need to determine if a car is worth buying or a movie is worth seeing. You'll also find lots of evaluations in business, in which they are used to determine an employee's eligibility for promotion or a manager's effectiveness at overseeing an important project.

This chapter[5] will tell you all about evaluative writing and the strategies you'll need to do it right.

21.1.6 Argumentation

Some people think of arguments as a lot of shouting and cursing (but that's not what college professors mean when they use the term "argumentation"). What they have in mind

---

2   Chapter 23 on page 107
3   Chapter 24 on page 117
4   Chapter 25 on page 123
5   Chapter 26 on page 129

is a clear-headed, logical, and convincing style of speaking or writing that makes a valid point and supports it with good evidence. An argument isn't just summarizing or restating what others may have said about an issue. You'll need to research the issue, evaluate the evidence, reach a conclusion, figure out the best way to support it, and arrange your thoughts effectively. Writing a good argumentative paper is probably the most difficult of all types of writing assignments, but we'll give you advice and discuss some strategies that will get you on the right track.

This chapter[6] describes what college professors mean by the term "argumentation," and discuss some methods that will earn good grades on these common but challenging assignments.

---

6   Chapter 27 on page 133

22 Analyzing Assignments

22.1 Snowflakes, Fingerprints, and Assignments

Writing assignments in college differ as much as instructors. There is no one guidebook, approach, or set of rules that college teachers will consult when putting together their coursework. Since each assignment will always be unique, it is important to devote time to thoroughly understanding what is being asked of you before beginning. Don't wait until the night before the work is due to begin asking questions and delving in. The sooner you understand and approach the assignment's requirements, the less time you will spend second-guessing (and needlessly revising) your writing.

22.2 Analyzing an Assignment

You will likely encounter many different kinds of writing assignments in college, and it would be nearly impossible to list all of them. However, regardless of genre, there are some basic strategies one can use to approach these assignments constructively.

- **Read the assignment sheet early and thoroughly.** An assignment sheet may be lengthy, but resist the temptation to skim it. Read every word. It would be unfortunate to hand in an incomplete or misguided assignment because you did not properly read and understand the guidelines. Since you can easily overlook details on the first reading, read the assignment sheet a second time. As you are reading, highlight areas where you have questions, and also mark words you feel are particularly important. Ask yourself why your professor has given this assignment. How does it relate to what you are studying in class? Pay attention to key words, such as *compare, contrast, analyze*, etc. Who is your audience? Should the paper be written in a formal or informal tone? Is there documentation required? If a specific number of sources are required, how many must be books vs. online sources? What type of citation is called for: APA, MLA, Chicago, etc.? Is there a page or word count minimum/maximum? Are you required to submit a draft before the final copy? Will there be peer review?
- **Get answers to your questions.** After thoroughly reading the assignment sheet, you might not have questions right away. However, after reading it again, either before or or after you try to start the assignment, you might find that you have questions. Don't play a guessing game when it comes to tackling assignment criteria--ask the right person for help: the instructor. Discuss any and all questions with the person who assigned the work, either in person or via email. Visit him or her during office hours or stay after class. Do not wait until the last minute, as doing so puts your grade at risk. Don't be shy about asking your professors questions. Not only will you better your understanding and the outcome of your paper, but professors tend to enjoy and benefit from student

inquiry, as questions help them rethink their assignments and improve the clarity of their expectations. You likely are not the only student with a question, so be the one who is assertive and responsible enough to get answers. In the worst case scenario, when you have done all of these things and a professor still fails to provide you with the clarity you are looking for, discuss your questions with fellow classmates.

- **Writing Centers.** Many colleges and universities have a writing center. Tutors are helpful consultants for reviewing writing assignments both before and after you begin. If you feel somewhat confident about what you need to include in your writing assignment, bring your completed outline and/or the first draft of your paper together with your assignment sheet. Tutors can also review your final draft before its submission to your professor. Many writing centers allow you to make appointments online for convenience and may also have "walk-in" availability. It is a good idea to check out the available options a week or so in advance of when you will actually need the appointment, or even longer if it will be during mid-term or finals week.

- **Create a timeline.** Set due dates for yourself, whether they be to have a topic picked or a whole rough draft completed. Procrastination rarely results in a good paper. Some school libraries offer helpful computer programs that can create an effective assignment timeline for you. This is a helpful option for new, inexperienced writers who have not yet learned the art of analyzing assignments, and who are not familiar with the amount of time that is required for the college writing process. Remember, late papers may or may not be accepted by your instructor, and even if they are your grade will likely be reduced. Don't sell yourself short with late submissions.

22.3 Prewriting and Brainstorming

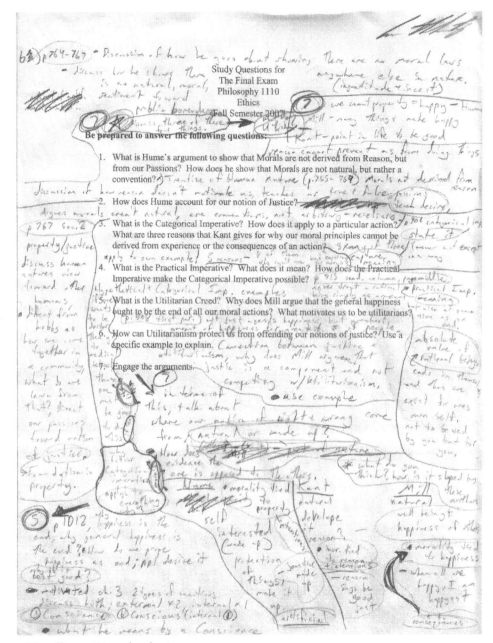

Figure 13   Prewriting Analysis

Every writing assignment from every discipline requires the formulation of complex ideas. Thus, once the assignment guidelines have been thoroughly considered, you should begin to explore how you plan structure your work in order to meet them. While this is often considered to be the start of the writing process, it is also an essential part of assignment analysis, as it is here that the assignment is broken down into the most digestible parts. Such a process can be done either individually or in a group, depending on the situation.

- **Prewriting.** The first and foremost stage of the individual writing process is that of Prewriting. Often overlooked by inexperienced writers, this is essentially the architectural stage of the writing/analysis process, where the foundations of an assignment are first laid out and constructed. *Free-writing, outlining, diagramming*, and *mapping* are all possible approaches to this stage of development, where the goal is to organize one's ideas around the requirements of the task at hand. Many people begin this right on the assignment sheet, as it can be helpful to highlight what the instructor is specifically asking for while simultaneously adding one's own understanding to the ideas. Eventually though, you will want to move to a separate page. If you are *free-writing*, you should start by writing out an assignment related question or main concept, and then proceed to freely (with or without punctuation or formality) write anything that comes to mind in relation to it. If you are *outlining*, you are essentially breaking down the main ideas of the assignment and your response to them in a linear format (by paragraph, subject, section, subsection etc.). If you are *diagramming*, your prewriting can take many different forms, but always as a visual representation of your response to some/all of the assignment constituents. Lastly, if you are *mapping*, you are essentially *outlining* in a more visual way, using both linear and non-linear representation to organize your ideas about the assignment. *Research* can also be conducted during this stage of the writing/analysis process, as it is sometimes helpful to know more about a topic before you make the commitment to writing about it. You may even choose to use more than one of these approaches if you find it helpful in developing your understanding of the assignment.

- **Brainstorming.** Similar to prewriting, brainstorming takes place in the space between analysis and drafting, the difference being that brainstorming generally involves group discussion. The size of a brainstorming group varies according to task, but ideally consists of smaller odd numbers (3, 5, or 7) when there is no assigned mediator present. There are obviously many pitfalls to such group discussion, and many divergent possibilities (distractions, freeloading, repetition, etc.) that can lead to counter-productivity. Nonetheless, if all members are devoted to the task of analysis and development, the variety of perspectives can prove to be most rewarding. If all goes well, each member of the group takes turns posing questions related to the assignment being discussed, to which the other members respond openly and freely. When positive attitudes and constructive criticism can manage to be maintained, each member of the group will have his or her own critical thinking expanded upon and enriched by the understanding of the other group members.

22.4 Sample Assignments

As discussed earlier, instructors will come up with any number of assignments, most of which will stress different types of composition. In each section below, there are sample assignment directions and suggestions on how to proceed. What follows is not meant to be a comprehensive list of assignments, but rather a short list of the most common assignments you can expect to see in an introductory English course. Many assignments not listed here are simply creative variations of these basic directives. For example, you could approach a visual analysis the same way you would a rhetorical analysis; an argument paper is similar to a research paper, perhaps with a shorter argument. The techniques you use in writing a narrative can also translate into writing a short story or observational essay.

22.4.1 Research Paper

For this paper, you will take a position on a topic of either local or national interest. Research the topic thoroughly, making sure you know all sides of the debate, and decide what your position will be.

Your task is to write an 8 to 10 page research paper convincing your audience of your point of view. You are required to use at least 8 sources, 4 of which should be scholarly (peer reviewed). You will use MLA format for your in-text citations and Works Cited page. Remember, the key to a good debate is knowing the opposition. Therefore, some of your sources and paper should be dedicated to such. Use this as an opportunity to show how your viewpoint is conclusive.

You will likely have to write a research paper of a significant length during college. Students are usually overwhelmed by the page count and the struggle to come up with a paper topic. Sometimes, in an attempt to make sure he or she reaches the page minimum, students choose very broad research categories like welfare or the death penalty. Believe it or not, these extensive topics generally do not make for great papers, simply because there is too much information to cover. Narrow topics allow for more in-depth research and writing. Choosing a topic takes time and research, so don't be surprised if your instructor requires your topic ahead of time. This is to make sure you do not leave all of your research until the last minute. Look online for topics that interest you and write down a few notes about what is going on in that field. Since a research paper generally involves an argument, you must pick a topic that has two sides. One-sided, fact-based arguments such as "smoking is bad for your health," are not suitable for research papers.

Look at the assignment sheet for key words. What is the purpose of the paper? To argue. What are your requirements? Not only are there page requirements, but also source requirements. What are scholarly sources? How do you judge the credibility of a source? Are you familiar with MLA?

There is one mistake that is very easy to make: confusing an argumentative research paper with an expository one. Don't let your argumentative research paper become an informational report where you simply list information on a topic (expository writing). Unless explicitly stated, that is not your assignment.

22.4.2 Narrative

A narrative can be defined as a story or account of an experience or event. Think of a moment or experience that you found to be particularly important, meaningful, humorous, etc., and describe this event. Events do not have to be extraordinary large or dramatic to be important and fun to read--a snapshot of what happened while you were sitting at a stoplight can be just as entertaining as a story about being in a tornado.

Narratives are a favorite first assignment for instructors, as it is assumed that most people find it easiest to write about what they are familiar with. At the same time, the idea of self-reflective writing can be very intimidating. Most students have fantastic stories to tell, but inevitably edit themselves too early by worrying that their stories might not be "important" enough.

However, the assignment clearly states that you should not worry about your narrative concerning a large event. One of the key words is "describe." Therefore, the most important part of the assignment is your use of description ("show, don't tell"). Prewrite and describe a few ideas you might want to talk about. Pick one of them and start writing down as many descriptive details as you can think of about the event. Who were you with? Where were you? What was the weather like? What did the building look like? What were you thinking? How did you feel? What did you learn? Recording these concrete details will help guide you through your narrative. Don't forget to include as many sensory perceptions (taste, touch, sight, sound, and smell) as possible to paint the clearest picture of what you are trying to describe to your reader.

At this point, you still might be worried about the "importance" of the story. While it is true that your story should come to some sort of point, themes usually develop naturally in a story. If you begin your story with an agenda, you'll often find yourself describing the theme and not the event itself. Allow the themes to develop, and do not try to force them unto the page.

22.4.3 Rhetorical Analysis

A rhetorical analysis calls for students to closely read a text and determine several characteristics about it (author, context, purpose, emotional appeal/effects, etc). For this assignment, you will read "A Modest Proposal" by Jonathan Swift and write a rhetorical analysis. Remember, this is not a reflection piece, but rather a deep look at the tone, style, and intended audience, as well as ethos, logos, and pathos.

At first, a rhetorical analysis sounds somewhat difficult. However, analyzing just means making a conscious effort to read each word carefully and think about what the author is doing. The first step would be to read the piece, not once, but two or three times. Highlight important passages and take notes. For this assignment, the instructor wanted students to write about ethos, logos, and pathos, which are rhetorical terms you should become familiar with. Pay attention to specific word choices that may evoke emotion, or any facts the author may have put forward in the text. Look at the background of the author as well as the time period in which he or she was writing. Consider the tone of the piece. Is it formal/informal/serious/humorous? These are all things to keep in mind while reading. Make an ongoing list of the author's rhetorical techniques that you may want to discuss in your paper.

Remember to be mindful of your essay's organization. It is easy to discuss three different topics in one paragraph and jump back and forth from one idea to the next, but this makes it difficult for your reader to follow. Also, do not forget that this is not a reflection. For this assignment, the instructor isn't concerned with your reaction to the text, or your ability to summarize; he or she wants to gauge your analytical skills.

22.4.4 Summary/Response Paper

> Read Martin Luther King Jr.'s "Letter from Birmingham Jail." Give a brief summary of the article and a response. Cite specific examples and avoid generalizations.

Before writing a summary, it is important to use your critical reading skills. First, read the article carefully. It might help to write down the main point of each paragraph in the margin next to it. Next, reread the article and look carefully for the main points the author is trying to get across. Look for things the author states explicitly, as well as what is implied by things that are not clearly stated. Look for any biases or missing information. Ask yourself questions while you read, such as "what is the big picture here? What is the author really trying to get across with this or that example?" The title will often provide a clue about the author's main point. Most of all, slow down and take the time to reread the article several times. In summarizing an article, think about how you would explain its message to someone who hasn't read it. What are the main points of the piece? What is necessary to know about the work in order to understand it?

While writing a summary is a familiar assignment from grade school, in college, summaries are no longer enough, and instructors will frequently require a response. Writing a response is giving your opinion about the text. However, statements such as "I did/did not like it" are not sufficient. Not only must you be more descriptive with your opinions, but you need to support them. If you do not think that an author provided enough information to prove his or her point, state the specific flaws and what could be done to improve them. The same rule applies for any emotions felt while reading the text. Instead of just saying the writing made you sad, point out a specific passage in the text that made you feel that way. Talk about the word choices the author used and how that affected your reading.

It is important to note the word "brief" in the assignment sheet. The instructor does not want a two-page summary and then a paragraph of reflection. Your response should take up the bulk of the paper.

22.5 Finishing the Assignment

Remember, no matter what the assignment, identifying key words in guidelines can help you determine what type of thinking and ability the professor wants you to demonstrate. The following six areas of competencies are from Bloom's Taxonomy. To learn more, visit: `http://jerz.setonhill.edu/writing/style/taxonomy.htm`.

- **Knowledge**: This becomes evident in how well you remember the subject matter, such as the major ideas, dates, places, events, etc. Questions may begin with: Identify, describe, examine, when, where, who.

- **Comprehension**: How well you understand the information presented. Can you describe the information in your own words? Questions may begin with: Interpret, contrast, predict, discuss.
- **Application**: Can you use the principles learned to solve other problems in different situations? Questions may begin with: Illustrate, examine, modify, experiment, relate.
- **Analysis**: Can you recognize hidden meanings, see patterns, identify the underlying parts? Questions may begin with: Separate, order, connect, classify, divide, explain.
- **Synthesis**: Can you relate knowledge from different areas to draw conclusions? Questions may begin with: Modify, rearrange, substitute, design, invent, generalize.
- **Evaluation**: This involves verifying the value of the evidence when solving controversies, developing opinions, etc. Questions may begin with: Decide, convince, select, compare, summarize.

If you need clarification on what your instructor is looking for, do not hesitate to ask. After you have finished your paper, be sure to double-check that you have fulfilled all the requirements. Proofread your paper multiple times before handing in the final copy.

23 Description

23.1 What is Description?

Description is the process by which a writer describes things he or she senses in order to communicate those senses to the reader. Descriptive language frequently makes use of sensory language, or language that appeals to one or more of the five senses (touch, sight, smell, taste, and sound). As a descriptive writer, the more vividly you are able to describe what you have sensed, the more engaged audience will be with your text.

Grammatically speaking, descriptive language is the use of nouns and adjectives in order to most specifically describe the experiences of a particular sense. By making the language you use more powerful, you may use description in order to allow your reader to truly sense what you are writing about. To this end, one of description's main goals is making the abstract seem more concrete.

Specific descriptive language has uses outside of describing sensory experience. For example, the abstract idea of freedom may have many evoke different definitions and feelings for different readers, but when described in terms of the freedom given slaves through the Emancipation Proclamation the idea of freedom becomes much more concrete and more uniform among readers. Description is used by writers in order to encourage their audiences to have a more specific reading of a text.

23.2 Why Write a Descriptive Essay?

A descriptive essay allows writers to engage their reader through the use of specific language and imagery. If the writer is trying to convey something that is scary or exciting, a concrete description is usually more effective than a vague or abstract one. These concrete descriptions create specific, vivid images in readers' imaginations. Think of a descriptive essay as being similar to writing a movie. At no time can a movie show beautiful. It must show what 'beautiful' is through the use of images.

A writer usually begins an essay with an objective. If a writer wanted to persuade the reader that ice cream is a tasty treat, what are descriptions that could cause the reader to want to eat ice cream? Would *sweet* sound appetizing? Would comparisons to other foods, such as a cherry, be used to convince the reader that the ice cream is worth trying? When you have begun to think in this fashion, then you are ready to start your essay.

23.3 Abstract Descriptions Versus Concrete Descriptions

Try to avoid vague, abstract descriptions. For example, a writer may write *beautiful* to describe a tree. However, *beautiful* is too vague. Instead, a concrete adjective or modifier would be stronger and gives greater impact. The reader needs details for a picture to form in their heads, abstract concepts like *beautiful* lack a real-world analog. Here's a reworked description of the tree: "the sun's rays glistened off the rain-slick leaves, even as the afternoon sky dipped towards evening." The *beautiful* qualities of the tree are "shown" through concrete details instead of merely told through abstraction. This gives the reader the illusion of immediate experience, as opposed to the dictionary variety

Abstract Descriptions

Figure 14   How would you use concrete language to describe this "cute" dog?

Abstractions are often ideas that cannot be seen, heard, touched, or smelled.

Examples of abstract descriptions:

- the sad man
- the happy woman
- the beautiful dog
- a lovely house
- an amazing sight

Concrete Descriptions

A concrete description can be seen, heard, touched, or smelled.

Examples of concrete details:

- the crunching sound
- the melted candy cane
- the burnt toast
- the flashing light
- the smooth butter

There are appropriate times to use abstractions. For instance, if the reader is already aware of the circumstances (i.e., a writer is referring to a passage from a novel, in which the audience knows of a certain event) then the writer can generalize the emotion. However, especially in creative works such as fiction and poetry, it is best to turn the abstract into the concrete.

23.4 Similes and Metaphors

Another way to add descriptive language is to use similes and metaphors, creating a picture in readers' heads by comparing two objects to one another. Similes and metaphors help to make connections between two ideas, concepts, or objects that clarify or give new meaning.

A simile is a comparison using the words like or as. It usually compares two dissimilar objects. For example, the bread was as dry as a bone. The comparison links a piece of bread that has become hard and white to a bone that is also hard and white. Bones often dry out, and so does bread. These similar characteristics are what make the simile effective.

A metaphor states that one thing is something else. It is a comparison, but it does NOT use like or as to make the comparison. For example, the athlete's stomach was a bottomless pit. The comparison implies that the athlete's stomach will not fill up easily or quickly. The athlete can eat lots of food.

To make a simile or metaphor, identify an object like a sunset, tree, or river, or a concept like love, peace, or anger. Then think of another object that has some similar traits. Decide whether the words "like" or "as" will help make the connection more understandable. A good simile or metaphor will make the reader look at both objects in a new perspective.

By adding similes and metaphors to a description paper, the writer can appeal to the readers' imagination and make the writing more interesting to read. Similes and metaphors add spark to descriptions.

23.5 How to Write Description

In order to write descriptively, you must take a topic and decide how to make that topic vivid for your audience. If the topic of the piece is merely to describe a particular place, you must decide what elements of that place, when described in text, will become most vivid for your audience. The first step in any descriptive writing is to choose a topic and begin to work out a thesis statement. As was suggested in the previous sections, you may choose to describe a particular place.

23.5.1 Thesis

Sample Thesis Statement: *Although Minnesota may seem drab and cold to outsiders, natives of the state find it a wonderful place to live.*

We can see in this thesis statement that the writer will attempt to show the aspects of Minnesota that make it a great place to live. After detailing a thesis statement, you should come up with a list of sensory words that provide vivid detail and support the thesis. You may start by thinking about the five senses. How does your particular place look, smell, feel, taste, and sound like? How can you best describe these senses so the reader feels what you feel? By organizing the elements of descriptive language into easier to handle sections, like the five senses, you are able to more specifically engage in what elements of the description are most useful.

23.6 Examples of Sensory Words

Examples of Sound Imagery

- Quiet solitude
- Grasshoppers chirping at night
- Trees rustling in the wind
- The howl of a wolf
- Birds singing
- Leaves crunching
- Fire crackling

Examples of Smell Imagery

- Chlorine at a pool
- Freshly cut grass
- Flowers in spring

- Morning dew,
- Freshly baked banana bread,
- Acrid-campfire smoke.

Examples of Touch Imagery

- Cold, wet snowflakes falling on your nose
- Corse sandpaper
- Rough, dry tree bark
- Wet sand beneath your feet
- Hot pan on the stove

Example of Visual Imagery

- The brilliant rays of sunset
- The churning blue waterfall
- Powerful deer racing across the field
- Clean snow falling softly in the sun
- Corn stalks rustling in the breeze

Examples of Taste Imagery

- Lutefisk or lefsa during the holidays
- Steaming, bitter black coffee
- Fresh, succulent strawberries
- Crunchy chocolate chip cookies
- Cotton candy, sweetly melting in your mouth

After deciding what senses you wish to invoke, make a list of all the words you wish to include. You should also begin to plan a way to present the information that will drive home the thesis statement in the most profound way.

23.7 Order of Presentation

The writer in this case could choose to present the positive aspects of Minnesota in terms of the seasons and weather changes. The details could be presented linearly, starting with spring and going through the winter, highlighting the aspects of each season that most closely support the thesis, that Minnesota is a great place to live.

Prior to starting the essay, give some thought as to whom the audience of your piece will be. Who is going to read the essay, and what effect would you like it to have upon them? An awareness of audience is important to choosing the level of formality you take with your writing. Knowing your audience will also help you distinguish which details to include throughout your essay. Assume that your audience knows very little or nothing about your subject matter, and include details that may seem very obvious to you.

23.7.1 Audience

Example Audience: In this particular essay, the writer wants to show an outsider to the state why Minnesota natives are so happy to live there. The essay should help break down stereotypes for those outsiders about Minnesota's cold weather and apparent drabness. Because the essay is designed for those who do not live in Minnesota, and maybe have never been there, it is important to include details about the state that may seem obvious to a native.

With the preparatory work complete, it is time now to begin writing your essay. Use your thesis statement to begin to construct an introductory paragraph. The introduction should set up the basis for your essay, and the thesis statement should state its purpose.

23.7.2 Introduction

Example Introduction: *Many who have not traveled to the state of Minnesota only hear of its cold weather and boring reputation. They are sure missing out on the great opportunities that Minnesota affords. Each season offers different senses that native Minnesotans and tourists know and love. Although Minnesota may seem drab and cold to outsiders, natives of the state find it a wonderful place to live.*

With the introduction complete, it is time to start constructing the body paragraphs of your essay. Each body paragraph should have a central theme in itself, and that theme should be represented in a topic sentence. Consequently, each sentence of the paragraph should relate to and support the topic sentence. The body paragraphs are where the majority of the details should be given. When writing the first draft of your descriptive essay, include as many details as is reasonably possible. You can always eliminate the ones that do not serve the essay as well when you are revising your draft. In the case of the Minnesota nature essay, we have decided to set up the body paragraphs in terms of season, starting with spring.

23.7.3 Body

Example Body Paragraph:

Spring in Minnesota brings new life to the state after the long winter season. The rain washes the landscape clean, leaving its fresh aroma for all to enjoy. The flowers soak up the golden sun's rays and begin to show their vibrant colors. The first birds can be seen and heard throughout the woods and fields, telling their stories in beautiful songs. The lakes begin to show their glossy finish as the ice melts away slowly under the heat of the season.

With the body paragraphs complete, it is time to bring the essay to a close with the conclusion. The conclusion should return back to the thesis and provide coherence to the essay. The conclusion should restate the main points of the essay in order to give the reader a final sense of what the essay was meant to portray. There should not be any new material introduced in the conclusion, and the way it is worded should give the reader a sense of finality.

23.7.4 Conclusion

Example Conclusion:

By examining what each of the seasons in Minnesota has to offer, it becomes clear that the state is a truly wonderful place to live or visit. Minnesota is much more than the cold and drab state that many people give it credit for. One visit to the state and anyone can see the great things about Minnesota.

With the essay complete, it is time to reread and revise your essay (also see revision sections of this textbook). Read your first draft and pinpoint all of the descriptor words you used. If possible, go back and add more after the ones you already used in the essay. If you can, read your essay out loud to a friend and have them tell you what images are vivid for them and what images are a little more cloudy. Rework any images that are cloudy with more descriptions. Also check to see if your descriptions have made use of all of the five senses: sound, smell, texture, sight, and taste. Repeat these steps as many times as necessary until you are happy with your product.

23.8 A Second Sample Descriptive Essay

23.8.1 First Draft

In recent years, many of St. Cloud's residents have congregated to Waite Park's stores and businesses for entertainment. However, people who focus their attention entirely on the flashy Crossroads Mall or the giant Parkwood 18 theater are depriving themselves of the fun and tradition of downtown St. Cloud. The downtown bars, stores, and restaurants provide a rich experience that is unlike all others in Minnesota.

Downtown St. Cloud's bars are always overflowing with cheek-stretching smiles, live music, and professionally made beverages. The Tavern on Germain boasts a cozy environment with drinks such as Vodka Sours and Captain Cokes. However, if one is tired of drinking the night away, he/she can go next door for live music ranging from the acoustic-guitar stringing of Leonard Mills to the horn-blaring excitement of Test Tube and the Tuba Players.

Entertainment is not unique to the over twenty-one crowd, especially when visitors can stop by coffee houses such as the Java Joint and the Meeting Grounds. Relax with friends while dining on coffee cakes and drinking them down with cappuccinos. As the laughter of your group erupts, and your nose inhales the aroma of coffee beans and melting chocolate, it becomes easier to take those few extra minutes for a lunch break.

When dinner time arrives, the options of the hungry people are plentiful. Cheese melts while sausage sizzles on the crust of pizza at the House of Pizza. When hungry individuals take a taste of the pie from the House, it melts in a mouth with layers of tickling pepperoni. If pizza is not what's in a person's mind, order a burger at the Green Mill or devour a calzone. Either one will gladly fill an empty stomach.

When dinner concludes, one can travel to some of the shops. Drum beats pound like gorilla dance moves at the Electric Fetus. From the slipperiness of the CD cases featuring covers with Pete Townshend driving his hand across the strings of his guitar, or other records with Mariah Carey singing on the windy stage, a music lover finds it all the Electric Fetus.

From music to tasty treats, St. Cloud's residents can find all that they desire downtown. Choose it instead of an over-crowded mall. It is meant for exploration, and with a little digging, anyone can find what they are looking for.

First Draft of a Sample Descriptive Essay

23.8.2 Second Draft

In recent years, many of St. Cloud's residents have congregated to Waite Park's stores and businesses for entertainment. However, people who focus their attention entirely on the Crossroads Mall or the Parkwood 18 theater are depriving themselves of the fun and tradition of downtown St. Cloud. The downtown bars, stores, and restaurants provide a rich experience that is unlike all others in Minnesota.

For those who seek quiet conversations and steaming-hot drinks to start off your day, downtown St. Cloud can provide them with cozy coffee houses like the Meeting Grounds. Inside, groups of friends unwind with frosted coffee cakes, and individuals with books and newspapers recline with a new mug of cappuccino. As the sun rises in the back of the Meeting Grounds, visitors inhale the aroma of coffee beans and melting chocolate, and it becomes easier for them to take a few extra minutes before leaving for work.

As those work days dip into evenings, hungry downtown patrons, with their stomachs growling in unison, march to any one of the many eateries. Mexican Village spreads the aroma of spices and peppers rolled into a tortilla wrap with thick cuts of beef down the street. However, not to be outdone, House of Pizza strolls out its smell of pepperoni that tickles the nose, but then sends a message to the mouth that says, "Come this way." A wind gust brushes through the downtown area carrying the Green Mill's calzone aroma, which leaves those hungry patrons without an easy answer.

With their stomachs filled, downtown patrons wander down the street to the retail shops. Some of the customers step into the Electric Fetus where the drums beat like avalanches, and the songbirds are in flight with microphones pressed against their lips. Further north, another sound rattles through each person's eardrum: the flipping of smooth pages from Books Revisited, where used literature is sold, stacked, then discovered by bookworms digging through each level. Books may be flipped and songs may blare, but shoes scuff the tile floor of Herbergers—a two-story department store where jewelry and clothing are yanked from the rack just as quickly as they are hung on.

The sun sets and the moon rises, but that just means that St. Cloud's downtown bars will be overflowing with cheek-stretching smiles, wall-shaking music, and lip-licking beverages. The Tavern on Germain rapidly serves drinks such as Vodka Sours and Captain Cokes to customers sitting at their table. Along with the constant guzzling, he/she can go next door for live music ranging from the acoustic-guitar stringing of Leonard Mills to the horn-blaring excitement of Test Tube and the Tuba Players.

Whether their hands are sorting through thin page of paperback books, or their mouths are chewing on the gooey cottage cheese of lasagna, downtown patrons are always on the go to the next hot spot. As the customers reach the end of the downtown St. Cloud district, most are ready to turn around and visit all the stops again. St. Cloud is bustling with retailers that will cause anyone's eyes to take a second glimpse.

Second Draft of a Sample Descriptive Essay

23.9 External Links

- A Brief Guide to Writing Descriptive Essays[1]

---

1   http://www.rscc.cc.tn.us/owl&writingcenter/OWL/Describe.html

- [http://leo.stcloudstate.edu/acadwrite/descriptive.html Checklist of Things to Consider when

24 Narration

24.1 What is Narration?

Narration may serve a variety of purposes in writing. It may serve as the primary mode in a narrative. Narration may also be used just like reasons and examples to support a thesis, based on either fact or invention. Often, it is used to increase reader interest or dramatize a point the writer wants to make. For example, Aesop wrote fables for his clients to use in their legal defense. They were short, easy to remember, and illustrated the client's argument. Traditionally, narration was used to recount the facts of a legal case, in order to put them into context and structure them in the best possible light for the speaker's purpose. Plutarch used narration as the basis for his comparison of Greek and Roman notables. In his 1989 history of the Civil War, *Battle Cry of Freedom*, James MacPherson uses narration to support the theme of the contingency of history. In short, narration has been used as proof for a long time.

24.2 What is Narrative?

A narrative is a constructive format (as a work of speech, writing, song, film, television, video games, photography or theatre) that describes a sequence of non-fictional or fictional events. The word derives from the Latin verb narrare, "to tell", and is related to the adjective gnarus, "knowing" or "skilled". [Oxford English Dictionary Online, "narrate, v.". Oxford University Press, 2007]

- First Person Narrative: A mode of narration where a story is told by one character at a time, speaking from their own perspective only. "I" "My"

- Second Person Narrative: A mode of narration where a story is told with the use of "You" "Your" EXAMPLE: You went to the store before you bought yourself a flower.

- Third Person Narrative: A mode of narration where a story is told with the use of "She" "He" "They" "They'll"

- Multiple Narratives: A mode of narration where a story is told with the use of several narrators which tell the story from different points of view. The task, for readers, is to decide which narrator seems the most reliable for each part of the story.

- Unreliable Narratives: An unreliable narrator is a narrator whose credibility is in question or has been compromised. This narrative mode is one which is developed by an author for various reasons, but is usually done so as to deceive the reader or audience. In most circumstances, unreliable narrators are first-person narrators, but third-person narrators can also be unreliable.

24.3 Elements

The minimum requirements of narration include:

- A beginning, middle, and end
- A main character, perhaps others as well
- A setting in time and place
- Motivated (or caused) action
- Supports the thesis ("It is best to prepare for the days of necessity.")

"The Ant and the Grasshopper"[1]. One example of narration requirements - Aesop's Fables

24.4 Classical Arrangement

The classical arrangement indicates how narration may be used:

- Introduction
- Narrative
- Proposition (thesis)
- Confirmation (more examples, reasons, or narration)
- Refutation (of competing explanations)
- Conclusion[1]

24.5 Modern Practice

Today, writers commonly begin their essay with a short narrative which leads to the thesis:

- Short Narrative
- Thesis
- Supporting examples and reasons
- Opposing viewpoints
- Conclusion

Or, they may use narration to support their argument:

- Introduction
- Thesis
- Supporting examples and reasons
- Narrative
- Conclusion

Many organizational methods exist for incorporating narration into writing. In the end, it will depend on your purpose and audience as to how and where (and even "if") you use it.

- "Shooting An Elephant by George Orwell"[2]

---

1   http://www.bartleby.com/17/1/36.html
2   http://www.online-literature.com/orwell/887/

- "Walden, Chapter 12"[3]

24.6 Student Essay

Below is a description of the process one might go through to write an essay supporting the thesis with narration.

Answer the following questions:

- What is the purpose of your essay? What point do you want to make?
- What specific statement (thesis) do you want your story to support?
- What audience do you wish to address? Your professor? Your classmates? Some fictional audience? This will determine how formal or informal you can be, what assumptions you have of what your audience knows and likes.
- What is your setting, in time and place? Or, where and when does the story take place?
- Which events best illustrate your purpose in telling the story? Which events are clear in your mind, and will be most easily related? What is the best order to relate the events? Treat this question like a brainstorming process, and list as many events as you can remember. Then narrow your list to the most pertinent to your thesis statement and inherent purpose.

In our example essay, the writer may start with the events of his freshman year, going all the way through to his senior year.

- Freshman:
  - I learned to manage my time with practice, schoolwork, and my social life.
  - I learned what it means to earn your status within a group atmosphere.
- Sophomore:
  - I learned to deal with adversity, as I was injured throughout most of the season.
  - I learned to ask for and rely on the help of others when I could not do things on my own.
- Junior:
  - I learned to truly work together to achieve team goals, as we had a very successful season.
  - I learned to present myself as a role model, as I gained some community notoriety.
- Senior:
  - I learned how to present myself as a true leader of a group, as I was elected team captain.
  - I learned to take pride in everything I do because it is the most rewarding.|caption=Events of the Narrative

---

Once you have stated the purpose of your essay, formulated a thesis, selected an audience, identified a setting, and brainstormed the events of your story, it is time to begin writing.

---

3   http://ebooks.adelaide.edu.au/t/thoreau/henry_david/walden/chapter12.html

Keep in mind that the more detail and description you can fit into your essay, the more the story will come alive for the reader. Also, your conclusion should relate how the events in the story changed you as a person with regard to your purpose.

AGLUYA, CRESCINTI BSA-1-C

My experience playing High School basketball taught me skills which will benefit me throughout the rest of my life. It all started during the fall of my freshman year at Otucan Bila National High School, when I quickly found out how important time management is. I had my schoolwork, which was fourteen credits including an extremely difficult Mathematics class. I had basketball, which included meetings and practice every day and running and lifting a couple times of week. I also had my social life, another important aspect, especially to a twelve year old.

My sophomore year taught me how to deal with adversity. I broke my leg during the second game of the season against Team Angels, and I learned how something that seems devastating can be seen in a positive light. I learned that life will always have something unexpected in store, but learning to deal with it makes us stronger people.

My junior year taught me how to set goals and achieve them in a team atmosphere. Our team that year had a mission to make the playoffs, and we were not going to let anything get in our way. We really came together that year because we all had a common goal. I learned that a group can achieve wonderful things if all of the group members work together and believe in each other.

My senior year in basketball taught me how to be a leader. I was elected team captain by my teammates, which showed me that my peers respected me and knew they could rely on me. Leadership does not come easily however. I learned that leadership must not only be earned, but it also must be kept. I was always conscious of the way I acted and spoke, because I knew my teammates were looking to me for strength.

Each year I played High School basketball taught me something not only about myself but also about the nature of the world and the people who inhabit the world. I learned how to balance my time, deal with adversity, the true meaning of teamwork, and how to be a respected leader. These skill-building activities will benefit me throughout the rest of my life.

Sample Narrative

24.7 Revision Hints

As with any form of essay, it is always important to go back and revise the first draft. Proofread the essay carefully, and look for ways to improve its overall appearance. In the case of narration, make sure the story flows for the audience. Do the events of the story make sense? Also, look to make sure that each event relates directly back to the purpose and thesis. Does this particular event reinforce my thesis? When writing a narration, it is also important to look for ways to make the story more vivid for the audience. Go back and include as many descriptive words and details as possible. Once you are satisfied with your product, make a clean and neat final copy.

24.8 External Links

- A Brief Guide to Writing Narrative Essays[4]
- Narrative Essays[5]

[1]D'Angelo, Frank J. *Composition in the Classical Tradition.* Boston: Allyn & Bacon; 2000; p. 22.

4   http://www.roanestate.edu/owl/Describe.html
5   http://leo.stcloudstate.edu/acadwrite/narrative.html

25 Exposition

25.1 What is Exposition Writing?

Exposition can be either oral or written. It is used to explain, interpret, inform, or describe. An expository writer must assume that the audience has no prior knowledge regarding the topic being discussed. So the topic must be written in a clear manner explaining how things work (you can however, leave out *common knowledge*--you probably are not writing for first graders).

As most academic terms, exposition can acquire various definitions depending on the context in which a writer is using the word. The HarperCollins Collins English Dictionary defines exposition in seven different disciplinary contexts.

1. Within the Communication Arts / Journalism & Publishing discipline exposition is defined as: a systematic, usually written statement about, commentary on, or explanation of a specific subject

2. The act of expounding of setting forth information or a viewpoint

3. (Business / Commerce) of a large public exhibition, especially of industrial products or arts and crafts

4. The act of exposing or the state of being exposed

5. (Performing Arts / Theatre) the part of a play, novel, etc., in which the theme and main characters are introduced.

6. (Music / Classical Music) Music the first statement of the subjects or themes of a movement in sonata form or a fugue

7. (Christianity / Roman Catholic Church) RC Church the exhibiting of the consecrated Eucharistic Host or a relic for public veneration (Harper Collins Dictionary)

25.1.1 Types of Exposition

- Description - The author explains a particular topic by showing characteristics, features, and examples.
- Comparison - The author shows how two or more topics are alike.
- Contrast - The author shows how two or more topics are different.
- Cause and Effect - The author demonstrates the cause while showing the effects of the cause.
- Problem and Solution - The author explains a problem, then explores possible solutions.
- Analytical - The author evaluates a topic or argument revealing its strengths and weaknesses.

- Classification - The author sorts things into useful categories, makes sure all the categories follow a single organizing principle, and gives examples that fit into each category.
- Sequence - The author lists items or events in numerical or chronological order.

25.1.2 Where Do I Begin?

Find a Topic and Research

First you must find a specific aspect of a topic that would interest you. You will have to research the topic extensively so that you can explain it—what exposition is all about. Research your topic extensively. You will probably have to spend quite a bit of time, but remember that the researching can be exciting. The general initial researching may even provide some valuable information that you want to explain. Researching is like exercising: at first it hurts, but with time you become stronger and it's easier to flex your researching muscles. After you have decided upon a topic, you can create a thesis.

Thesis

An expositional paper is most easily written when you have a "tight" thesis. This means that the focus of your topic is extremely specific. When your thesis is concise, you can write at length because you know exactly what you should be writing about. But when you have a sloppy, vague thesis, you can become lost and your writing reflects this. This goes back to choosing a topic focus that deals with something specific, and not overly general. A thesis makes a claim regarding your focus and is supported by details and facts. It is written in one or two complete sentences. An example of a thesis would be: "Gardening can be a rewarding hobby because of the creativity involved, the variety of plants, and the many uses of plants."

Create a Sketchy Outline

After you write your thesis, create a sketchy outline so that you have a game plan for your paper. Your outline should have information that you want to include for each part of your thesis. For our thesis example, we could find lots of information that could support the different parts of gardening. Notice the word *could*--just because we have the information doesn't mean we must use it in the paper. This is a rough outline after all.

Start Writing

Too often we don't begin writing because we are stuck—don't be, just start writing. You can begin anywhere. Start writing where you feel the most comfortable. When you have your outline, as sketchy as it may be, it reminds you of ideas that you want to include in your paper. Remember though that readers are interested in what YOU have to say—they don't want to read regurgitated quotes and opinions of others, so make sure that your point is being heard.

25.2 Structure

The structure of an expository piece consists of first an introduction that contains the most crucial element—the thesis—the main point you wish to convey. After the introduction is the body, in which you clarify the different aspects of the thesis in great detail. The final piece, the conclusion, restates and rephrases (using different words) the thesis and ties up any "loose ends".

25.2.1 Introduction

The very first part of your introduction should have an attention-grabbing device (a hook) to engage your readers. Hooks can be statistics, facts, questions, or unusual details. Don't make general statements such as "it is clear that..." because you are trying to explain something that perhaps your reader doesn't know, so it would not be clear to them. Instead be informative. The introduction will also contain your thesis. Good topic referring to Rhetoric. One can check it at the essays writing companies and already written essays accomplished by writing service writers.

25.2.2 Body

Now that you have your specific thesis, along with your sketchy outline, you must support your thesis claim by using concrete evidence and examples. You should exfoliate your thesis. Remember that expositional writing assumes that your readers have no prior knowledge regarding your topic, so you must explain things very clearly. Parallelism can be very important in your paper. It can give the readers a feeling of structure and importance. Pick a method of organization and stick with it.

In our example, we would explain in detail how much creativity is involved in gardening. We could write about the style of impressive European or Oriental gardens. Next, we would show how there are a variety of plants. We could write about plants found in different climates. Finally, we would explain the many uses of plants. We could write about floral bouquets and vegetables.

Because exposition's purpose is to inform, you will want to establish common ground with your readers. You should write objectively, which will fulfill the purpose of explaining things.

25.2.3 Conclusion

A conclusion wraps up your paper by recalling your main points, but do not use the identical words that you used in your introduction. Conclusions and introductions are like frames, they should tie your whole paper together. You should explain your main points briefly and freshly. Don't be sloppy--this is the last impression you are making.

25.3 Sample Exposition Assignments

Here are some sample assignments to prepare you for a real exposition paper or essay. Remember that your audience has very little previous knowledge of your topic!

UNKNOWN TEMPLATE Sample

Sample Assignments

- Write an informative exposition essay on the many uses of duct tape.
- Compose a descriptive exposition essay about your room.
- Type an analytical exposition essay that analyzes your computer keyboard and the how effective it is at its job.
- You can also use other subjects to write about, such as your favorite food or drink or your hobbies.

25.4 Sample Exposition Essay

Assignment: Explain an aspect of cellular phones.

UNKNOWN TEMPLATE Sample

Sample Exposition Essay "Words are, of course, the most powerful drug used by mankind." - one of the best ways to spread this "powerful drug" is through the simple act of talking to another person. Everybody wants to talk and everybody also wants to listen and learn. How is one man or woman supposed to communicate with another from across the city, state, or even country without a very powerful tool? This powerful tool, while seemingly simple, is called a cellular phone, or cell phone for short. The cell phone has revolutionized the way that the world communicates with each other and spreads the good word. One might be asking just what a cell phone is--well, listen up and find out. The cell phone has its roots with the telegraph and telephone. These are both devices that are able to send messages through land-based wires called phone lines. That means that a coded message or a voice is sent through phone lines in order to make it to its destination. The receiving person can then translate the code or listen to the voice on the other end. On a telephone, people were capable of having a conversation from across the nation while it sounded like they were in the same room as each other. In order for them to be able to make a call to each other, though, there would have to be a web of phone lines connecting them over thousands of miles of land. Laying all of these phone lines was very cumbersome, as was only being able to send or receive calls from a stationary place, like a house or office. While the Telephone made broad communication more accessible, it still did not have entirely enough freedom for the people. This was all changed in the year 1973. A man named Martin Cooper invented the first Cellular Phone while working for Motorola. It was about the size of a brick and weighed over 30 ounces (or 1.8 pounds). While big in size, it was even larger in potential. Cooper made his first call on his cell phone while walking in the middle of a New York street. There were no wires connected to his phone. There was nothing restricting his movement and could send or receive calls from anywhere. How does a cell phone work if it is not connected to the phone lines? The short answer to that question is: satellites. The cell phone emits a signal to one of the many satellites that are orbiting Earth. The satellite catches the signal and sends it back to Earth to the person that was meant to receive it. This does not mean that cell phones cannot communicate with land-line telephones. If a cell phone calls a land-line, the signal is sent to the satellite and then back to a satellite dish on Earth where it is then re-sent through landlines to the house or office. This also works in reverse for a land-line that is calling a cell phone. The cell phone is much more than just a unwired phone in the present day. It has evolved much since Cooper's phone of '73 and they now weigh an average of 3 ounces. Cell phones can now store all of the phone numbers that a person needs. There is no more having to find the list of phone numbers on a piece of paper and to dial the number every time a call is placed to somebody. With cell phones, one simply just has to find a person's name on the phone and press send. They can even store schedules, set sleep alarms, take pictures, play music, browse the Internet, and much more. The cell phone has come a long way in 30 years to set a world free of wires. There is nothing holding anybody back from walking down the middle of the street while having a conversation with somebody 2000 miles away anymore. The cell phone is a marvel beyond what was imagined when Alexander Graham Bell first invented the telephone. It is a very powerful tool for getting our words around, and will take us places in the future that we have never dreamed of.

- Information in this essay was provided from About.com[1].

25.4.1 Why Is This Good?

First the introduction, a surprising and interesting quote, immediately catches your attention since it equalizes words and drugs. The introduction has a tight thesis, "The cell phone has revolutionized the way that the world communicates with each other and spreads the good word."

The body explains the revolution of cell phones. Notice how the writer clearly defined what a phone line is and how it works. The writer transitions into another topic by asking a question, "How does a cell phone work if it is not connected to the phone lines?" Asking questions is an easy rhetorical device that can make your paper flow more smoothly.

Finally, this conclusion ties together the paper since it recalls the main themes. By using different words, the conclusion is fresh and not predictable. It is future looking. "It is a very powerful tool for getting our words around, and it will take us places in the future that we have never dreamed of."

25.5 External links

- Information about Expository Writing[2] With writing samples.

---

1   http://inventors.about.com/cs/inventorsalphabet/a/martin_cooper.htm
2   http://www.stanford.edu/~arnetha/expowrite/info.html#what

26 Evaluation

26.1 What is Evaluative Writing?

Evaluative writing is a type of writing intended to judge something according to a set of criteria. For instance, your health might be evaluated by an insurance company before issuing a policy. The purpose of this evaluation would be to determine your overall health and to check for existing medical conditions. The better your evaluation, the less the insurance company might charge you for coverage.

26.1.1 Criteria

The key to effective evaluative writing is starting off with a clear and precise argument. Your main argument is what you will use to perform the evaluation. You may want to argue that a Chevy Tahoe is better than a Ford Expedition based on its horsepower, gas mileage, capacity, warranty, etc. Other evaluators might argue the difference between their towing capability. Whatever the main argument may be for your evaluative essay, make sure that your argument is clear.

- Make sure you have a well presented subject. Without one, you will lose your readers.
- Create a thesis statement. Thesis statements help you stay focused and help your reader to understand what is being evaluated or judged.
- Give only information that is imperative to the decision making process. If it looks like unnecessary information, it probably is.
- Do not be biased when creating an evaluative essay. Give both good and bad examples of the topic.
- You are the "expert" in an evaluative essay. Support your opinions with facts, not whims.

Things to Remember

26.1.2 How to Evaluate

A big question you might have is: how do I evaluate my subject? That depends on what your subject is.

If you are evaluating a piece of writing, then you are going to need to read the work thoroughly. While you read the work, keep in mind the criteria you are using to evaluate. The evaluative aspects may be: grammar, sentence structure, spelling, content, usage of sources, style, or many other things. Another thing to consider when evaluating a piece of writing is whether the writing appeals to its target audience. Is there an emotional appeal? Does the author engage the audience, or is the piece lacking something? If you can, make notes directly on your work itself so that you remember what you want to write about in your essay.

If you are evaluating anything else, use your head. You **need** to try, use, or test whatever thing you are evaluating. That means you should not evaluate a 2005 Chevrolet Corvette unless you have the $45,000 (or more) to buy one, or the money to rent one. You also need the know-how of driving a car of that power and a base of knowledge of other cars that you have tested to make a fair comparison.

On the note of comparisons, **only compare things that are reasonably alike**. People don't care to know how an apple compares to a backpack; that is for a different type of essay. Compare different types of apples to each other and different types of backpacks against each other. That is what people are looking for when reading comparisons in an evaluation essay.

Whatever you are evaluating, make sure to do so thoroughly. Take plenty of notes during the testing phase so that your thoughts stay fresh in your mind. You do not want to forget about a part of the subject that you did not test.

26.2 Structure of the Essay

26.2.1 Introduction

In the introduction of your evaluative essay, you should clearly state the following: - what you are evaluating (the subject -- like a 2009 Toyota Prius) - the purpose of your evaluation - what criteria you are evaluating your subject on (mileage, price, performance, etc.)

For example, you should not just write that you are judging the taste of an apple. You should explain that you are judging the sweetness, bitterness, and crispness of the apple.

26.2.2 Body

Unlike some types of essays, the introduction is **not** the most important part of an evaluative essay. Most readers already want to read about the subject that you are writing on, so you don't need to draw them in with a fancy intro. Your audience just wants the information!

Be sure to be very descriptive and thorough when evaluating your subject. The more you leave out of the essay, the more unanswered questions your readers are left with. Your goal should be to cover all aspects of the subject and to tell the audience how good or bad it is. Consider, for example, not only what quality the subject possesses, but what is missing. Good evaluations measure the quality or value of a subject by considering what it has and what it lacks.

26.2.3 Conclusion

The conclusion for an evaluative essay is pretty straightforward. Simply go over the main points from the body of your essay. After that, make an overall evaluation of the subject. Tell the audience if they should buy it, eat it, use it, wear it, etc. and why. After that is done, your essay is over. Good job!

26.3 Sample Assignments

Here are some sample assignments to get your brain pumping:

- Evaluate the plans for a new Minnesota Twins ballpark (found here: New Ballpark Plans[1]). How does it compare to the current Metrodome in Minneapolis in terms of seating, concessions, cost to build, etc.? In the end, is it a good idea to build their proposed park?

- Evaluate your backpack. Test its durability, comfort level, ease-of-use, storage capacity, fabric quality, manufacturing quality, etc. Compare it with one or more of your former backpacks and/or one of your friend's backpacks. Also, compare it to a different type of backpack (example: duffle bag VS. two-strap backpack). Take notes on each backpack and rate them against each other. Is your backpack the better one?

26.4 External Links

- A Brief Guide to Writing Evaluation Essays[2]
- Useful Phrases for Use in Evaluative Writing[3]
- Important Elements to Consider[4]

---

1   http://minnesota.twins.mlb.com/NASApp/mlb/min/ballpark/index.jsp
2   http://www.rscc.cc.tn.us/owl&writingcenter/OWL/Evaluation.html
3   http://home.ku.edu.tr/~doregan/Writing/evallangpanova.htm
4   http://kerlins.net/bobbi/education/writing/critiques.html

27 Argument

27.1 What is An Argument?

When you hear the word "argument," what do you think of? Maybe you think of a shouting match or a fist fight? Well, when instructors use the word "argument," they're typically thinking about something else. What they're actually referring to is a written or spoken form of defense.

More to the point, they're talking about defending a certain point of view through writing or speech. Usually called a "claim" or a "thesis," this point of view is concerned with an issue that doesn't have a clear right or wrong answer (e.g., four and two make six). Also, this argument should not only be concerned with personal opinion (e.g., I really like carrots). Instead, an argument might tackle issues like abortion, capital punishment, stem cell research, or gun control. However, what distinguishes an argument from a descriptive essay or "report" is that **the argument must take a stance**; if you're merely summarizing "both sides" of an issue or pointing out the "pros and cons," you're not really writing an argument. "Stricter gun control laws will likely result in a decrease in gun-related violence" is an argument. Note that people can and will disagree with this argument, which is precisely why so many instructors find this type of assignment so useful -- they make you think!

Academic arguments usually "articulate an opinion." This opinion is always carefully **defended with good reasoning and supported by plenty of research**. Research? Yes, research! Indeed, part of learning to write effective arguments is finding reliable sources(or other documents) that lend credibility to your position. It's not enough to say "capital punishment is wrong because that's the way I feel."

Instead, you need to adequately support your claim by finding:

- facts
- statistics
- quotations from recognized authorities, and
- other types of evidence

You won't always win, and that's fine. The goal of an argument is simply to:

- make a claim
- support your claim with the most credible reasoning and evidence you can muster
- hope that the reader will at least understand your position
- hope that your claim is taken seriously

If you defend your argument's position with good reasoning and evidence, you should earn a high grade, even if your instructor personally disagrees with the views you are defending.

We will be covering the basic format of how to structure an argument. This includes the **general written argument** structure, and the **Position** and **Proposal** variations of that basic form. If you want to make a claim about a particular (usually controversial) issue, you can use the Position argument form. Alternately, if you would like to offer a solution to a particular situation that you see as problematic, such as the rising cost of education, you can get your idea across using a Proposal argument. By adapting one of these three methods, you will be well on the way to making your point. The great thing about the argument structure is its amazingly versatility. Once you become familiar with this basic structure of the argumentative essay, you will be able to clearly argue about almost anything!

| "If you can't annoy somebody, there's little point in writing." |
| --Kingsley Amis (1922 - 1995) |

27.2 Basic Argument Essay Structure

27.2.1 Introduction

The first paragraph of your argument is used to **introduce your topic** and the issues surrounding it. This needs to be in clear, easily understandable language. Your readers need to know what you're writing about before they can decide if they believe you or not.

Once you have introduced your general subject, it's time to **state your claim**. Your claim will serve as the thesis for your essay. Make sure that you use clear and precise language. Your reader needs to understand exactly where you stand on the issue. The clarity of your claim affects your readers' understanding of your views. Also, it's a good idea to highlight what you plan to cover. Highlights allow your reader to know what direction you will be taking with your argument.

You can also mention the points or arguments in support of your claim, which you will be further discussing in the body. This part comes at the end of the thesis and can be named as *the guide*. The guide is a useful tool for you as well as the readers. It is useful for you, because this way you will be more organized. In addition, your audience will have a clear cut idea as to what will be discussed in the body.

27.3 Body

27.3.1 Background Information

Once your position is stated you should **establish your credibility**. There are two sides to every argument. This means not everyone will agree with your viewpoint. So try to **form a common ground** with the audience. Think about who may be undecided or opposed to your viewpoint. Take the audience's age, education, values, gender, culture, ethnicity, and all other variables into consideration as you introduce your topic. These variables will affect your word choice, and your audience may be more likely to listen to your argument with an open mind if you do.

27.3.2 Developing Your Argument

Back up your thesis with logical and persuasive arguments. During your pre-writing phase, outline the main points you might use to support your claim, and decide which are the strongest and most logical. Eliminate those which are based on emotion rather than fact. Your corroborating evidence should be well-researched, such as statistics, examples, and expert opinions. You can also reference personal experience. It's a good idea to have a mixture. However, you should avoid leaning too heavily on personal experience, as you want to present an argument that appears objective as you are using it to persuade your reader.

There are a couple different methods of developing your argument. Two variations of the *basic argument structure* are the **Position Method** and the **Proposal Method**.

Position Method

The **Position Method** is used to try to convince your audience that you are *in the right*, and the other view of your argument is *wrong*.

---

1. **Introduce and define your topic.** Never assume that your reader is familiar with the issues surrounding your topic. This is your chance to set up the premise (point of view) you want to use. This is also a good time to **present your thesis statement**.
2. **Background information. Do your research**! The more knowledgeable you are, the more concise an argument you will be able to give. You will now be able to provide your reader with the best information possible. This will allow your audience to read your paper with the same knowledge you possess on the topic. Information is the backbone to a solid argument.
3. **Development.** You have your argument, and you may have even stated your thesis. Now, start developing your ideas. Provide evidence and reasoning.
4. **Be prepared to deal with the "Other Side."** There will be those who oppose your argument. Be prepared to answer those opinions or points of view with knowledgeable responses. If you have done your homework and know your material, you will be able to address any opposing arguments with ease and authority.
5. **In conclusion...** Now is the time to drive home your point. Re-emphasize your main arguments and thesis statement.

Position Method

Proposal Method

The **Proposal Method** of argument is used when there is a problematic situation, and you would like to offer a solution to the situation. The structure of the Proposal method is very similar to the above Position method, but there are slight differences.

---

1. **Introduce and define the nature of the problematic situation.** Make sure to focus on the actual problem and what is causing the problem. This may seem simple, but many people focus solely on the effects of a problematic situation. By focusing on the actual problem, your readers will see your proposal as a solution to the problem. If you don't, your readers might see your solution as a mere complaint.

2. **Propose a solution, or a number of solutions, to the problem.** Be specific about these solutions. If you have one solution, you may choose to break it into parts and spend a paragraph or so describing each part. If you have several solutions, you may instead choose to spend a paragraph on each scenario. Each additional solution will add both depth and length to your argument. But remember to stay focused. Added length does not always equal a better argument.

3. **Describe the workability of the various solutions.** There are a variety of ways that this could be done. With a single-solution paper you could break the feasibility down into short and long term goals and plans. With a multiple-solution essay, you may instead highlight the strengths and weaknesses of the individual solutions, and establish which would be the most successful, based on your original statement of the problem and its causes.

4. **Summarize and conclude your proposal.** Summarize your solutions, re-state how the solution or solutions would work to remedy the problematic situation, and you're done.

Proposal Method

27.3.3 Dealing With the Opposition

When writing an argument, expect that you will have opposition. Skeptical readers will have their own beliefs and points of view. When conducting your research, make sure to review the opposing side of the argument that you are presenting. You need to be prepared to counter those ideas. Remember, in order for people to give up their position, they must see how your position is more reasonable than their own. When you address the opposing point of view in your essay and demonstrate how your own claim is stronger, you neutralize their argument. By failing to address a non-coinciding view, you leave a reason for your reader to disagree with you, and therefore weaken your persuasive power. Methods of addressing the opposing side of the argument vary. You may choose to state your main points, then address and refute the opposition, and then conclude. Conversely, you might summarize the opposition's views early in your argument, and then revisit them after you've present your side or the argument. This will show how your information is more reasonable than their own.

27.4 Conclusion

You have introduced your topic, stated your claim, supported that claim with logical and reasonable evidence, and refuted your opposition's viewpoint. The hard work is done. Now it's time to wrap things up. By the time readers get to the end of your paper, they should have learned something. You should have learned something, too. Give readers an idea to take away with them. Conclude = to come together or to end (not restate what has already been said in your paper). One word of caution: avoid introducing any new information in your conclusion. If you find that there's another point that you wanted to include, revise your essay. Include this new information into the body of your essay. The conclusion should only review what the rest of your essay has offered.

27.5 Strengthening Your Argument

27.5.1 Phrasing

It is important to clearly state and support your position. However, it is just as important to present all of the information that you've gathered in an objective manner. Using language that is demeaning or non-objective will undermine the strength of your argument. This destroys your credibility and will reduce your audience on the spot. For example, a student writing an argument about why a particular football team has a good chance of "going all the way" is making a strategic error by stating that "anyone who doesn't think that the Minnesota Vikings deserve to win the Super Bowl is a total idiot." Not only has the writer risked alienating any number of her readers, she has also made her argument seem shallow and poorly researched. In addition, she has committed a third mistake: making a sweeping generalization that cannot be supported.

Use phrasing that does not:
• Alienate any part of your audience
• Make an argument that is poorly researched or shallow
• Make an unsupported generalization
Mistakes that could ruin your Argument

27.5.2 Objective Language

You should avoid using "I" and "My" (subjective) statements in your argument. You should only use "I" or "My" if you are an expert in your field (on a given topic). Instead choose more objective language to get your point across. Consider the following:

I believe that the United States Government is failing to meet the needs of today's average college student through the under-funding of need-based grants, increasingly restrictive financial aid eligibility requirements, and a lack of flexible student loan options.

"Great," your reader thinks, "Everyone's entitled to their opinion."

Now lets look at this sentence again, but without the "I" at the beginning. Does the same sentence becomes a strong statement of fact without your "I" tacked to the front?:

The United States Government is failing to meet the needs of today's average college student through the underfunding of need-based grants, increasingly restrictive financial aid eligibility requirements, and a lack of flexible student loan options.

"Wow," your reader thinks, "that really sounds like a problem."

A small change like the removal of your "I"s and "my"s can make all the difference in how a reader perceives your argument-- as such, it's always good to proof read your rough draft and look for places where you could use objective rather than subjective language.

27.7 The Fallacies of Argument

Okay; your paper is filled with quality research. You're feeling good about your paper. But when you get the paper back your instructor has left a comment like, "This is an argument fallacy". So now you're left wondering what is "false" about the argument; and what is this "argument fallacy"?

Argumentative fallacies are sometimes called "logical fallacies". Usually these "fallacies" are created when the reasoning behind the argument lacks validity. A lack of validity weakens your argument, and then leads to a failure to provide a sufficient claim.

Don't feel badly if your paper says "fallacy of argument" on it. This is a common error in argumentative papers. In fact, a detailed list of "logical fallacies" can be found in the "Common Errors" section of this book (just below "Run-On" sentences and "Sentence Fragments". If you would like to see the list of logical fallacies, please visit The Writers Handbook[1].

"Argumentative fallacy" can be caused by your 'negligence' or lack of rigor and attention while making a certain argument. In other words, a very general argument, not followed through rigorously, can end up in something as an 'argumentative fallacy'. So, never generalize; don't just say and leave -- pursue your point to its logical termination.

27.8 A Side Note

Many topics that are written about in college are very controversial. When approaching a topic it is critical that you think about all of the implications that your argument makes. If, for example, you are writing a paper on abortion, you need to think about your audience. There will certainly be people in each of your classes that have some sort of relationship to this topic that may be different than yours. While you shouldn't let others' feelings sway your argument, you should approach each topic with an open mind and stay away from personal attacks. People may be offended by something you say, but if you have taken the time to think about the things that go into your paper, you should have no problem defending it.

27.9 Further Reading

- *Argumentation and Advocacy*

  This scholarly journal covers the various areas of argumentation. Although the information that could be valuable to certain persons is scattered, an in-depth read of all articles

---

1   http://en.wikibooks.org/wiki/Rhetoric_and_Composition/Logical_Fallacies

spanning 1989 to today would be valuable to any person studying argumentation and rhetoric. You may be able to access it from an educational facilities database.

27.10 External Links

- Effective Academic Writing: The Argument[2]
- Essentials of Effective Persuasive Essays[3]
- Logical Fallacies[4]
- Support Your Argument[5]
- Paradigm Online Writing Assistant[6] Occasions for Argumentative Essays.
- Logic in Argumentative Writing[7]

---

2   http://www.unc.edu/depts/wcweb/handouts/argument.html
3   http://www.hamilton.edu/academics/resource/wc/Effective_essays.html
4   http://leo.stcloudstate.edu/acadwrite/logic.html
5   http://www.wooster.edu/writing_center/resources.html
6   http://www.powa.org/argumentative-essays/
7   http://owl.english.purdue.edu/owl/resource/659/01/

28 Advanced Topics

29 Overview of Advanced Topics

29.1 Overview: Advanced Topics

Now that you have learned some of the basics of college writing, it is time to dive into the advanced topics of writing. The tools you have learned from previous sections will help you to be a more successful writer with advanced topics. There are many different reasons for which one writes. It could be for school, work, or even the community. The topics discussed in this section are writing for the humanities, sciences, and business. Each chapter will highlight the unique features that separate these genres and give practical examples of how each uses writing to achieve goals.

29.1.1 Writing in the Humanities

Writing in the Humanities includes theoretical writing, creative writing, interpretive writing, and analytical writing. Each of these qualifies as writing in Humanities, but each uses a significantly different style.

Theoretical writing includes historical and philosophical writing. This topic focuses on the ideas of past cultures and people. It also includes writing about your own theories.

---

*Thomas Paine's "Common Sense"

- The philosophies of Buddha

- Einstein's theories on Nuclear Physics|caption=Sample Theoretical Writings

---

Creative writing uses a more imaginative approach and can include storytelling, personal expression, or even free association. Poetry, song lyrics, short stories, non-fiction, and fiction novels are all included under creative writing. In creative writing, there is more freedom for the writer to explore feelings or ideas. Some forms of creative writing, like sonnets, do include formatting concerns or restrictions. Creative writing is more concerned with personal expression than adhering to tradition, however.

*A science-fiction story

- A biography of what the US would have been like if it lost WWII

- A story about your future life|caption=Sample Creative Writings

Interpretive writers do more than simply summarize the text they study. Interpretive writing improves understanding by asking a series of good questions. The interpretive writer introduces their own ideas about a text, but they must always back up claims by referring to the text they analyze, or another appropriate source.

Analytical writing is much like interpretive writing, but also goes a bit further. Not only will you provide information, but you will also analyze it. This includes asking "how" and "why." You will need to take a critical approach to develop an understanding of the topic before writing about it.

This chapter[1] will expand on the differences of theoretical, creative, interpretive, and analytical writing, and will share tips on how to write successfully while using those different approaches.

29.1.2 Writing in the Sciences

Writing in the sciences focuses on informing the reader of new discoveries, and assisting readers in discovering truth through facts. This form of writing should not leave anything open to interpretation by the reader. Information should be presented with solid data given in detail. Science writing is generally written in past tense and should be concise. Common forms of science writing includes lab reports and literature reviews.

Writing in science includes two main categories: natural sciences and social sciences. Natural sciences include pure science and applied science. Pure sciences are life sciences, physical sciences, and earth sciences. Applied sciences include medical sciences, engineering sciences, and computer science.

Social sciences focus on human behavior and societies. Social sciences involve documenting actual events as they happen as with case studies. Categories of social science include psychology, anthropology, political science, sociology, education, business, and economics.

* Story regarding global warming

- Story based on the research of estrogen
  |caption=Sample Scientific Writings

---

1   Chapter 30 on page 149

This chapter[2] will explain the distinct features of writing for the sciences.

29.1.3 Writing in Business

Business writing has a practical bent to it. Writing in business often means explaining a situation, event, or change. The author typically has a very specific action they wish the audience to take, and that action often contains time concerns as well.

Good business writing is concise and focuses directly on the stated purpose. A business document needs to be organized in a manner that directs a reader's eye to the most important points. A well-written business document should allow the reader to quickly scan for purpose, time constraints, and a contact person who can answer further questions.

Writing in business can include: memos, cover letters, resumes, project reports, proposals, thank-you letters, emails, and business plans.

This chapter[3] will give you the techniques needed to build a resume as well as many important documents used in a business setting.

---

2   Chapter 31 on page 161
3   Chapter 32 on page 173

30 Writing in the Humanities

30.1 Introduction

> "All great literature addresses directly or indirectly two questions: *What kind of world is this?* and *How should we live in it?*"
>
> --Christopher Clausen

Writing in the humanities includes posing questions dealing with human values. The ultimate goal in writing in the humanities is to explain/share the human experience, to use writing as a tool to reflect upon life, and to tell how life should, or should not, be lived. "Humanities" as a discipline includes not only literature, but also philosophy, ethics, performing arts, fine arts, history, aspects of anthropology and cultural studies, foreign languages, linguistics, jurisprudence, political science, and sociology. In a humanities class, you might be asked to attempt the analysis of a poem, a performance or a play, a painting, a film or even a musical performance.

There is often a difference in feel between writing in the Sciences and writing in the Humanities. Writing in the Sciences is often convergent (meaning oriented toward finding or articulating a specific answer to a specific question). Writing in the Humanities is often divergent (meaning oriented toward exploration of multiple answers to multiple questions).

30.2 Categories of Humanities Writing

Writing in the Humanities falls into three categories: theoretical writing, creative writing, and interpretive and analytical writing. Term papers and research papers are included in this discipline of writing when their topics pertain to the field of humanities.

30.2.1 Theoretical Writing

Theoretical writing involves writing on a topic from a theoretical perspective. In physics, for example, there is a theory on how the galaxy operates called the "string theory." A physics paper centered around the string theory would be considered a theoretical paper.

30.2.2 Creative Writing

Creative writing attempts to achieve, or create, an affect in the minds of the readers. The intended affect differs depending on the goals of the writer. The intention may be to expound on the grieving process (catharsis), or to make a person laugh or cry. The potential results are unlimited. Creative writing can also be used as an outlet for people to get their thoughts and feelings out and onto paper. Many people enjoy creative writing but prefer not to share it. Creative writing can take place in a variety of forms. Poems, short stories, novels, and even song lyrics are all examples of creative writing. Viewpoints regarding what exactly is encompassed under the term *creative writing* differ. To some, non-fiction can be considered creative writing because it is done from the author's point of view and may be written in an individual style that engages the reader. In fact, many universities offer courses in "Creative non-fiction." Others like to separate non-fiction from creative writing because it deals with details that actually took place, even if viewed subjectively. Regardless, the outlook of the writer is what matters, and whether something is considered creative writing or not is less important than producing a product that you can be proud of.

Narrator

A narrator is the voice or person who tells the story. One must never assume that a narrator of a story is related to the author in any way. Even if we, as an audience, are aware that the author of the story once had a similar experience to that of the narrator, we cannot make assumptions that there is any truth to the text. When writing or discussing criticism, the intent of the author is also off limits because regardless of the author intent, the value of a text is determined by reader response alone. An example of an author having a similar experience to the narrator of a story she'd written, is Charlotte Perkins Gilman's short story *The Yellow Wallpaper*. Because the author had released statements revealing that she'd had a smilar medical treatment in her life to the narrator of her story, we still cannot assume that the narrator and Gilman are one in the same person.

A **First-Person** narrator is when one person narrates the story. Thus, a reader will recognize a first-person narrator because the pro-nouns "I" and "my" will be used. Because the story is narrated by one person, we are limited to the thoughts and observations of that person. There are many reasons that an author may choose to use a first-person narrator, but the reason is mainly to demonstrate the changes within one particular character, and also to build suspense. For example, if an author were to suddenly swith a first-person myself novel to a third-person narrator, the "who-done-it" aspect of the story would be ruined because we would suddenly be able to dive into the minds of multiple characters.

There is also **Third-person limited** and **Third-person omniscient.** Third-person limited is when the narrator is limited to the thoughts of one particular character, but there is a little more freedom than with a first-person narrator because the narrator can more easily observe the behavior of others. Finally, a third-person omniscient narrator is when the lens of the storyteller is pulled back even further, but we are able to dive into the minds of any and all characters. Therefore, a third-person omniscient narrater is rather God-like in that it enables us to know absolutely anything and everything that is happening in the novel. This may sound like the most enjoyable way to compose, but as stated earlier, there are drawbacks to this kind of narrator in that it may be harder to create an element of surprise for the reader.

Literary Periods

Deconstructionism is an approach to literature which suggests that literary works do not yield a single, fixed meaning because we can never say what we truly mean in language.

Early Modern Era Period extending from about 1500 to 1800, marked by the advent of colonialism and capitalism.

Modernism Writing and art roughly made in at the start of WWI (1914) through the end of WWII (1945).

Postmodernism is a literary and artistic movement that flourished in the late twentieth century, partly in response to Modernism. A common theme in this kind of work is self-reflexiveness.

1

30.2.3 Interpretive and Analytical Writing

Interpretive Writing

- An interpretation involves the discovery of meaning in a text (or film or painting, etc.) or the production of meaning in the process of reading a text. Therefore, interpretive writing must address many questions. It tries to assist the reader in understanding specific events (literary, cultural, or otherwise) rather than just engaging in summary. For example, a student writing an interpretive paper about a specific book may try to explain the author's attitudes or views on a specific subject matter. The writer of the paper then uses the evidence found in that book to back up his or her claims. A poor example of interpretive writing is a book report. A good example of interpretive writing is a scholarly article about another text.

Writing might ask questions such as, "Why did these events happen?" or "What was the significance of these events to the author or main character?" as opposed to, "What happened" or "How did these events come about?" The former questions encourage writers to explore their own thoughts or to delve into the mind of the writer of the text, or even attempt to put himself in the shoes of the protagonist. The latter is less challenging, as the book or piece of literature will plainly lay this type of information out for the reader.

Analytical Writing

- Analytical writing examines the components of a text. Writers of analytical essays or articles consider information, break it apart, and reconstruct it in order to describe the information so another reader can make sense of it. Writers must make sense of a work before they can begin to describe its constituent parts.

- Analytical writing focuses on the words "how" and "why." A writer often uses each of these two terms to give proof of their current analogies. By using these strong terms, a reader can feel that the writer is confident in their work and know "how" and "why" they should react.

- Analytical writing happens in four steps. The *first* step is to clearly identify the problem, the question, or the issue. The *second* step is to define the issue. The *third* step is the

---

actual analysis of the topic. Finally, the *fourth* step defines the relationship between the issue and the analysis of that issue.

Analyzing and Interpreting Literature

- There is a lot of overlap in the processes of analysis and interpretation, especially when writing about literature. Writing about literature (poems, short stories, plays, etcs) often involves making an argument that can be backed up with specific examples from the text. When interpreting a poem the writer should expect that they will have to include specific references to the lines, words, or phrases to which they are referring. A writer analyzing the main character in *The Great Gatsby* should include specific references that explain why they have reached a particular conclusion.

- An essay dealing with literature should not be a summary of the text. It doesn't always hurt to give a few background examples, but the writer should focus on talking about the portions of the text that emphasize their points, not summarizing the entire piece for the reader. If the reader isn't familiar with the primary text, they can go back and read it themselves. The interpreter's job isn't to recap, but to make an argument, and hopefully provide some sort of illumination of the work.

- A piece of literature should always be referred to in the present tense.

- Take a look at this sample essay on the play *A Midsummer Night's Dream*

Fairies, Duality, and Conflict

It's hard to read A Midsummer Night's Dream without noticing at least some duality within the play. While it's relatively easy to spot in the "lamentable comedy" performed by the mechanicals, there are also more nuanced examples that are introduced in Act 2, Scene 1. This scene reveals some of the play's duality, specifically in regards to the fairies, as it continues to build on Act 1's theme of conflict between lovers.

The start of this scene opens with Puck talking with another fairy. This is the first appearance of any fairies and it adds a fantasy, or dream-like, element to the play. The unnamed fairy announces that, "I serve the Fairy Queen, / To dew her orb upon the green" (2.1.8-9). This fits the idea that many people have of fairies; they are pleasant folk associated with nature. Nothing about this fairy is threatening or even mischievous. This is directly at odds with the character of Puck. Puck spends his time pretending to be footstools that women can sit on, "Then I slip from her bum, down topples she, / And 'Tailor' cries, and falls into a cough" (2.1.53-54). He "frights the maidens of the villagery" (2.1.35) and does things like, "mislead night wanderers, laughing at their harm?" (2.1.39). While the unnamed fairy is out spreading dew upon blades of grass, Puck is out spreading mischief. The unnamed fairy represents the good within fairy-kind, while Puck represents the potentially threatening. An examination of Puck's name adds to this. According to the unnamed fairy, Puck is also known as Robin Goodfellow (2.1.34); but, he doesn't go by that name, he goes by Puck. If Puck were a more good-natured fairy, he might prefer to go by the name Robin Goodfellow. However, his decision to play a darker role than the other fairies mirrors his decision to go by a less pleasant sounding moniker. Puck is more of an imp than a fairy. He has a trickster mentality that isn't present in the other fairies.

Puck and the unnamed fairy are representative of two larger factions, which are each headed by a more powerful fairy. At the beginning of the scene the unnamed fairy says she serves the fairy queen, and Puck later reveals who he serves by saying, "I jest to Oberon and make him smile" (2.1.44). Later in this scene Oberon will ask Puck to run an errand for him, and the sensitivity of the errand suggests that Oberon wouldn't trust just anyone with it. In addition to being Oberon's jester, Puck is also his confidant.

Oberon's entrance into the scene matches the more threatening demeanor that Puck embodies. Puck notes that, "Oberon is passing fell and wrath, / Because that she as her attendant hath / A lovely boy, stolen from an Indian king" (2.1.20-22). Oberon and all he represents is at odds with Titania and all that she represents. Oberon and Titania's conflict is in addition to the other conflicts in the play between couples: Theseus and Hippolyta and the Lysander/Hermia/Demetrius/Helena quartet. It's also fitting that Oberon and Titania are arguing over a human boy. The human world has created conflict in the fairy world, just as the fairy world will later on intensify the conflict of the human world of the four lovers.

Oberon and Titania are shown in this scene as having emotions like any ordinary human. This reinforces the bond between the two worlds in the play; the world of fantasy and the more concrete world that the humans live in. Oberon and Titania both have other lovers. Titania notes that Oberon has been spending time with Phillida and Hippolyta (2.1.66-71), while Oberon counters that Hippolyta has been intimate with Theseus (2.1.76-80). They argue over infidelity like any humans would in a similar relationship. The fact that they both appear to have cheated on one another may not entirely add up since Titania appears to represent a kinder, gentler fairy demographic, as opposed to Oberon's more threatening one. But Titania says why she cheated. She calls her infidelities, "the forgeries of jealousy" (2.1.81). Titania is arguing that she only cheated because Oberon drove her to it. Perhaps, she needed more attention than Oberon was willing to give. Perhaps, she was trying to hurt Oberon like he had hurt her. These are very human reactions and impulses.

Yet, these are not mere humans, but fairies: not just fairies, but fairy royalty. Because of this wrinkle, their actions, and their discord, has a marked effect on the world around them. Once Oberon started cheating on Titania,

> The winds, piping to us in vain,
> As in revenge, have sucked up from the sea
> Contagious fogs which, falling in the land,
> Hath every pelting river made so proud
> That they have overborne their continents.   (2.1.88-92)

In addition to the floods there are also droughts, famine and a host of other issues (2.1.93-114). The relationship of these two is clearly the reason for the disturbance in nature. This is shown when Titania says, "And this same progeny of evils comes / from our debate, from our dissension. / We are their parents and original" (2.1.115-117). The trouble that has overtaken the natural world is at odds with the preparations concerning the festival that are taking place within Athens. Much as the forest world is a different place than the stone walls of Athens. Yet, despite their differences, nature and the civilized world will interact. It's impossible to keep them completely apart despite their separate natures.

It's also worth noting how the relationship between Oberon and Titania was prior to their discord,

> Met we on hill, in dale, forest, or mead,
> By paved fountain or by rushy brook,
> Or in the beached margent of the sea,
> To dance our ringlets to the whistling wind.   (2.1.83-86)

They were like two young lovers, who met everywhere and couldn't get enough of each other before Oberon ruins things. Titania says to him, "But with thy brawls thou hast disturbed our sport" (2.1.87). Certainly, many relationships encounter problems after an initial period of bliss; but, it should also be noted that abusive people often appear to be sweet and caring before their true colors show. Oberon may just be that cruel. He only wants the Indian boy because Titania has him; perhaps, specifically because Titania loves him. After all, Oberon wants the boy to be a, "Knight of his train, to trace the forests wild" (2.1.25). As the fairy king Oberon must have plenty of others whom he could get to fill that type of position. Titania, on the other hand, genuinely cares for him. We know this because she, "Crowns him with flowers, and makes him all her joy" (2.1.27). Oberon can't quite comprehend why Titania shouldn't do what he says and he says so, "Why should Titania cross her Oberon?" (2.1.119). Because Oberon can't comprehend why Titania would cross him, he sends Puck to get him a juice that will allow him to force Titania into submission (2.1.169-174). Oberon's unwillingness to allow Titania's free spirit to go unpunished is a perfect example of the cruel and threatening demeanor of his. The element of fantasy that the fairies add can be dreamlike, but dreams can become nightmares, and Oberon is a darker personality to counter Titania's light.

This scene also has Demetrius and Helena in it, and provides us great insight into their characters. Demetrius is brushing off Helena and she says,

```
        I am your spaniel; and, Demetrius,
        The more you beat me I will fawn on you.
        Use me but as your spaniel, spurn me, strike me,
        Neglect me, lose me; only give me leave,
        Unworthy as I am, to follow you.  (2.1.203-207)
```

This works on a variety of levels. For one, it brings into the play a darker, more masochistic, idea of love that is at odds with the pure notion of love that the audience may assume that Lysander and Hermia share. It also reveals Helena as a woman who acts the opposite of Titania. Titania handles her abusive relationship by seeking love in another's arms, by spending time with the people who care for her, and by devoting her time to a boy. She separates herself from her abuser, Oberon, rather than seeking his company. Hermia seeks the abuse out. She views any attention, no matter how negative, as positive simply because it's some sort of attention. If Demetrius gave her positive attention, perhaps she wouldn't be happy for long. Demetrius, on the other hand, tells Helena that looking at her makes him sick (2.1.213). He talks to her as if he hates her, and it takes a hard-heart to look so cruelly on someone so pathetic. Oberon happens to witness the exchange between these two and he sends Puck to put Demetrius under the same spell that he wants Titania put under (2.1.259-266). It's this part of the scene that sets into motion the rest of the play, as Titania is put under the spell's effects, and Puck inadvertently finds Lysander instead of Demetrius. In addition to setting the stage for the action that will come afterward, this scene reveals much about the characters within it. It introduces the fairies and their duality, and it builds up a darker aspect of the play through the continuation of conflict that acts to counteract some of the lightheartedness of the play.

Sample Essay

Here the writer has chosen to focus on one specific scene in the play, and how it fits their argument about the duality and conflict present within the play. Notice that throughout the entire essay there are numerous examples from within the text. Had the author not included these, or had they just summarized everything briefly, the essay wouldn't be as strong as it currently is. Here the reader can see exactly what lines make the writer think the way they do. Also, notice that the paper isn't a summary of what happens in the scene. When the writer gives details about what happens in the scene, it is because these details relate directly to the topic of their paper.

30.2.4 Research Papers and Term Papers

Term papers have a variety of elements that make them stand out from other papers. They carry three distinct characteristics. First, there is a large amount of research that goes into a term paper. The research contains various findings such as: facts, statistics, interviews, quotes, etc. Researching and gathering data must include understanding that information once it is compiled. The second characteristic is the amount of preparation it takes in gathering, compiling, analyzing, and sorting through everything in order to create a draft of your data. Finally, the third characteristic involves knowing the rules that must be followed when writing a specific term paper in the humanities discipline. These rules will generally be conveyed by your instructor.

Writing the research paper involves a bit of detective work. While there is much reading to be done on the chosen topic, reading is not the only pathway to gain information. As a writer in the humanities, you can also conduct interviews, surveys, polls, and observation clinics. You should research and discover as much information as you can about the given topic so you can form a coherent and valid opinion.

30.3 Elements of the Humanities Paper

Many styles of documentation are used when writing the humanities paper. Choosing the style depends on the subject being addressed in the paper and the style your instructor may prefer you use.

When it comes down to actually writing your paper, be sure to include the following elements: an introduction, a thesis statement, the body of the paper (which should include quotations, and, of course, the citations), and the conclusion.

30.3.1 Introduction

Like most papers and essays, an introduction is absolutely necessary when writing in the humanities. There can be some confusion as to which should come first; the introduction or the thesis statement. This decision could probably be clarified by asking your instructor. Many writers include the thesis statement in their introduction. Generally speaking, however, the introduction usually comes before the thesis statement.

The introduction should grab your reader and make them interested in continuing to read your paper. Ask a question, say something powerful, or say something controversial. Be specific, not vague. Say something interesting, not mundane. Relay something the reader may not know, not something that is public knowledge. The idea is to get the reader's attention, and keep it.

A good intro may go something like this:

> "Imagine yourself walking out of class feeling refreshed and relaxed because your day is almost done. You race down the stairs and out the doors just to take in the amazing scent of fresh outside air when suddenly you smell something completely wretched. You notice something that resembles a small grey cloud coming out of a fellow student's mouth. Then your throat begins to feel clogged and just when you can't take it any longer, your lungs give in and you feel as if you can no longer breathe. You think to yourself, 'What's happening to me? Am I dying?' No, not exactly. Your lungs and the rest of your body have just been affected by what is commonly known as passive smoking, which is becoming one of the leading causes of death in the United States."

After the introduction has been written, you can then go into your thesis statement. Many people regard the thesis statement as a continuation of the introduction, only in the next paragraph.

30.3.2 Thesis Statement

The thesis statement should come at the beginning of the paper. It will introduce the reader to the topic you intend to address, and gives them a hint of what to expect in the pages that follow. Thesis statements should avoid words and phrases such as, "In my opinion..." or "I think that..." Start your thesis by taking a stand immediately; be firm in your statement, but not pushy. You'll either be given your topic for your paper or you will choose it yourself. In either case, after the topic is chosen, write a thesis statement that clearly outlines the argument you intend to address in the paper. The thesis statement will be the center of your paper. It should address one main issue. Throughout the paper, whatever you write will be focused on the thesis statement. As your paper develops, you may find you will want to, or need to, revise your thesis statement to better outline your paper. As your paper evolves, so does your thesis. In other words, when writing your thesis statement, keep your paper in mind, and when writing your paper, keep your thesis statement in mind. Your paper will defend your thesis, so write your paper accordingly.

For example, if the topic is "Analyzing Mark Twain's 'Huckleberry Finn,'" your thesis statement might address the social implications or meanings behind the characters chosen for the story. Keeping the thesis statement in mind, you would then write your paper about the characters in the story. Let's say you are writing a philosophy paper. Your thesis statement might include two opposing arguments, with the hint that you intend to argue or prove one side of the argument. Many thesis statements are written in such a way as to try to prove an argument or point of view, but challenge yourself; make your thesis statement a statement of how you plan to *disprove* an argument. Maybe you want to attempt to show your readers why a specific point of view does *not* work.

Your thesis statement should address one main issue. It takes a point of view or an argument, and the paper is the development of this argument. If your thesis statement is too simple, obvious, or vague, then you need to work on it a little more. You should try to write it in a way that will catch your reader's attention, making it interesting and thought-provoking. It should be specific in nature, and address the theme of the entire paper. The thesis statement may be written to try to convince the reader of a specific issue or point of view. It may also address an issue to which there is no simple solution or easy answers; remember, make it thought-provoking. Many thesis statements *invite* the reader to disagree.

Don't be alarmed if you find yourself midway through your paper and wanting to change your thesis statement. This will happen. Sometimes a writer will start out thinking they know *exactly* the point they want to make in their paper, only to find halfway through that they've taken a slightly different direction. Don't be afraid to modify your thesis statement. But a word of caution; if you modify your thesis statement, be sure to double check your paper to ensure that it is supported by the thesis. If you have changed your thesis statement, it would be wise, even advisable, to have a third party read your paper to be sure that the paper supports the thesis and the revised thesis describes the paper.

30.3.3 Body

The "body" of your paper contains the *evidence, analysis,* and *reasoning* that support your thesis. Often the topic of the paper is divided into subtopics. Typically, each subtopic is discussed in a separate paragraph, but there is nothing wrong with continuing a subtopic throughout multiple paragraphs. It is good practice to begin each paragraph with a *topic sentence* that introduces the subject of the new paragraph and helps transition between paragraphs. A topic sentence will help keep you focused while writing the paragraph, and it will keep your reader focused while reading it.

30.3.4 Conclusion

The purpose of a conclusion is to "wrap up" the discussion of your paper. Especially if the paper is a long one, it is a good idea to "re-cap" the main ideas presented in your paper. If your paper is argumentative, you'd likely want to re-enforce the standpoint introduced in your thesis statement; however, rather than repeating your thesis, offer closing statements that make use of all the information you've presented to support your thesis. Try to "echo" your thesis so that your reader understands that you have fulfilled the "promise" a thesis statement implies, but give your reader a sense of *closure* rather than simply restating everything you said above just ending it.

Here are some strategies for closing your discussion:

After summing up your main points/thesis you might

- Comment on the significance of the topic in general: why should your reader care?
- Look to the future: Is there more work to be done on the topic? Are there predictions you can make about your topic?
- Ask something of your reader: Is there something your reader can do? Should do?

30.3.5 Argumentative Research Papers

One of the main things that differentiates a college level research paper from research papers below the college level is they almost always will be argumentative; that is, they will be taking a stance. The research is then used to back up the argument of the writer, or to put their argument into context. Students new to college will often attempt to simply provide information that makes the research paper becoming stale and unnecessary. If all the paper is doing is repackaging old information, why not just go back to the original source? Papers that just provide information risk unintentional plagiarism. If none of the information provided contains your own insights, then failing to cite everything means that it is plagiarized. Yet, most students would be reluctant to cite the entirety of their paper.

30.3.6 Plagiarism

Plagiarism results from including non-trivial information (ideas, facts, etc) from another source without acknowledging its source. Plagiarism is one of the most serious offenses that can be committed in academia and it involves varying degrees. Plagiarism at its most blatant includes handing in an entire paper that is not one's own; it also includes failing to document one's sources. When writing a research paper, avoid unintentional plagiarism. Because almost no knowledge other than eye-witness accounts is truly original, be sure to find sources for all non-trivial information. Plagiarism can be grounds for failing a paper or the course as a whole.

30.4 Resources To Use

The humanities category offers many good sources from which to gather information. The Internet is fast becoming an important source of information for humanities writing. There are many history sites, journalism and news sites, sites focusing on the history of film, sites dedicated to womens' issues, and so on. More traditional physical resources include dictionaries, encyclopedias, biographies, indexes, abstracts, and periodicals, and our old friend, the library.

As you can see, there are many resources from which to choose when writing your paper. Start at the most basic level and progress from there. For example, if you are writing about a specific work of a famous author, the obvious place to begin is with a careful reading of the work in question. Once you are done, try to articulate what you know to be true, what you think is *probably* true, and what is open to question: that is, what you might need to find out. It is helpful to actually go through the physical process of writing out two or three key questions that you would like to focus on.

At that point, you may want begin your further researches with a search through an encyclopedia, or do an online search for available resources, including interviews. After you have found the information you need there, you might then search a through a card catalog in a library for specific books. You may find that while searching for one specific book you will stumble upon many other useful books on the same subject. You can then begin to look through book reviews for information on your subject. Book reviews can be especially informative in that they will often will identify important themes, raise new questions, and broaden your sense of what is at stake in the text. Next, you may want to try searching for articles in periodicals, and even abstracts of articles, which will provide a summary of the content of the potential article.

30.5 External Links

- Academic Writing Support Materials for Humanities Students[2]
- Four Keys to Writing in the Humanities[3]
- Conventions of Writing Papers in Humanities[4]

---

2   http://www.dartmouth.edu/~writing/materials/student/humanities/write.shtml
3   http://darkwing.uoregon.edu/~munno/Writing/FourWritingIdeas.html
4   http://www.geneseo.edu/~easton/humanities/convhumpap.html

31 Writing in the Sciences

31.1 Introduction

Writing in the sciences fulfills one of two purposes:

1. Inform the reader of new discoveries
2. Assist the reader in clarifying the truth using new facts or perspectives

A comparison: While writing in the humanities is used to explore the human condition, writing in the sciences is used to examine nature, human experience, and/or technology.

This leads to the two major types of papers written in the sciences:

1. Lab report
2. Literature review

Writing in the sciences requires elements not necessarily needed when writing in the humanities. It requires data, evidence, facts, and precision, which in turn require intimate attention to detail. The goal of writing in the sciences is to clearly present what you have discovered or what you did. This generally requires the writing to be done in the past tense. The language used should allow no room for interpretation by the reader. The nature and subject matter of the ideas in your paper must be presented in a factual style, leaving out figurative or emotional language.

Besides lab reports and literature reviews, writing in the sciences also includes reviews for a peer or textbook, or grant proposals and equipment or facility requests. It is easy to get caught up using jargon and highly technical language. While this language may be appropriate in certain cases, you should know your audience and avoid using words they will not understand (also including definitions where appropriate).

Space occasionally becomes an issue when writing in the sciences. For example, grant proposal applications and abstracts require the text to be limited to a short paragraph. Therefore, an indispensable tool for the scientific paper is the ability to summarize quickly and get to the point. An example grant proposal may include the following sentences:

"Our preliminary research shows a high probability of success if allowed to develop. This requires us to find additional monetary help, as well as a facility to use long term. We are asking for your company's help."

Although you may include a few facts or numbers to back up your claim of success, this is the general format for such a request.

There are basic tips to keep in mind while writing your scientific paper.

- Be detailed
- Remain focused on your topic

- Leave figurative language out
- Be precise
- Define jargon based on assumed audience knowledge

There are two categories of sciences writing; **social sciences** and **natural sciences**.

31.2 Social Sciences

When writing in the social sciences, the writer will spend less time in the library researching data, and a majority of time documenting actual events. Writing in the social sciences is the study of human behavior, the value systems of people, and the interactions between people, whether in the family unit or simply in a group setting.

Writing in this discipline can be a very challenging experience. Gathering the data and interpreting the information can be tedious. Interviews are conducted, and attitudes must be examined and recorded. But recording data gathered from studying human beings is difficult because the human mind is an ever-changing thing.

One key element to writing a paper in the social sciences is the art of taking a stand. Choose your topic, make your claim, provide evidence to support your claim, and finally, convince your reader that your claim is the one with which to side. Take a hard look at both sides of the issue you intend on addressing. Doing so will prepare you to defend arguments in opposition to your viewpoint. Because issues in the social sciences are subjective, the writer should expect some degree of opposing opinions and even, possibly, some controversy. This is why it is suggested that when you write a social sciences paper you choose a topic that you either possess first hand knowledge, know a great deal of information on, or simply a topic about which you are passionate.

Charts and graphs are common elements included in the social sciences paper. A valuable source of information for the social scientist is a government document. These documents contain the most up-to-date information in a variety of fields.

Writing in the social sciences uses a technical vocabulary.

Social sciences attempt to study and describe human behavior and societies. The social sciences can be broken down into further into the following categories:

31.2.1 Psychology

The case study is one of the main writing choices in psychology. These are often studies of a patient seeking help through psychotherapy. These types of case studies can generally be divided into five sections:

1. Background Information

   This section describes the person based on information a therapist would get from the person during an intake interview. This would include, but is not limited to: demographic information, family history, and history of symptoms.

The following three sections will consider how a person would react to three general categories of psychotherapy. In each section, the following questions should be answered:

- What is the therapy like?
- What does the person talk about or do in that therapy?
- What is the therapist's role?
- How would this person react to that therapist role?
- Would the person benefit from this therapy? Why or why not?

2. Psychoanalytic Therapy

This type of treatment could be a traditional or contemporary style of psychoanalysis. In other words, the typical patient laying on a couch and talking about his or her feelings, or a more contemporary approach of question and answer, or another setting in which the patient feels more comfortable. A form of psycho-dynamic therapy (changing up the environment for the patient) could also be used.

3. Behavioral Therapy

This could be a form of behavioral therapy, cognitive therapy, or a mixture of both.

4. Humanistic Therapy

This could be existential therapy, gestalt therapy, Zen therapy, or whatever style seems to fit the patient. This is a very progressive form of psychotherapy.

5. Conclusion

This section should draw an overall conclusion of how the person in question would react to each kind of considered therapy. The patient's feelings do need to be taken into account when recommending the best treatment, as no one can be helped when they do not want to be. A final recommendation is made, and the case study is usually reviewed by colleagues, or a board or some kind, to comment and recommend a course of action to the psychologist.

Places you may want to look for current information include psychology encyclopedias and abstracts and mental health journals.

(Further resources to consider follow at the end of this section.)

31.2.2 Anthropology

Presenting a case study is a common form of presenting the anthropology paper. The writer is looking at and analyzing the past.

There are specific guidelines to follow when writing an anthropology paper. Stick to the facts and document these thoroughly in the reference list. Quotations are important, but not as important as data.

Because anthropology is such a specialized field, be sure that you re-read your paper several times to be sure that it is comprehensible to a person who may not be a specialist in the field. In other words, can your average college student understand what you are talking about? The trick here is to find a balance in this paper; it must be scholarly, yet understandable.

31.2.3 Political Science

Writing case studies is the main type of writing in this discipline. When writing a paper in political science, you will probably be analyzing how different political organizations function, both individually and as a group. While many of the other categories of the social sciences involve directly observing the group dynamics, writing a paper for political science involves indirect observation. You will pick one specific behavior to observe and focus your paper on that chosen behavior.

Writing for political science can include any level of the government; city, state or federal. Places you may want to look for current information include government documents and newspaper articles. You should expect to be able to support and defend the chosen topic or argument that is the subject of your paper, and do so in a convincing and scholarly manner. If you accomplish all this, and make it a sound political argument, you have then written a solid political science paper.

31.2.4 Sociology

Writing a good sociology paper includes a clear thesis statement. While this is important in all papers requiring a thesis statement, the field of sociology carries with it a potential danger; taking sides.

Writing about sociology is about studying human behavior and the interaction between individuals or groups. An effective sociology paper will analyze these interactions and remain objective. The pitfall that many writers fall into when writing a sociology paper is that they take sides, and as a result they will slant their terminology toward one view or another. This is the trick to a successful sociology paper; staying on the median.

The case study to be the primary focus in sociology writing. In this discipline, writing about group dynamics is a key element.

31.2.5 Education

Many topics are covered in the education section of the social sciences, including students with special needs and child development. The instructor may choose to assign a topic for each individual student or the class as a whole. This gives the group the opportunity to work together and developed a more refined paper. The case study is a common type of paper chosen for a group assignment. Other times, the education instructor may allow each student to choose his or her own topic related to the education field. If that is the case, choose a topic that is of interest to you. You may not have a lot of knowledge about your chosen topic, but if you are genuinely interested in it, the information will be easy to come by and just as easy to understand.

Some of the possible types of papers you may be required to write include literature reviews, an analysis paper, case studies, research papers and lab papers. There are many more types of papers to write in this discipline, so be sure to clarify with your instructor what he or she expects.

31.2.6 Economics

When writing a paper in the economics discipline, the goal is to provide the reader with a clear understanding of the different (or specific chosen) areas of economics. It also seeks to define the many areas of economics, such as goods, services, and simple the state of economics in our society.

The economics paper may be as simple as a journal review (the Wall Street Journal, for example). Academic journals will be used often, as will statistical data from government sources.

One important thing to remember when writing in this discipline: be sure your vocabulary reflects the nature of the subject. Use topic-specific words and avoid personal observations. Be as factual as possible, avoiding jumping to unsubstantiated conclusions.

31.2.7 Elements of the Social Sciences Paper

When it comes down to actually writing your paper, be sure to include the following elements: an introduction, a thesis statement, the body of the paper, and the conclusion. Many social scientists use these headings in their paper.

One element of the social science paper that greatly differs from the humanities paper is that it should be written in such a way that the reader can take any section from the paper and read it independently from the rest of the paper, without having to look back at any other section. It is this type of technical writing that sets the social sciences paper apart from the humanities paper; each section is its own mini-paper. Knowing your audience members will greatly assist you in writing your social sciences paper.

A social science paper include many elements such as a title page, an abstract, thesis statement, introduction, body, conclusion and bibliography.

Your **title page** should include the subject or title of your paper, your name (and, if required, your address and phone number), and the current date. Some instructors also require you include the name of the course along with course number. An *abstract* is a short summary of the ideas you will be proposing in your paper. It is the place to state the argument you intend to address. You can do so by writing an outline of the background information for the paper. When writing your abstract, consider what experiments you did and what kinds of interviews you conducted. The abstract will be set aside from the rest of the paper, usually in the beginning. It will be the only element of the paper on its own page. An effective abstract will be able to summarize the paper with anywhere between 100 and 300 words.

The **thesis statement** will also come at the beginning of your paper. It will state the purpose of your argument and will introduce your claim to a specific type of human behavior. Your thesis is generally a part of your introduction. Your *introduction* will introduce your paper's main ideas. Keep them succinct, but make them interesting. Some questions to answer in your introduction may include: Why did you choose this topic? Is there a need for the general public to know about this issue, and why? How does this issue affect you, if at all? Define the problem clearly. Give examples so the reader knows exactly why this is a problem and how it affects society. Your instructor may want your introduction to be a separate element of the paper or a part of the body of your paper.

Toward the beginning of the **body** of your paper you will put your hypothesis. If you conducted experiments, what did you think would happen when you first began them? Working through the body of the paper you should cover the testing of the hypothesis, along with the discussion of any research conducted. The body of the social sciences paper will include many elements: the background of the problem or issue you are addressing (which addresses the issue of topic importance), your rationale (which justifies your choice of topics), your statement of qualification (which outlines why you, as a writer, as qualified to write on the subject), a survey of literature (which denotes the sources you used in forming your hypothesis), the methods of research used, the time estimate outline (for completing your experiments/projects), and any information about budget limitations. The body is where you will include any charts or graphs that will assist you in reporting your information. Supporting discussion should be written to explain these elements.

In the **conclusion** of the social sciences paper, you should recap the information you addressed in the body of the paper, keeping in close contact with the thesis. Did your test results differ from your hypothesis? If so, why? The conclusion should explain how the data supported or did not support your hypothesis. During your entire conclusion, you should always back up the main theme of your paper.

You will certainly need to include a works cited page (**bibliography**) to credit any sources used in your paper. Also, many education research papers include an appendix. You may include charts, graphs, and definitions. Most social sciences papers use the APA (American Psychological Association) format for documentation style, however, you will want to discuss style with your instructor before you begin your paper.

31.2.8 Resources to Use

Different resources you will use in order to complete your social sciences paper will provide different levels of information. An encyclopedia will provide basic information in pretty general terms. The information here will be in a the form of a summary, and will not be very comprehensive in nature. This is where books, a better source for information, will be beneficial. When you search for one specific book, this search may lead you to several other valuable books that you find you will want to reference in your paper. Finally, journal articles should be the final source you should rely on for information. Journal articles will provide the most comprehensive and up-to-date information in the subject you are researching. This is one of the reasons that it is important to use the journal article as your *last* source of information; the journal article is written in such a way that it assumes the reader has prior knowledge on the subject matter. So read your encyclopedia first (general and summative information), then research your subject in books (dedicated material), and finally in journal articles (comprehensive and scholarly).

In any case, you should steer yourself away from the mainstream media for your information. Stick with the scholarly print sources.

31.3 Natural Sciences

Writing in the natural sciences means writing about the natural aspects of our world. Theories are tested in order to solve problems. The natural sciences paper is used to evaluate and conclude from this testing.

Writing in this discipline is a detailed, tedious process. Specific steps must be taken to ensure you have gathered accurate data. Once you have gathered enough data, you must organize it into a coherent flow of ideas, ending with your evaluation or conclusion. One of the critical parts of the natural sciences paper is the presentation. You have your data, you have organized it, so now it is time to present it in a factual, knowledgeable way.

Natural Sciences can be broken down into 2 categories; **pure sciences** and **applied sciences**.

Pure Sciences include the life sciences, physical sciences, and earth sciences. Life sciences focuses on how plants, animals, and organisms (living things) relate to each other and how they interact with their surroundings. Biology is one area of the life sciences. Others include ecology, molecular biology and genetics, and food sciences.

To write about the physical sciences is to write about matter (anything that occupies space) and energy (what causes matter to move), not living things. There are many topics in the field of physical science. The list includes aerodynamics, thermodynamics, chemistry, and even astronomy.

Earth science, quite simply, is the study of the earth and its history. There are four main areas of earth science: *geology* (the study of the structure of the earth and how it formed), *meteorology* (the study of weather), *oceanography* (the study of the ocean and the creatures living in it), and *space science* (the study of the planets, stars, and everything else out there). Possible earth science topics may include volcanoes, tornadoes, the study of rocks, our atmosphere, earth minerals, or the solar system.

Applied Sciences include medical sciences (i.e. forensics, pharmaceuticals), engineering sciences (i.e. electrical/mechanical engineering) and computer science.

31.3.1 Elements of the Natural Sciences Paper

Keep in mind that when writing in the sciences, fact is preferred over flair. Write about the facts - the experiment outcomes, the process of information gathering, or a succinct hypothesis. Focus *on* the "what" and keep away from *describing* the "what."

It is good pedagogic practice to require student write ups to be near in style to what would be expected in a published paper. There is a tradition in science of using a neutral tone, the third person and the passive voice, and some institutions may require this style for high marks. It can however lead to rather stilted writing and other institutions encourage the use of the 1st person in write ups. It is necessary to be aware of the requirements of the course, the potential audience of the article and perhaps even the personality of the marker.

There are seven steps to writing in the Natural Sciences:

1. The problem being addressed must be stated in an objective fashion.

2. Unbiased relevant information must be gathered.

3. The information gathered must be analyzed.

4. A hypothesis is formulated.

5. Experimentation (the fun stuff) to prove your hypothesis. Remember that keeping a journal of experiment outcomes is important for your final steps, so be detailed.

6. Analyze your journal notes.

7. Arrive at your conclusion, which may or may not prove your original hypothesis.

When it comes down to actually writing your paper, be sure to include the following elements:

Title

The title of the natural sciences paper is very important. It should be concise and clearly describe what your paper is about. You may choose to introduce what you tested. For example:

"Synthesis of 2-phenyl-2-butanol via a Grignard Reaction"
Sample title for a natural sciences paper

This title describes the molecule of interest and the reaction of interest, making it easy for the reader to determine if this paper is one they would want to read.

Abstract

This is a brief description of your paper. Take the main ideas and summarize them in 250 words or less. For example, this is an abstract for a paper written in the organic chemistry field.

"This experiment synthesized 2-phenyl-2-butanol using a Grignard reagent under reflux conditions. Learning to utilize Grignard reagents is an important skill for any future chemist. After performing the experiment, it has been concluded that there was a moderate to poor yield of 2-phenyl-2-butanol produced. Unwanted oxidization of Magnesium metal during the formation of the Grignard reagent is a possible explanation. However, the characterization of the product using IR spectroscopy and 1H NMR spectroscopy has reinforced the production of a pure product."
Abstract containing 80 words

There is little to no explanation of the details of the experiment or results. If the reader is interested in this synthesis, they now know that this experiment showed a poor but pure yield, and used both IR and NMR spectroscopy to analyze the product. This is important in scientific writing because of the massive amounts of information available to a researcher. The nature of modern computer searches has meant that the abstract of a *published* paper is of paramount importance. There may be a hundred people reading the abstract for every single one who actually ever reads the full paper. Anything useful which the paper contains therefore **must** be mentioned in these 250 words. Abstracts help research scientists to weed through papers to find information pertinent to their specific interest.

Introduction

The paper should begin by introducing and forming a question in the introduction. The introduction should include relevant theories and equations used in your experiment. If other scientists have conducted similar experiments, give recognition to these predecessors of your work. Any hypotheses you have formed should be stated here. A brief description of the experiments conducted should be outlined in the introduction also, saving the intimate details of the experiments for the body of the paper.

"The reaction itself was developed by Victor Grignard of France in the late 1800s. His preparation of magnesium alkyl halides (now referred to as Grignard reagents) was first presented to the Académie des Sciences in France on May 11, 1900. (Nobel Prize.org) The reaction uses Magnesium metal to create an electron rich carbon atom from an alkyl or aryl halide. This is the Grignard reagent. The electron rich carbon atom becomes a nucleophile, attacking any other molecule that is electron poor. If placed in solution with a molecule containing a ketone, the Grignard reagent will attack the ketone carbon, creating a new carbon-carbon bond connected to a negatively charged oxygen atom. That oxygen is then easily turned into an alcohol using any weak acid. ..."
Sample Introduction Text

This introduction goes into detail regarding the synthesis used and what is synthesized in the experiment. This provides ample background information for the reader who may not be an expert in the experiment performed.

Thesis Statement

The thesis statement of a scientific paper is a clear and concise statement of your topic of study. This could be included in your introduction.

"The compound synthesized in this reaction, 2-phenyl-2-butanol, is a chiral molecule."
Thesis statement for sample paper

This thesis statement clearly defines what is being accomplished (or trying to be accomplished) through this experiment. Notice that this particular example does not include a hypothesis. For a synthesis-type experiment, there may not be any predictions to be made. Not all scientific papers need to include a hypothesis.

Body

Since the goal of the scientific paper is to present facts supported by evidence, there are general rules to follow in the paper. Avoid adjectives and adverbs (being descriptive), and instead focus on the nouns (the focus of the paper) and the verbs (how it acted).

Structure your sentences so that they are clear and easy to understand. Keep your audience in mind when using technical jargon. Limit yourself to words and jargon that your audience should be familiar with. Overuse of unfamiliar jargon will not make you sound smarter, it will only thoroughly confuse your readers.

The body of the paper will include the following

Experimental

This section contains all of the reagents you used in your experiment, most likely accompanied by any hazard warnings they might carry. If a colleague wants to reproduce your experiment, they need to know what they are getting themselves into. Also described here should be all of the equipment used in your data collection process, including specific equipment names and numbers.

Procedure

This section contains the steps taken during your experiment. If you used a procedure previously recorded elsewhere, feel free to simply reference that procedure to save time and precious space for data. If you are using a self-written procedure, you need to meticulously write every step down so that your experiment could be repeated in exactly the same way by a different team of scientists.

Results

Here you would record all of the numerical data you generated during your experiment. Refrain from drawing conclusions. Simply enter tables, graphs, and numbers that are pertinent to your conclusions.

Conclusion

In your conclusion, you should focus on the data you presented. Share and discuss your results. Here you are allowed to give your opinion on what the results mean. Although you are given the freedom to interpret your data how you see fit, avoid linking your findings with other, unexplored subject matter. If you didn't cover it in your introduction or experiment, leave it out of the conclusion!

Acknowledgments

Sometimes, but often not, you will need to put this section in. Examples are if you have used a service to run spectra or analysis for you, or someone has given you help by lending some part of their apparatus made for a different experiment. Acknowledgment sections are very appropriate and recommended for academic writing, as all equipment utilized usually belongs to the university. Some scientific service providers **require** a specific form of words in the acknowledgment as part of their regulations. These will be provided along with the results of your submitted sample.

References Cited Page

Follow the specific documentation style chosen or required. If citing, for example, a huge reference book of analytical and preparatory chemistry, give the page or chapter number so the reader stands a chance of finding the text you used. It is a good idea to make sure you cite any important references already cited for you in the laboratory instructions and add some more to show that you have looked further than just reading your assignment brief.

Appendix

This section is reserved for boring calculations and notes that you made during the actual experimentation process. No one really wants to see your hand written notes, but you are still required to present them to prove that you did observe what you claim in your paper. This section, therefore, usually contains a photocopy of the laboratory notebook page, or pages, that contain data and comments relevant to your paper.

31.3.2 Resources to Use

Seeing as writing in the natural sciences is technical in nature, you will find that your resources are going to have to be scholarly, comprehensive, and up-to-date (the only time you should use a reference that is several years old is to do comparisons). The first step is to educate yourself on your topic by locating information through a simple search. Information and data can be compiled by doing a search and writing down the information you find to familiarize yourself with the subject. When you feel comfortable with the level of knowledge of this information, you can move on to the next step in the research process.

That next step is finding encyclopedias, textbooks, reference books, and the like to continue filling in the details on your topic. These resources will be dedicated to the chosen topic. They will provide more detailed information and help you fill in any holes in your research or to simply answer questions that may have popped up during the information gathering stage. A good way to find if there are newer articles than your favorite reference is to use the *citing references* feature of many search systems. These might well give you a link to a more comprehensive and up to date reference.

Finally, you will turn to review articles, lab reports, and research reports to get the most up-to-date information. This is the most important resource you will use, and the most challenging. These articles and reports provide information that reveal the most recent discoveries on the chosen topic. However, they also tend to be technical in nature and are written in a way that assumes the reader is familiar with technical jargon associated with the field or subject. While keeping this in mind, review articles and research reports will round out your resource selection nicely.

Don't be afraid to search the Internet for information. There is a great deal of good stuff out there, but you should be careful in what you use. Be sure to gather any Internet information from a scholarly source, such as an educational site or a non-profit site. Use the Internet as a *secondary* or even better a *tertiary source* and preferably cite a review article or a *journal of record*. The citing of either the Internet or encyclopedias is sometimes expressly forbidden so you need to check on institutional policy here. (Despite this some book series, though they have *encyclopedia* in the title, such as Wiley's *The Encyclopedia of Nuclear Magnetic Resonance* are actually review journals and are eminently citable.) Internet articles change and so a citation should include the date accessed, for example:

| EDEXCEL http://www.edexcel.org.uk/Qualifications [accessed 27th October 2004]. |
| Example citation for internet article. Note that the date accessed has been included. |

31.3.3 Acronyms and Abbreviations

Science abounds in acronyms and abbreviations, which can be very irritating if you are not in the know. Even common ones like IR for infrared spectroscopy or MRI (Magnetic Resonance Imaging) should be named in full followed by the abbreviation the first time they are mentioned and then the abbreviation used from then on.

...the first sessions on Computer Aided Design (CAD) come in the General Computing Laboratory in year 1 (GCLy1). Subsequently CAD teaching is embedded in the course work./caption=Correct use of an Acronym}} Acronyms do not always mean the same to different people. A RAS can be either a *Reusable Asset Specification*, or in a system performance context *Reliability, Availability and Serviceability* or many would guess it is a *Random Access Something-or-other*

Longer reviews in subjects like biochemistry which have to name numerous macromolecules and cell constituents might require a separate *acronyms glossary* after the references and bibliography.

31.4 External Links

- Writing Guidelines for Engineering and Science Students[1]
- The Mayfield Handbook of Technical and Scientific Writing[2]
- Online Technical Writing: Online Textbook[3]
- EServer Technical Communication Library[4]
- Writing Lab Reports[5]
- The National Academy of Sciences[6]
- Exercises in Science: A Writing Course[7]
- Standard and Descriptive Sample Lab Reports[8]

---

1   http://www.writing.eng.vt.edu/
2   http://web.mit.edu/course/21/21.guide/Demo/web/
3   http://www.io.com/~hcexres/textbook/
4   http://tc.eserver.org/
5   http://www.rpi.edu/web/writingcenter/labs.html
6   http://www.nas.edu/
7   http://fauxpress.com/kimball/w/logo.htm
8   http://www.ncsu.edu/labwrite/res/labreport/res-sample-labrep.html

32 Writing in Business

Writing for business includes multiple types of formats including, but not limited to, cover letters, resumes, memos, e-mails, letters, proposals, business plans, and formal reports. This section will focus on how to be a successful business writer.

32.1 Purpose of Business Writing

The main purpose of business writing is to *convince*. For example, as a professional business writer, you often find yourself explaining the value of a complex idea in order to obtain agreement among readers. Or, you find yourself crafting a document intended to persuade people and rouse them to action.

In other respects, business writing is much like any other form of writing that includes pre-writing or brainstorming, writing and revising. The most important aspects of business writing are clear and concise writing and getting the message across in the best way. As with all writing, it is important to keep the audience in mind when coming up with the best format to get the message across.

32.2 Audience

The most important concept to keep in mind when writing for business is who your target audience is. You need to tailor your writing to fit different audiences in different situations. If you address the document's specific target audience in terms it understands, your document will have a better chance of achieving its goal.

Every business document has a purpose. You could be trying to persuade your boss that you are due a raise in one instance, and trying to persuade the HR Department that the company picnic would have more participation if it were held at a lake in another instance. In both instances, the language and way you would approach each is going to differ.

32.3 Deadlines

Much, if not all, professional business writing is performed against a deadline. In fact, making a deadline with time to spare is the hallmark of a pro. That act alone inspires a sense of confidence in a business that is often as persuasive as the document itself. So, a good rule of thumb for business writers would be 'better a B+ document that arrives on time than an A that's late.'

32.4 Memos and E-mails

Writing memos and e-mails in a business setting is slightly different than writing to a friend or family member. The biggest difference is that in a business setting, the writing must be professional or formal. A big misconception about e-mailing in business is that formality is not important. Grammar and composition are both important aspects. However, should you receive an email of memo which contains compositional and grammatical flaws, it may be rude or unwise to point these out to the author. Memos and e-mails have a similar approach. The purpose of both is to get a certain message across. This section will cover deciding when it is appropriate to use either a memo or e-mail, content, pre-writing techniques, and effectiveness.

32.4.1 Memos

The memo or memorandum has a few types. The memos can be short notes, reports, plans or proposals. The standard memo is most effective when attempting to inform many people within the same organization of upcoming events, changes, thoughts, or ideas.

Most memos will have five basic elements:

- The organization's logo or letterhead
- The "to" line
- The "from" line
- The subject line

Note: When writing your subject line, make sure it is called something accurate, unique and specific. Name your memo something informative.

- The date line

The first sentence of your memo you should clearly state your purpose. Be concise and direct.

Example: An example from "How to write it? (pp.167)"

```
To:    All Department Heads
From:  Joan Alexander
Date:  May 10, 2007
Subject:Weekly Department Head Meeting, May 30, 2007, 8:00 am. Room
108
Agenda:
    1.Vote on the vacation policy.
    2.Elect a media spokesperson.
    3.Introduce the new vice president of marketing, Mark Halpern.
```

Example: The purpose of this memo is to request authorization to travel to Minneapolis to visit the Museum of Natural History to learn more about dinosaur fossils.

Use headings throughout your memo to help the reader decide what they want to read and understand the information they are being presented. Headings can also help the reader understand the purpose of the section (i.e. summary).

If your memo has a lot of information or if it is really long, you may consider summarizing the memo. This can help readers understand the body of the memo, allow readers to skip information that is not relevant to them or to remind the reader of the memos main points. A good memo will record the clear main ideas and every important decision.

Keep in mind your audience when writing your memo. You may need to provide background information or explain the events that led to the situation to which the memo is regarding.

32.4.2 E-mails

Emails are fast, cheap, easy to use and digital. Because of its widespread use, here are some things to keep in mind when writing "business" emails.

- Use an appropriate level of formality.
- Keep messages brief. If you are replying to an email, don't repeat information from the email, instead establish a general context of the email. Also, if sending the email to more than one person, you may want to consider blocking the original author's name for privacy's sake (BCC = Blind Carbon-Copy).
- Be careful when writing. Because email is often informal, it is easy for them to become sloppy. Make sure you read your email before sending it.
- In formal business email, avoid the use of characters to create emotion faces, such as :), Orz, or > <.
- Use the subject line. All business emails should have a subject so the reader can decide quickly whether or not they need to read the email.
- Don't use all capital letters or use annoying backgrounds. Keep your emails simple. Try to stay away from using italics, bolds or underlining. Even if your email supports these options, others may not.
- Don't forward a message without the permission of the author.
- Above all, have something to say. Don't send emails just for fun or just to reply agreeing with the writer (unless this is requested or expected). In other words, don't send a message just to feel like you are part of the conversation.
- Remember, if you are writing a memo or email during working hours or on a company computer, the company OWNS this material (and has the fully legal right to inspect it). Avoid overtly personal and/or sensitive content in your email while at work. If you are concerned about this possibility, look into message encryption.

32.5 Cover Letters and Resumes

Writing a resume or a cover letter is basically a sales pitch to a potential employer. You need to acknowledge that they have a need (an empty position), and that you are *the* perfect fit for them or at least close enough of a fit to bring into their office for an interview.

32.5.1 Cover Letters

The cover letter and resume will form employers' first impressions of a potential employee. These documents will be the first thing the employer sees, therefore, make every attempt to ensure the documents are without errors (grammatical, spelling, punctuation, etc.). Mistakes in the resume and cover letter are one of the biggest reasons why job seekers fail to secure an interview. If the potential employer finds mistakes, they will have the feeling that the applicant probably will not take the time to be careful with their work when they are on the job.

The cover letter is an opportunity to expand on any specific points in the resume that deserve more attention and can be connected to aspects of the desired position. Remember, there is likely a large pool of people applying for the same position. Use the cover letter effectively to present yourself and distinguish your application from the rest.

Any time a resume is sent in the mail, it must be accompanied by a cover letter. The cover letter is an important factor in getting your resume past the first barrier. The cover letter must be customized for each opportunity. It can also be an opportunity to explain any problems,questions, and things that may not be clear in your resume (such as gaps in employment).

Why is the cover letter so important?

The cover letter:

- is your opportunity to personalize your resume and target your skills to the specific employer;

- connects your past experiences listed on your resume to your potential future position at a new job;

- highlights your strengths, accomplishments, and sparkling personality;

- can be tailored to the needs of the specific company to which you are applying.

Cover Letter Formats

Employer Invited Letter: Use the employer invited letter when an employer has requested a resume. This is often in response to a classified ad or publicized listing. This style focuses on matching your qualifications to the advertised requirements of the position.

Uninvited or Cold Contact Letter: Use the uninvited letter to contact employers who have not advertised or published job openings. The focus is on matching your qualifications to the perceived needs of the employer based on labor market research. This strategy requires that a phone or personal contact with the employer either precede or follow the sending of the resume and cover letter.

Referral Letter: Use the referral letter to contact employers to whom you have been referred. The effective job seeker will receive referrals to many job opportunities through networking and informational interviews. The referral may be to a specific job opening (advertised or unadvertised) or to an employer who may not be hiring. In a referral letter the individual who provided the referral is mentioned in the letter.

Specific points to address in the cover letter.

- Let the company know why you are contacting them. Your intent may seem obvious, but tell the employer you are interested in a job at their company. Opening a letter without stating you intent may seem awkward. Whenever possible address the cover letter to a specific person by name and title.

- Let the employer know how you heard about the open position. For example, "I am interested in X position. I heard about/discovered the opening online/in the newspaper/from one of their a current employees. It is likely that the company has more than one open position so make sure to identify the specific position in which you are interested.

- Include a detailed description of your educational and work experience. Be sure to highlight the areas in your work or educational history that apply directly or closely to your desired position. You can put either paragraph first, but put your strongest information first. If you have a lot of work experience related to the job, then put your work experience first. If your educational experience makes you more strongly qualified, consider putting that information first. Remember, extra-curricular activities can be very valuable, if they are applicable to the position.

- Use terms from the ad that are clearly relevant to you and your experience. Take a cue from the job ad and emphasize how you are specifically qualified for the position. If the job requires a degree in Management and you have a Master's Degree in Management, emphasize that point. Writing your cover letter specifically for the job for which you are applying, will stand out more than a person who has a generic cover letter. Utilize action words and descriptive statements to convey your qualifications and career objectives.

- Reemphasize your interest in the position. Include a polite, but also confident request for an interview. Ask that they contact you and be sure to include how you'd like to be contacted (i.e. give your phone number and/or your email address.

You may also want to state the best time you can be reached. It is also a good idea to reference your resume, if you haven't already done so.

- Remember, be confident! If you don't sound like you think you are qualified for the position, why should a potential employer? Your cover letter needs to persuade the employer that you have skills and abilities that are useful to the company.

Cover Letter Outline

Insert Date Here

Ms. Catherine Smith

Human Resources Director

St. Mary's Hospital

123 Southview Drive

Minneapolis, MN 55555

Dear Ms. Smith,

First Paragraph: Introduction

1. Explain why you are writing and the position you are applying for

2. Where you learned of the position

3. Who referred you to the job (if someone did)

4. Explain your interest in the employer, company, product/services

Body: Two to four paragraphs

1. Explain why you are qualified for the position

2. Link your cover letter to your resume; expand upon highlights of your resume with specific examples

3. Discuss your most relevant and distinguishing characteristics

Close: One paragraph

1. Indicate that your resume is enclosed/attached

2. Mention your desire for an interview

3. Notify the employer of a day and time you will follow up

4. Express your appreciation for their time and consideration of your application

Cover Letter Example

1234 Spring Drive

Anytown, MN 55432

May 25, 2005

Northern Newspapers, Inc.

5678 Fall Way

Othertown, MN 56789

Dear Ms. Nelson:

I am interested in applying for your Administrative Assistant opening I found posted on the Career Builder website. Please accept the enclosed resume as my application for the position.

I am accustomed to a fast-paced environment where deadlines are a priority and handling multiple jobs simultaneously is a requirement. As a Committee Legislative Assistant for the MN House of Representatives, I demonstrated my ability to multi-task jobs for two representatives and the committee for which I was responsible. I enjoy a challenge and work hard to attain goals. Constant communication with all levels of management, as well as constituents and customers, has strengthened my interpersonal skills.

I know I can contribute to the success of the Northern Newspapers.

I would welcome an opportunity to expand on my qualifications, which include:

- Extensive editing and proofreading skills
- Working both independently and as part of a team
- Substantial computer experience
- Having held various positions that emphasized problem-solving, multi-tasking and attention to detail; and
- Bachelor of Arts degrees in English.

  I am enthusiastic about and genuinely interested in this position. I know that my background and skills fit the qualities you are looking for in a candidate. Please contact me at (555) 555-5555 or at my e-mail address (j-j-doe@msn.com) to set up a time for us to meet in person.

  Thank you for your consideration.

  Sincerely,

  Jane Doe

Sample Cover Letter

Other Tips:

The cover letter and resume should be no more than a page.

Be creative, original and professional. Avoid using templates and standardized cover letters from books or websites.

If you are asked to supply additional materials or references, do so promptly.

Double check spelling and triple check any names and titles.

32.5.2 Resumes

Figure 15 Hourglass in wooden stand

Unlike cover letters, resumes are a brief outline used by hiring managers to *scan* a potential employee. Think of the resume as a "snapshot" of your most relevant work and educational experience. Just like your cover letter, you want to bring out aspects of previous positions that relate to the one you are hoping to obtain.

Resumes need to be brief and descriptive at the same time. How are you going to manage that? You will need to be very selective in your word choice. Each resume usually gets under a one minute chance to make an impression. You should generally be able to get everything that you need to say in one page. Make sure the pertinent information really stands out. If you glance at your resume and can't find what's important right away, someone else will have a hard time finding the information that's important.

Hiring managers expect that your resume be typed or printed, neat, easy to read, clearly outlined. Don't use bright colors of ink or paper. Make sure it looks professional.

There are several elements to a resume:

- Identification - Include your name, address, e-mail, phone number.

- Objective - Write a clear goal, avoid generalities. Objectives are not necessary, but they are really helpful when applying for a volunteer position, internship or other positions that are a little more vague than a job opportunity. If your objective states you want a job, don't include it, but rather specify the particular field of employment.

- Employment - Include your skills and responsibilities, with what equipment you worked. The most important thing to include here is what you gained from your employment, the results of your experience. Use an active voice and strong verbs.

- Education - Include information about your degree and the institution. Again, make sure you talk about the results of your education, not just that your received an education.

- Interests and Activities - Make sure these are relevant to the job and demonstrate the personal impact you made as part of the group or working on a project. Don't just include random hobbies.

- References - There are a variety of opinions about whether or not to include references on the resume. Most employers are aware that they can request references from the job applicant at any point throughout the interview and hiring process. The job application itself, also may ask for references and their contact information. It is important to utilize the "white space" on your resume most effectively. You can list your references or write "available upon request". If you choose to list your references on a separate sheet of paper, make sure your name is on all sheets in case the pages get separated. To provide continuity between your cover letter, resume and references list, consider using the same header with your name and contact information on all three documents.

How to get started:

1. **Define your objective.** What position do you want to be hired for with the resume you will be working on? Resumes should always be customized to reflect the skills related to the desired position. A resume for a human resources position should look different than a resume for a counseling position.

2. **Identify and evaluate your audience.** Who in the company will most likely be viewing your resume first: a human resources representative, the CEO or the district manager? What skills, qualities and knowledge will your audience look for?

3. **Prioritize your selling points.** You have considered who your audience is going to be and what they will be looking for, now consider what areas in your work and educational experience best match the desired skills, qualities and knowledge. Brainstorm the key buzz words and action verbs that would best highlight your relevant qualifications.

4. **Showcase your successes.** Every employer wants a winner on their team. Demonstrate your successes (e.g. college degrees, educational honors, scholarship winnings, job promotions, leadership and community involvement and any other relevant awards/recognition).

5. **Choose your resume format and layout.** What resume format (chronological, functional or combination) will best showcase your qualifications for the job. How can the layout be designed to best highlight so that the employer will quickly notice your selling points?

6. **Create, Critique and Revise.** Nothing good is ever written. It is always rewritten. Start the resume writing process as early as possible. Although your resume will always be a work in progress, revising will continually improve the final product. Ask a career advisor, professor, parent or room mates seriously edit your resume. Any typo, spelling and grammatical error or spacing mistake should be improved. Your goal should be to have your resume error free.

7. **Ensure the printing looks professional.** Typing your resume is an absolute must. Print your resume on a laser printer and use a heavier paper stock.

Questions to help jog your memory about your college activities for your resume:

• Did you win any academic scholarships? What were the winning criteria?

• Were you on the Dean's list?

• Do you have a high GPA?

• What major (s) and/or minor (s) did you complete?

• Worked while a student to help fund your education?

• Completed an internship?

• Active in student organizations? Held any positions of office/leadership? If so, what were your responsibilities?

• Played sports? Captain? All conference?

• Volunteer/community service?

• Summer employment?

• Student newspaper, radio station, or television station?

• Wrote articles for a publication? Had work published?

• Created a web site?

• Conducted original research?

• Presented papers, served on panels?

• Helped organize a special event or conference?

• Research assistant or teaching assistant?

• Theatre production? Debate team? Choir? Band?

• Individual tutoring?

• Field service/practicum as part of your major?

Using Key Action Verbs

What is an action verb? Action verbs describe achievements or results in a concise and persuasive manner.

The following job description uses a non-action verb:

Was the supervisor of ten employees.

The next job description uses an action verb:

Supervised ten employees.

The job description using the action verb is more concise (three words shorter). Concise writing is easier for the reader to understand and carries more impact and power.

Use action verbs as the first word of each bullet point in your resume to emphasize job descriptions in your resume. Examples:

• Developed and wrote content for the organization's website

• Created and coordinated special events generating product awareness and increased sales

• Evaluated company's marketing and public relation campaigns' impact & implementation.

It is common for students to be too brief in their description of their skills, qualities and traits. Key action words will help you best describe and sell your skills and abilities.

1. First read through the entire list below and write down the action verbs (skills) employers look for in your field or particular position.

2. Next, read through the entire list a second time and write down the action verbs you have used in the experience you are describing on your resume.

3. Look back at your written list and highlight the words that appear on both lists. Incorporate these words into your resume and cover letter.

Accelerated Corresponded Exhibited Judged Predicted RevampedActivated Counseled Expanded Launched

There are a few different forms of resumes. One gives a chronological breakdown of your work experience while the other shares your skills and prior positions based on function.

Resume Examples

Jane Doe

Summary of Qualifications:

- Exceptional interpersonal skills
- Extensive experience assessing needs and referring people to agencies and departments who can service them
- Energetic, Competent, Flexible and Motivated with a Positive Attitude
  Work Experience:
  May 2004-present Company A Smithtown, MN Pension Service Phone Representative
- Field questions in an inbound call center regarding pension payments
- Provide customers with necessary paperwork for specific concern.
- Assist departmental leaders in various time sensitive projects
  Nov. 2001-May 2004 Company B Jonestown, MN Editor
- General editorial work, including proofreading, formatting publications and layout design
- Work with products through all stages—from conception to publication
- Experience with working under deadlines
- Opportunity to work on projects both independently and with small groups
  Nov. 1999-Nov. 2001 Company C Hugestown, MN Committee Legislative Assistant II
- Met with individuals or groups to identify needs and briefed the Representatives on meeting details
- Organized volunteers to campaign for state representative candidate
- Maintained successful constituent relations, which lead to the continued support of my Representatives
- Assisted in scheduling people to testify at committee hearings
- Arranged travel information for representatives and committee
- Worked as part of a team
- Learned importance of time management, supervisory, selling, and organizational skills
  June 1998-Nov. 1999 Company B Jonestown, MN Customer Service Representative
- Facilitated and communicated effective solutions to internal and external customers
- Received customer appreciation notice in the form of letters to my manager
- Acquired better people and organizational skills
- Opportunity to sharpen quick-thinking, problem-solving skills
  Sept. 1996-May 1998 College Y Sharp, MN Peer Tutor
- Provided writing instruction and acted as a resource for college and graduate students
- Served as a liaison between faculty members and students
  Education:
  May 1998 College Y Sharp, MN English with a Political Science minor (cumulative GPA 3.6)
  References available upon request. |caption=Chronological Resume.

Jane Doe

Career Objective: Obtaining a challenging position as an administrative professional

Education: B.A. awarded May 1998 College Y, Sharp MN Major: English Minor: Political Science Cumulative G.P.A 3.6

Administrative Experience:

Nov. 1999-Nov. 2001 Company C Hugestown, MN Legislative Assistant II

- Met with individuals or groups to identify needs and briefed the Representatives on meeting details
- Organized volunteers to campaign for state representative candidate
- Maintained successful constituent relations, which lead to the continued support of my Representatives
- Assisted in scheduling people to testify at committee hearings
- Arranged travel information for representatives and committee
- Worked as part of a team
- Learned importance of time management, supervisory, selling, and organizational skills

Other Experience:

May 2004-present Company A Smithtown, MN Pension Service Phone Representative

- Field questions in an inbound call center regarding pension payments
- Provide customers with necessary paperwork for specific concern.
- Assist departmental leaders in various time sensitive projects

Nov. 2001-May 2004 Company B Jonestown, MN Editor

- General editorial work, including proofreading, formatting publications and layout design
- Work with products through all stages—from conception to publication
- Experience with working under deadlines
- Opportunity to work on projects both independently and with small groups

June 1998-Nov. 1999 Company B Jonestown, MN Customer Service Representative

- Facilitated and communicated effective solutions to internal and external customers
- Received customer appreciation notice in the form of letters to my manager
- Acquired better people and organizational skills
- Opportunity to sharpen quick-thinking, problem-solving skills

Sept. 1996-May 1998 College Y Sharp, MN Peer Tutor

- Provided writing instruction and acted as a resource for college and graduate students
- Served as a liaison between faculty members and students

Interests and Organizations:

- Administrative Assistants of America
  - member 1997 – current
  - secretary 2003 – current
- Big Brothers/Big Sisters volunteer

References:

Betty Smith Manager Company C 135 Lane Road Hugestown, MN 55559 (555) 444-3333

John Bill Department Leader Company A 246 Street Lane Smithtown, MN 55558 (555) 666-5555

Professor Nancy File Department of English College Y Sharp, MN 33562

Functional Resume

32.6 Follow up or Thank you letters

After an interview, take that time to write a thank you letter. The follow up letter can do more good for you in less time than most other aspects of the application/interview process. Thank the interviewer for taking time out of their schedule to meet with you. Also, make sure to emphasize your particular qualifications and/or restate your interest in the position. This letter puts your name in front of the interviewer again and also shows that you are truly interested in the position. Plus, if you are basically **tied** in contention for the job with another person, the thank you letter may tip the scales in your favor.

Mail the thank you letter within a day of your interview. Not only will this help you in remember the details of your interview, it will also help to ensure that your potential interviewer **sees your thank you letter** before making a final decision about the position.

When to Write Thank You Letters:

A thank you letter should be written after an interview, when someone provides or sends you information at your request, when a contact was particularly helpful to you, or any other contact that you would like to express thanks and develop a good relationship with.

Writing Your Thank You Letter:

The body of your thank you letter is really a "sales" letter. It is an opportunity to restate why you want the job, to reiterate your best qualifications that match the job requirements, and how you will make significant contributions to the establishment. A thank you letter is also the perfect opportunity to discuss anything that your interviewer neglected to ask you or that you neglected to answer as thoroughly as you could have.

Customize Your Thank You Letters:

It's very important to keep your audience in mind when writing your thank you letter. Typically your thank you letters are typed but research suggests that managers like hand written thank you notes also.

In addition to thanking the person you talked with, thank you letters also reinforce the fact that you want the job.

Follow Up Letter to Recap Important Information:

Remind individuals who attended the meeting of the main events and important dates that were discussed. Remind individuals who attended an important business event of the discussions that were made. This helps keep the work flowing and everyone on the same page. This also promotes further discussion and collaboration.

Follow-up Letter to announce a special Offer:

This type of letter helps improve your relationship with a new customer. Remind the customer that you are willing to help them by stating the advantages that your company can offer. Thank the customer, or announce the special sale or limited time offer. Remind the customer why you are a good business to work with.

Follow-up Letter to Remind Readers of Important Events:

Make sure to include the date, time, location of the event, and any other important information that the reader needs to have in order to attend the event.

32.6.1 Thank you letter example

1234 Spring Drive Anytown, MN 55432 May 26, 2005 Northern Newspapers, Inc. 5678 Fall Way Othertown, MN 56789 Dear Ms. Hall, I would like to express my appreciation for your courtesy in extending to me an interview this Monday for the position of Administrative Assistant with your Editorial Department. As a result of our interview, I am convinced that the position of Administrative Assistant at Northern Newspapers, Inc. is exactly the kind of challenge and opportunity I am seeking. As you may recall, my experience in editorial work at Company B coupled with my Legislative Assistant expertise with Company C will be a real benefit to you and the rest of the Editorial Department at Northern Newspapers, Inc. Thank you again for your time and consideration. I am looking forward to hearing from you soon. I can be reached at (555)555-5555 for another interview or to answer any more questions you may have for me. Sincerely, Jane Doe
A sample Thank You Letter.

32.7 Other business letters

Besides writing a letter to express appreciation for an interview, there are several other types of follow up letters. Here are some tips for these types of letters.

- Letter accepting a job offer - Express appreciation for the offer. Show enthusiasm for the position. Repeat the major terms of your employment such as start date, job title, or salary.

- Letter of rejection in response to a job offer - Again, express your appreciation for the offer. If it's appropriate, explain your reason for declining the offer. Remember, at some point in the future, you may want to work for this company, so be polite with your rejection.

- Letter acknowledging a rejection - Why bother? This letter maintains good relations with the company. You might get a phone call later on saying that the first choice candidate wasn't able to take the position.

32.8 Proposals, Business Plans and Formal Reports

Proposals, business plans and formal reports can be a critical part of your business career. All of these may deal with important outcomes. The goal of all of these is to persuade the readers into agreeing with your ideas. Often times, you are trying to gain something from the readers, such as money, equipment or help.

32.8.1 Considerations

When starting a proposal, the first thing to consider is what your goals are. If you are asked to write a proposal for someone, make sure you are clear on what their goals and requirements are.

There are four main elements that must be considered with your goals.

1. What are the immediate goals and how do they relate to the long-term goals?
2. What costs or risks are involved with writing the proposal? This includes time and people needed. Do not forget to explore hidden cost opportunities.
3. What kinds of resources are you going to need? Are those resources readily available?
4. What will come from an unsuccessful proposal? Will it be helpful if only some goals are met?

After considering your goals, there are still many more things to think about. You must take into consideration the readers, your argument, feasibility, and action.

32.8.2 Readers

The more you know about your readers, the more you can tailor your report to appeal to them. If you are lucky, you already know a lot about the reader because they wanted you to write the proposal and have given you specific guidelines. However if you do not know much about your readers, then you better do some research on them. It is important to know what form of research they will be the most receptive to. Surveys may satisfy one reader, while another reader may not find them to be as credible.

Argument

An argument can be summed up as what the main issue is and the importance of that issue. You need to prove to your readers the significance of the issue. You must convince your readers that your issue needs their attention or help. You need to inform them of the issue, tell them why they should care, what they can do to help, the benefits of their help, and why they should find you credible.

Feasibility

In your report, often as part of your argument, you will have to convince the readers of the feasibility of the issue. Included in this would be offering alternative plans, addressing the costs and risks involved, as well as the resources needed. You should be able to identify why your plan is the best option.

Action

You will also need to include a plan of action in your report. Most proposals are asking the readers for something. You will need to tell the readers exactly what it is that you want them to do.

32.8.3 What is included in a proposal?

Cover, cover letter, table of contents, executive summary, appendix, and graphics.

Cover

The cover page should include the title of the proposal, who the proposal is for, who the proposal is by, and the date.

Cover letter

The cover letter is used to introduce the formal report. It is often less formal than the report itself. The letter usually includes an introduction of the topic and how it was authorized, a brief description of the plan, highlights of the report's findings, conclusions, and recommendations.

Table of contents

The table of contents is just as it sounds, a table of the proposal's content and page numbers. In the table of contents you should include section headings/topics and the page they can be found on. Be sure to include leaders (numbers, dots or bullet-points) to link the section with the corresponding page number.

Executive summary

The executive summary is a brief overview of the proposal. You should summarize your main points, you should begin with your purpose and follow the order of your proposal. Make sure to avoid including non essential information. The executive summary should not be longer than 10 percent of the length of the proposal. With proposals that are 10 pages or less, it may not be necessary to include an executive summary.

Appendix

An appendix is pretty much any supporting material that you either reference in your proposal or may be supporting sources that be relevant to some readers and not others. You may choose to include survey forms, other reports, tables of data, or any related material. They are named Appendix A, B, C, etc.

Graphics

While graphics are not a must, they are greatly appreciated. Graphics help to break up all of the text in order to give the reader's eyes a little break. You may choose to include a few small charts or graphs in your reports also. Just be sure that the graphics are relevant to the proposal.

32.8.4 Some tips to consider while writing your proposal...

1. Be clear on your topic. Do not try to cover too many aspects in one proposal. Stick to the most important so that you can be clear and concise.
2. Create a phrase that will draw in your readers. Pick an aspect of your report that should interest you readers and mention it early on to gain their interest.
3. Make sure to include any background information that may be necessary in order to understand the proposal.

4. Give yourself enough time to finish the proposal to the best of your ability. You do not want to be in a time crunch while writing such an important document.

5. You should not start writing until all of your research has been conducted and you have reached all of your conclusions.

6. All basic writing standards apply... you should revise and edit, be consistent with verb tense, and avoid using "I" or "we" because you want the proposal to be objective and credible.

32.9 External Links

- Business Writing Introduction[1]
- Bull's Eye Business Writing Tips[2]
- Cover Letters[3]
- Guide to Basic Business Letters[4]
- Business Letter Formats[5]
- 10 Secrets of Business Letters[6]
- Letter Writing Rules[7]
- Resumes[8]
- Writing a CV Resume[9]
- Writing Memos[10]
- Business Report Writing[11]
- Tips for Writing a Business Proposal[12]
- http://www.brightexpress.com/follow-up-letters.html
- http://www.career.vt.edu/jobsearc/thankyou.htm#when

---

1   http://faculty.millikin.edu/~moconner.hum.faculty.mu/e201/index1.html
2   http://www.basic-learning.com/wbwt/tips-index.htm
3   http://www.wisc.edu/writing/Handbook/CoverLetters.html
4   http://esl.about.com/cs/onthejobenglish/a/a_basbletter.htm
5   http://www.wisc.edu/writing/Handbook/BusinessLetter.html
6   http://www.asu.edu/duas/wcenter/business.html
7   http://englishplus.com/grammar/letrcont.htm
8   http://www.rpi.edu/web/writingcenter/resume.html
9   http://www.soon.org.uk/cvpage.htm
10 http://www.rpi.edu/web/writingcenter/memos.html
11 http://business.clayton.edu/arjomand/business/writing.html
12 http://www.4hb.com/0350tipwritebizproposal.html

33 Oral Presentations

Oral presentations use many of the same techniques that are used in rhetorical writing. Planning your topic, researching, editing, reviewing, and revision are all important steps in producing a good oral presentation; the same as they are when writing an essay or research paper.

The best way to ensure that your speech is a success is to have enthusiasm for your topic and to give yourself adequate time to develop that enthusiasm into a workable talk.

33.1 Introduction

Once your topic has been decided upon and research is underway, it's time to think about how you plan to present your information.

33.1.1 Preparation

Of the several angles that need to be addressed in regards to delivering a speech, the most important thing to keep in mind is, "Who is my audience?" Never underestimate the importance of knowing your audience.

If you're planning to present information about new advances in interactive role-playing games on the Internet to a group of senior citizens, chances are you will need to use different terminology and examples than you would with a college-age audience composed of aspiring Software Engineers. If your audience can't understand what you're trying to say, you'll find it much harder to accomplish your objective.

Consider the following characteristics of your audience:
• Knowledge Base
• Age
• Race
• Gender
• Occupation
• Values & Morals
Who is Your Audience?

This brings us to consideration number two: what is the purpose of your speech? Is it a call to action? Strictly to inform? To persuade? Just as you will adjust your language for various audiences, so will you use different rhetorical strategies to achieve different goals.

In tandem with keeping your information audience-appropriate and on topic, your decision to use visual aids such as Powerpoint, charts, or any kind of props (in the case of demonstration presentations) will have a sizable impact on your audience, and as such should be given careful thought.

A question that you may want to ask yourself is, "How do I want to present the information?" You might want to give a bare-bones speech, have a Powerpoint presentation, or use exhibits to add character to your information. You also may ask, "How much information can I present in the allotted amount of time?" Sometimes starting a speech with something everyone can relate to helps to ease in the audience and make them more interested in what you will be discussing. Be sure to "trim the fat" off of your presentation if you are strapped for time. If you are running far over the amount of time that you have been allotted, you may need to re-assess your information and further narrow your scope. One of the most important things you should ask yourself is, "What ideas and thoughts do I want to leave the audience with?" These are the key points that you want to center your presentation around.

Knowing your audience gives you the key to gain and hold their attention, which is a central task for any presenter. Use your knowledge of the audience's demographics to draw them into the presentation from the very first sentence. By knowing what sorts of examples and illustrations you can use to make the contents of your presentation relevant and interesting, you have unlocked the door to understanding and persuasion.

33.1.2 Ways of Beginning a Speech

When you begin your presentation, you want the audience to feel interested and invested in what you have to share. The more interested you get them right off the bat, the more they are going to pay attention throughout the rest of the presentation. This can be done in a multitude of ways, but it is important to remember to keep your introduction relatively short; wordy introductions can lose your audience before you actually get to the speech itself. It is also important to remember that whatever opening line you choose, you must connect it to the content of your speech.

The use of quotations is a tried-and-true way of introducing a subject--if it is done correctly. Here is an example using Albert Einstein:

"After the nuclear bombs were dropped during World War II, the leading creator of this destructive force said, 'I know not with what weapons World War III will be fought, but World War IV will be fought with sticks and stones.' Albert Einstein stated this after finally seeing the bombs' full power; for he knew that he very well may have had a hand in the end of the world."
Opening with a quotation.

Startling statistics might help to open the eyes of your audience. Here is an example concerning incarceration rates:

"By the end of 2004, 724 out of every 100,000 U.S. residents were incarcerated. The United States of America has the highest jailing rate in the entire world."

Opening with a statistic.

Sharing a personal experience is an effective, but risky way of opening an oral presentation. Use this option only if it's the right fit for your audience. For example, if you are presenting to a group of Video Game Design students at your school on the topic of fun game play elements, you might use a personal experience like this:

"A couple years ago, there was this game that had just came out. Everybody was talking about how awesome this game was and how sweet the graphics were. So, I did what any gamer would do--drove directly to the store, picked up a copy of the game, brought it home, and popped it into my Xbox. My excitement heightened as the game loaded and the intro sequence played. When the game started, I was absolutely astonished ... at how bad the game play was. The game looked cool, but all you did was run around and hit the enemies in the head with a sword over and over again.   That game was not fun; Let's make a game that is fun."
Opening with a personal anecdote.

Using a joke to start a presentation is often a good idea. You just better hope that your audience thinks it's funny! In most cases, this means keep your joke clean. Also, try to make the joke pertain to the subject you are presenting on. Here is an example that you might use when doing a presentation on football:

"Anyone who makes a bad call against the Detroit Lions risks ticking off their last remaining fan."
Opening with humor.

If the presentation is more formal, you may just want to give an overview of the main topics you will cover in your speech. Here is an example using college dropouts:

"Today, I will be discussing college dropouts. I will be going over the current rate of dropouts as well as the many common reasons for it. I will also talk about the reasons to stay in college, like better knowledge, life experiences, and more pay in the future."
Opening with an overview.

33.2 Methods of Presenting Your Speech

When it comes time to present your speech, there are several methods of delivery to choose from. In most cases, your subject matter will be the main criteria for deciding whether to read verbatim, memorize your script, or work from cue cards. In the case of a scholarly presentation with an extensive amount of detail, you may choose to write out your speech and deliver it as written. If your goal is to persuade your audience through high-energy speaking and eloquent prose, you may choose to script and memorize your argument. When introducing an informal topic with which you are familiar, you may find that index cards and an outline will suffice. No matter which way you choose to present your speech, you need to be **prepared**!

Written preparation can include notecards or a fully spelled-out speech. In any case, it is essential that as a speaker, you provide clear talking points and transitions for your audience. When you write an essay, your audience or readers have the advantage of clearly seeing your paragraph, section, and page breaks; when you speak to an audience, you must recreate this experience verbally. To provide a recent example, President Barack Obama is known for numbering his extemporaneous responses to questions from the press or during election debates. When outlining a proposed solution, he will clearly mark its steps with one, two, and three. This rhetorical strategy is effective in helping his audience easily follow his logic and responses; though you can opt to use transitions that are somewhat more subtle, never forget that your audience cannot see the progression of your argument and you must visually outline it for them.

33.2.1 Manuscript Speaking

Writing the content of your speech out word for word may be appropriate for certain situations. For instance, when you are presenting critical facts or statistics, having the data at your fingertips helps to prevent errors. While misquoting information might sound like a minor offense, under certain circumstances it can have grave repercussions, such as being sued for slander. Though in most cases incorrect information will only confuse your listeners and embarrass you, it's good to remember that such mistakes won't be tolerated in many professions, including law and politics.

The drawback to a scripted speech is that the audience will almost certainly know that you are reading word for word. This has several drawbacks, including decreased eye contact and stilted delivery, both of which leech power away from your presentation and tend to create a feeling of disconnect between the listeners and the speaker.

If giving a manuscript speech is necessary, practice is the best way to avoid a bad presentation. By reading your speech aloud several times, you will become more comfortable with the rhythm and inflections of your writing. Make sure that you are thinking about where and when you can make eye contact with your audience to underscore your points and add emphasis to important parts of your speech. Particularly with a written speech, you can add visual cues to your speech to remind you when to look up or emphasize a certain point.

33.2.2 Memorized Speaking

When a presenter memorizes a speech, it's basically a manuscript speech minus the paper. Memorizing a speech can improve eye contact with an audience. Body language may also improve because the speaker has more freedom to move about the area, since papers/notes will not be used.

A problem posed by memorizing a speech arises when the presenter forgets the speech. This can cause an embarrassing, awkward situation and make the speaker appear inept. Plus, the speaker's tone tends to sound artificial and rehearsed.

If you choose to memorize a speech, you might want to have a sparse outline with you just to remind yourself of your talking points.

33.2.3 Extemporaneous Speaking

An extemporaneous speech (extemp speech) is delivered from a prepared outline or note cards. The outline and/or note cards include the main ideas and arguments of the speech. The only information that is typically copied word for word are quotes. Outlines and note cards should be used for keeping the presentation organized and for reminding the presenter what information needs to be provided.

Extemp speaking has many advantages compared to the other methods of delivery.

For one, an extemporaneous speech sounds spontaneous because the presenter is not reading word for word. Glancing at an outline or a note card that has key ideas listed allows the presenter to add detail and personality to the information being presented.

Second, similar to memorized speaking, eye contact and body language can increase. The speaker's head is not down, buried in a manuscript.

Third, the speaker is able to take in audience feedback and respond to it as it occurs. An audience tends to change moment by moment, and a good speaker can tell when more or less detail is needed for different parts of the presentation.

In order to ensure an extemporaneous speech's strength, it is important to practice presenting with the outline or note cards being used. Inexperienced speakers tend to worry that they will forget important information if they do not write it out on their outline/note card.

Practicing your speech, even if it's just to your pet or mirror, will help increase your confidence level in both delivery and knowledge of the subject.

```
Minnesota Twins History Note card #1
 I. Intro - Personal Experience
 II. Creation
     A.President of Org. - Calvin Griffith
     B.1960 - Move from "Washington Senators" to MN Twins
     C.Metropolitan Stadium, built in '56
     D.Show pic of 60's uniform
 III. Historic Twins' Players
     A.Killebrew
     B.Kaat
     C.Oliva
```

Note card Example for Extemp Speech.

33.3 Do's and Don'ts

Now that you have familiarized yourself with the various methods of preparing and delivering oral presentations, it's time to discuss the best way to present your information. You may be familiar with Marshall McLuhan's adage "the medium is the message." Don't forget that in the case of an oral presentation, you ARE the medium. In other words, no matter how well-researched and cunningly written, your speech will only be as professional as your look and manner suggest it is. Your appearance and delivery are just as important as the content of your presentation.

33.3.1 Dress Code

You've no doubt heard this from your high school guidance counselor, your parents, and a dozen brochures about successfully interviewing for employment, but it bears repeating: **First impressions are important**. It is imperative that you dress to impress. For most situations in which you will be delivering an oral presentation, this means "Business Casual."

For **men**, business casual usually consists of a button-front shirt, tie, dress slacks, and dress shoes (blazer is optional). Men should also be clean-shaven or else properly groom their facial hair. For **women**, business casual includes a button-front shirt (or professional-looking sweater or top- on this point, women tend to have more business casual options than men), dress pants or skirt (of appropriate length), and dress shoes. Both men and women should take care not to expose too much skin.

If the speech will be presented before an audience that will be dressed formally, *wear a suit*. You should try to get plenty of sleep the night before your presentation, so that you will be fresh and well rested. Before approaching the podium, take a quick look in the mirror--Hair tidy? Teeth clean? Tie straight? Under no circumstances should hats or anything that obstructs eye contact with the audience be worn.

As with other elements of public speaking, consider what your particular audience will expect of you. In some cases, dressing casually is entirely appropriate; in others, only a suit (for women and men) is acceptable.

33.3.2 Delivering The Message

When speaking to the audience, act poised and confident, even if that's not how you feel on the inside. Some of the most common "tells" that a person is ill at ease include fidgeting, throat clearing, and speaking too rapidly. Stand up straight and stay relatively still--don't shift your weight from foot to foot. Keep your hands quiet, and avoid putting them in your pockets. Also, try to prevent yourself from adjusting your shirt or glasses or from playing with your notecards, hair, or writing utensils. Concentrate on keeping your breathing slow and even, and try to relax. Most importantly, make eye contact with the audience, **not the floor**. You should be as confident in your vocal delivery as you are in your posture. Avoid saying "Um", "Uh", or "Like". These words make you seem uncertain, unprepared, and undermine your credibility. Vary the tone of your voice and talk at a steady, conversational rate. Last, but not least, do not chew gum or suck on candy while speaking. If you're afraid that your mouth will go dry, it is acceptable to have a small glass of water at hand to sip discreetly.

Again, the most important preparation you can do is to practice your speech several times to a mirror, your pet, a friend, or family member. The more comfortable you feel with your material, the more confident you will be when presenting it to an audience.

33.4 Conclusion

Figure 16   "WOW" your audience!

Leaving the audience with a bang is necessary in order to ensure a lasting impression. Remember, the last thing presented tends to be what the audience remembers the best. The ending of a speech can be as important as the beginning and body. The conclusion should do what the introduction did, except in reverse.

33.4.1 Ways of Ending a Speech

After completing the presentation, the presenter should summarize the main points again without repeating verbatim what was said in the introduction. After that, you want to "Wow" your audience again with one of the techniques for introducing your speech. This can include: a quotation, a startling statistic, a personal experience, a joke, or a formal closure. Particularly if you are presenting persuasive information, you may want to end your speech with a call to action. What are you asking of your audience? What can they do after listening to your speech? Finally, asking for questions is a good way to minimize any confusion that the audience might have or bring to light any relevant connections which you may have overlooked.

33.4.2 Thank Your Audience

While this is one of the most important things to do at the end of a presentation, it is also one of the most forgotten things. Remember that the audience has given up their time to listen to you. They could have been anywhere else in the world doing anything they wanted to do, but they were there with you. You should appreciate that. An example of thanking your audience could look like this:

"That is all I have for today. I appreciate you giving me your time. Thank you very much and have a great day."
Ending with a thank-you.

33.5 External Links

- General Information and Advice[1]
- Managing Nervousness During Oral Presentations[2]
- An Online Handbook[3]
- Presentation Tips for Public Speaking[4]

---

1   http://www.rpi.edu/web/writingcenter/presentation.html
2   http://www.learningcommons.uoguelph.ca/ByTopic/Learning/LearningGeneral/
    LearningGeneralLearningFastfacts/Fastfacts-ManagingNervousness.html
3   http://www.ecf.utoronto.ca/~writing/handbook-oral.html
4   http://www.aresearchguide.com/3tips.html

34 Grammar and Mechanics

35 *Understanding Grammar*

36 What is Grammar?

36.1 What is Grammar?

Grammar is the study of how words and their component parts combine to form sentences. Grammar is the scientific study of language that includes *morphology* (also "accidence" or the forms that words take) and *syntax* (the relation of the words to other words). Grammar also involves the study of the different parts or elements of speech (for example nouns, verbs, adjectives, etc.), the relations between those elements. A knowledge of grammar provides a vocabulary to discuss how the language works.

Need some help?

- St. Cloud State University has a great website that is very useful for writers called LEO: `http://leo.stcloudstate.edu`.

It is especially great because it is written based on college writing. It is quite in depth and is broken down into many categories so a writer can find what they need. Access is available for anyone, not limited to students of St. Cloud State University.

- A writer can use many different reference tools through St. Cloud State University's website. Among these references includes free access to the Oxford English Dictionary. Go to `http://lrts.stcloudstate.edu`.

Click the "Library" link then the "Online References Resources" drop down menu. Here, there will be a list of many useful resources. Some of these resources are limited to student only use.

Category:Rhetoric and Composition[1]

---

1   `http://en.wikibooks.org/wiki/Category%3ARhetoric%20and%20Composition`

37 Parts of Speech

37.1 Nouns

A noun is the part of speech that can fit into specific morphological and syntactic frames: A noun takes inflection suffixes for plural, singular possessive and plural possessive cases (-s;-'s;-s'). A noun appears after a determiner. Nouns refer to persons, places, things, states, or qualities.

Nouns appear: after adjectives, after articles, as a subject of a sentence, as an object of a preposition, as a direct object of a transitive verb, and as an indirect object of transitive verb.

There are different kinds of nouns in terms of their grammatical function. These can be classified into different categories:

Count nouns refers to discrete number of things that are countable. They can take the plural forms and can be preceded by articles. Examples: book, house, car.

Non count also known as *mass noun* and refers to things and objects that are indiscreet. Examples: rice, oil, weather.

Common nouns are any person, place, or thing. Common nouns are not capitalized. Examples: a city, the policeman, that desk.

Proper nouns are the name of a specific person, place or thing. Proper nouns are capitalized. Personal names are the best examples of proper nouns. Examples: Nicolas, Idaho, Daily News.

Collective nouns are used to name groups. Even when a collective noun is in the singular form, it can be used to refer to a group. Example: team, herd, jury

Concrete nouns words that represent objects one can see, hear, touch, smell or taste. *Abstract nouns* are anything one cannot see, hear touch, smell or taste.

Some examples of nouns are: Tom, table, classroom, desk, bottle, door, conscience.

37.1.1 Determiners

Determiners are used as modifiers of a noun phrase or words that occur before a noun. Determiners can be classified as articles, demonstratives, quantifiers, possessive noun and possessive pronouns.

Determiners form a closed class of words that number (exclusive of ordinals) about 50 in English and include: the teacher, a college, a bit of honey, that person, those people, whatever purpose, either way, your choice.

Articles: a, an, the.

Demonstratives: this, that, these, those, which, etc. (when used with noun phrases).

Possessives: my, our, your, her, his, its, their, whose, and possessive nouns (John's, the teacher's).

Quantifiers: all, few, many, several, some, every, each, any, no etc.

Cardinal Numbers: one, two, fifty, etc.

Ordinals: first, second, last, next, etc.

37.1.2 Articles

There is also a special class of determiners called articles. These are the words *a*, *an*, and *the* and sometimes proceed nouns or other words that come before a noun.

A Definite Article (English the) is used before singular and plural nouns that refer to a particular member of a group. (The cat on the mat is black.)

An Indefinite Article (English a, an) is used before singular nouns that refer to any member of a group. (A cat is a mammal.)

A Partitive Article indicates an indefinite quantity of a mass noun; there is no partitive article in English, though the words some or any often have that function. An example is French du / de la / des, as in Voulez-vous du café ? ("Do you want some coffee?" or "Do you want coffee?")

A Zero Article is the absence of an article (e.g. English indefinite plural), used in some languages in contrast with the presence of one. Linguists hypothesize the absence as a zero article based on the X-bar theory.

The words *a* and *an* are called indefinite articles, because they do not identify a particular person, place, or thing. *The* is called a definite article, because it does specify a particular person, place, or thing.

37.1.3 Using *a* and *an*

Determining which word to use, either *a* or *an*, is based on the first sound of the word that follows it. When a word starts with a consonant **sound**, use *a* before it. When the word begins with a vowel **sound**, use *an* before it. Be careful, sometimes the first letter of the word is not the first sound of the word (see *hour* and *unicorn* below).

- *a* show
  - *an* amazing show
- *an* octopus
  - *a* huge octopus
- *an* hour
  - *a* house
- *an* apple
  - *a* red apple

- *a* unicorn
  - *an* angry unicorn

37.1.4 Singular and Plural

In order to show whether a noun is singular or plural, change the noun's spelling. A noun will take the plural inflection '-s' for most words in English. But, there might be irregular plural nouns as well. Some of the examples of irregular nouns are given below:

- boy/boys
- child/children
- woman/women
- man/men
- syllabus/syllabi
- ox/oxen
- deer/deer

If you are unsure how to change a word into the plural form, check your dictionary.

37.1.5 Possession

Nouns also undergo a morphological change to express possession (ownership) by using an apostrophe followed by the letter "s" ('s). This can denote 'singular' or 'plural' possessive. Possession is having some degree of control over something else. Generally, to possess something, a person must have an intention to possess it. A person may be in possession of some property (although possession does not always imply ownership). Like ownership, the possession of things is commonly regulated by states under property law. Languages have several means to indicate possession.

EXAMPLES:

- girl/girl's (singular)
- children/children's (plural)
- man/man's (singular)
- woman/woman's (singular)

---If a singular noun does not end in s, add 's

The delivery boy's truck was blocking the driveway.

Bob Dole's concession speech was stoic and dignified.

The student's attempts to solve the problem were rewarded.

---If a singular common noun ends in s, add 's—unless the next word begins with s. If the next word begins with s, add an apostrophe only. (This includes words with s and sh sounds.)

The boss's temper was legendary among his employees.

The boss' sister was even meaner.

The witness's version of the story has several inconsistencies.

The witness' story did not match the events recorded on tape.

---If a singular proper noun ends in s, add an apostrophe.

Chris' exam scores were higher than any other students. --Usually singular proper nouns will be names like Chris, and Alyssa.

37.2 Pronouns

A pronoun is a word that often replaces a noun phrase, other pronouns, or other words functioning as a noun in a sentence. The word or group of words that a pronoun replaces or refers to is called the antecedent of the pronoun

Example #1 The dog is old. *It* walks slowly. In this sentence, the word *it* replaces *the dog.*

Example #2 Wow, that boy can throw a football. *He* must have thrown it 60 yards. In this sentence, the word *he* replaces *that boy.*

There are several types of pronouns: personal pronouns, possessive pronouns, intensive and reflexive pronouns, relative pronouns, interrogative pronouns, demonstrative pronouns and indefinite pronouns.

Personal Pronouns are those that refer to specific people or things. Examples: I, he, she, we, us, they.

```
After they finished shopping they put the groceries in the trunk.
```

Possessive Pronouns indicate ownership. Examples: My, mine, your, our, theirs.

```
My brother bought his car.
```

Intensive and Reflexive Pronouns Intensive pronouns emphasize a noun or another pronoun.

```
The President himself called to congratulate me.
```

Reflexive pronouns look the same as intensive pronouns but serve a different function. They name a receiver of an action.

```
We shopped ourselves to death.
```

Relative Pronouns introduce subordinate clauses and function as adjectives.

> The man *who* yelled at us to get off his lawn did not even own the
> property!

Interrogative Pronouns introduce questions.

> *Who* was that? *Who* will help me? *Which* do you prefer?)

Demonstrative Pronouns point out specific persons, places, things or ideas such as that, those, this, these.

> *This* is my dog.

Indefinite Pronouns refer to non-specific people or things. Examples: All, both, any, few, everyone, each, nobody, some, several, neither.

> *Several* people cheered after the solo.

Pronouns most often replace a noun but can sometimes function as a determiner. These are called pronoun/determiners because they are in the form of a pronoun but function as an determiner.

> *This* material was new to me.   *This* functions as a pronoun/adjective.

Pronoun Problems

Pronouns can cause many problems for writers. Here are some tips to help you.

- Make sure the pronoun and its antecedent (the noun or pronoun to which the pronoun refers) agree. They must both be singular or plural.

Examples: My *dog* finished her *food*. (Both are singular) The *dogs* fought for *their* food. (Both are plural)

-Collective nouns should be used as singular unless they are obviously plural.

Example: The *jury* gave *its* verdict.

-Compound antecedents connected by *and* should be used as plural.

Example: *Jack and Jill are* getting married.

-Some antecedents that are indefinite and morphologically singular (*anyone, each, everyone, nobody, somebody*) can take *they.*

Examples: And everyone to rest themselves betake - Shakespeare, *The Rape of Lucrece,* 1549 I would have everybody marry if they can do it properly - Jane Austen, *Mansfield Park,* 1814 ... the detachment and sympathy of someone approaching their own death - Alan Moorehead, *The Blue Nile,* 1962

-Make sure the antecedent is clear.

Example: When she set the picture on the glass table, *it* broke.

By using *it* after two nouns, the reference is unclear. Which item broke? The picture or the table? When reading your writing, ask yourself these questions. If you are unclear as to which noun is the antecedent, it will be unclear for the reader as well.

-Deciding whether to use we or us

If you are unsure as to which pronoun to use, try omitting the antecedent.

Example: *We/Us* workers would like to have more breaks. It makes much mores sense to say *We would* instead of *Us would*.

37.3 Verbs

A verb is the main word in the predicate of a sentence. It expresses an action, describes an occurrence, or establishes a state of being. Depending on the language, a verb may vary in form according to many factors, possibly including its tense, aspect, mood and voice. It may also agree with the person, gender, and/or number of some of its arguments (subject object, etc.)

an action would be: Josh *threw* the ball.
Jason *kicked* the football.

an occurrence would be: a hush *descended* on the crowd.
a feeling *warmed* his heart.

a state of being would be: Jill *was* serious.
The house *is* on the hill.

37.3.1 Principal Parts

The principal parts of verbs are the different forms that verbs take depending on how they are used in a sentence. For example, take the verb escape.

base form: to escape

past tense: escaped

present participle: am escaping

past participle: escaped

37.3.2 Subject-Verb Agreement

Verbs need to agree with their subjects in number (singular or plural) and in person (first, second, or third). Find the verb and ask "who or what" is doing the action of that verb.

To make verbs agree with compound subjects, follow this example:

A pencil, a backpack, and a notebook **was** issued to each student.

```
This sentence should be edited to say:
```

A pencil, a backpack, and a notebook **were** issued to each student.

Verbs will never agree with nouns that are in prepositional phrases. To make verbs agree with their subjects, follow this example:

The direction of the three plays **are** the topic of my talk.

```
This sentence should be edited to say:
```

The direction of the three plays **is** the topic of my talk.

The subject of my talk is *direction,* not *plays.*

In the English language, verbs usually follow subjects. But when this order is reversed, the writer must make the verb agree with the subject, not with a noun that happens to precede it. For example:

Beside the house **stands** sheds filled with tools.

```
This sentence should be edited to say:
```

Beside the house **stand** sheds filled with tools.

Because the subject is *sheds*; it is plural, so the verb must be *stand.*

===Verb Tenses===

Tenses in a verb help to show when the action expressed by a verb takes place. The three simple tenses are the present tense, past tense, and future tense. Verbs also take *aspect.* Aspect refers to progression or completion of an action. The 'aspect' affixes are denoted by '-en' and '-ing,'which forms non finite participle forms.   ---Present Tense Present tense expresses an unchanging, repeated, or reoccurring action or situation that exists only now. It can also represent a widespread truth.

```
Examples: The mountains are tall and white. Unchanging action
Every year, the school council elects new members.  Recurring
action
Pb is the chemical symbol for lead.  Widespread truth
```

---**Past Tense** Past tense expresses an action or situation that was started and finished in the past. Most past tense verbs end in -ed. The irregular verbs have special past tense forms which must be memorized.

```
Examples: W.W.II ended in 1945.  Regular -ed past
Ernest Hemingway wrote "The Old Man and the Sea." Irregular form
```

---**Future Tense** Future tense expresses an action or situation that will occur in the future. This tense is formed by using will/shall with the simple form of the verb.

```
Examples: The speaker of the House will finish her term in May of
2012.
The future tense can also be expressed by using am, is, or are with
going to.
The surgeon is going to perform the first bypass in Minnesota.
We can also use the present tense form with an adverb or adverbial
phrase to show future time.
The president speaks tomorrow. (Tomorrow is a future time adverb.)
```

---**Aspect:** Refers to the nature of the action described by the verb. There are three aspects: indefinite (or simple), complete (or perfect), continuing (or progressive).

The three indefinite tenses, or simple tenses, describe an action but do not state whether the action is finished:

the simple past ("I went") the simple present ("I go") the simple future ("I will go")

```
Progressive: He is reading a book
Perfect     : Mary has taken her work seriously
```

The simple tenses locate an action only within the three basic time frames that we've recognized, present, past, and future. There are also three complex aspects of time that can be expressed:

```
Progressive forms: express continuing actions.
Perfect forms: express actions completed before
    another action or time in the present, past, or future
Perfect progressive forms: express actions that
    continue up to some point in the present, past or future.
```

===**Transitive and Intransitive Verbs**=== Transitive verbs help to carry out the action of a specific subject, and are followed by a noun phrase. A transitive verb must be followed by a direct object.

```
For Example:
      He          ran          to school.
   (Subject) (did something)   (object-where?)
      She cuts her hair every month.
      The dog runs around the tree.
```

Intransitive verbs do not take any object, but they do express the actions that don't require the subject to do something to something else. The intransitive verbs can stand alone in a sentence.

```
For Example:
        Katie ran.
          -The intransitive verb ran is a complete
           action by itself and doesn't need an object
           to complete the action.
        Jack fell on the steps in the entryway.
```

37.3.3 Linking Verbs

Linking Verbs link the relationship between the subject and the rest of the sentence. This type of verb explains the connection between the subject and it's complement.

The most common linking verb is "to be." The *linking verb* forms the main verb in a sentence and is also known as the copula.

```
Example: The tea is hot.
         There are many books on the shelf.
```

In the above sentences, *is* and *are* serve as the linking verbs as well as the main verbs in the sentences.

```
        Common Linking Verbs:
            appear          become
            seem            taste
            continue        remain
```

A *true* linking verbs are any form of be {am, is, as, were, are being, might, etc.} The true linking verbs act as the main verb in a sentence.

example: The work was very tiring.

In this sentence, *was* function as the linking verb which is also the main verb in the sentence. This type of sentences cannot be transformed into passive sentences because the verbs do not have a direct object (non-transitive verbs).

In your writing you can also input verbs with multiple personalities. such as appear, feel, remain, smell.

37.4 Adjectives

Adjectives modify or limit the meaning of nouns or pronouns, usually by describing, quantifying, or identifying those words and is often described as determiners. An adjective answers the question *what kind, which one, how many* or *how much.*

A *describing* adjective would be... Josh threw the *yellow* ball.

A *quantifying* adjective would be... We caught *several* sunfish last weekend.

A *identifying* adjective would be... Carol tried hard to win *that* race.

The most widely recognized adjectives are those words, such as big, old, and tired that actually describe people, places, or things. These words can themselves be modified with adverbs, as in the phrase very big.

Besides being used to modify a meaning, adjectives can be used to compare items.

a comparative adjective would be: This year's graduating class was *smaller* than last year's class.

another comparative adjective would be: This year's offensive line was the *smallest* in the past few decades.

Finally, adjectives can be pronouns. Pronouns used as adjectives usually show ownership.

A pronoun used as an adjective would be: Shelia bought *her* first car yesterday. Another pronoun used as an adjective would be: The Smith's saw *their* dreams crumble when they were denied a mortgage.

37.5 Adjectival Phrase

An adjectival phrase is a phrase with an adjective as its head (e.g. full of toys). In English, an adjectival phrase may occur as a post-modifier to a noun (a bin full of toys), or as a predicate to a verb (the bin is full of toys and clothes).

37.6 Adverbs

Adverbs are modifiers or descriptive words, phrases, or clauses that bring detail to your sentences. An adverb answers the question *where, when, how* or *to what extent*. They modify verbs, adjectives, other adverbs, or entire clauses. Once you figure out what word you want to modify, you are able to choose which modifier you need. Many adverbs end in -ly except for always, never, very and well. The most commonly used adverb is *not*.

37.6.1 Difference between adverbs and adjectives

Adjectives and adverbs answer different questions. An adjective modifies a noun or pronoun and answers these questions:

- Which: the latest magazine arrived.

- What kind: a huge difference remained.
- How many: the three books were different.

An adverb modifies a verb an answers these questions:

- When: tomorrow, the storm will quit.
- How often: students change majors frequently.
- Where: the class is held here today.

When choosing between an adjective and adverb, determine the word being modified and then figure out its part of speech.

37.6.2 Forming adverbs

Often adverbs are formed from adjectives, but some are not derived from other words such as again, almost, always, never, here, there, now, often, seldom, well. The adverbs that are derived from adjectives can be formed by adding the suffix -ly to the ending.

- beautifully
- strangely
- cleverly
- respectfully

Remember that an -ly does not make the word an adverb. Some adjectives also end in -ly such as friendly and lovely.

37.6.3 Placement

The location of the adverb in a sentence can change the rhythm and emphasis dramatically.

- Formerly, Star Wars was just three movies.
- Star Wars was formerly just three movies.

37.7 Conjunctions

con·junc·tion Pronunciation Key -[kuhn-juhngk-shuhn]

Conjunctions join words, phrases or clauses within a sentence. They illustrate a relationship between the elements that are being joined.

Coordinating Conjunctions *for, and, nor, but, or, yet, and so* are coordinating conjunctions. These are conjunctions of two grammatically equal elements such as two nouns or two clauses. This can also be remembered through the acronym FANBOYS.

Example: I like apples *and* oranges.

Correlative Conjunctions come in pairs such as *either...or, neither...nor, not only...but also*. These conjunctions also connect two equal grammatical elements.

Example: I will have *either* pasta *or* pizza for dinner.

Subordinating Conjunctions *After, although, as if, because, even though, once, in order that, and rather than* are some common subordinating conjunctions. These are conjunctions that introduce a subordinate clause and illustrate a relationship with the rest of the sentence.

Example: Although I would rather party tonight, I will go to the library instead.

Conjunctive Adverbs are used to show a relationship between two independent clauses (complete sentences). Some examples are *accordingly, furthermore, therefore, however.*

Example: I always brush my teeth; *therefore,* I have no cavities.

37.8 Prepositions

Prepositions are words that come before a noun or pronoun that form a phrase that modifies another phrase within the sentence. This phrase, the prepositional phrase, usually functions as an adjective or adverb and often indicates a position or place.

Some examples of prepositions:

about, above, after, along, among, as, before, behind, below, beside, between, by, despite, during, for, in, into, like, of, onto, opposite, over, past, regarding, since, and with.

Example: He brought his furniture into the apartment.

Some common compound prepositions:

according to, except for, in front of, next to, as well as, instead of, due to, in spite of, because of, and with regard to

Prepositional Phrases begin with a preposition and most often end with a noun. The noun is known as the object of the preposition. There are several different types of prepositional phrases classified by the type of word it modifies.

Adjective prepositional phrases most often modify the noun directly before the prepositional phrase. These usually answer the questions *which one?* or *what kind of?*.

Example: The thoughts of the professor were closed minded. *of the professor* is the prepositional phrase which modifies *thoughts*. What kind of thoughts? Those of the professor.

Adverbial prepositional phrases modify a verb within the sentence. These usually answer the questions *When? Where? How? Why? Under what conditions?* and *To what degree?*

Example: You cannot judge a book *by its cover.* The prepositional phrase, by its cover, modifies the verb *judge.* How can you not judge a book? By its cover.

37.9 Interjections

inter · jection ---The word "interjection" literally means "thrown in between" from the Latin inter ("between") and iacere ("throw").

The part of speech that usually expresses emotion and is capable of standing alone. This uses an exclamation marker (!), also known as the exclamation point. Even when interjections are a part of a sentence, they don't directly relate to the grammar of that sentence. Interjections take on more than one of the following usages:

-sudden outburst -a form of salutation -to emphasize in the imperative mood

Words belonging to this part of speech, such as:

```
Ugh! or Wow! Oh! Hey! Ow!
```

Category:Rhetoric and Composition[1]

37.10 Active vs. Passive Voice

A shift between active voice and passive voice is confusing to readers and should be avoided at all times. If you do shift voice, justify it and have a reason for it.

Voice refers to the verb's ability to show whether a subject receives or acts the action received by the verb. When using the active voice, the subject performs the action.

```
For Example:
    The boy ran straight home at dinner time
        <The boy---the subject, did the action----he ran.
```

In writing, active voice is more dramatic and often users fewer words than passive voice in English. There will be introduced more in the "active and passive" section later.

37.11 Types of Sentences

In English there are three main types of sentences. They function according to the usage and pragmatics. They are also referred to as moods, in English. The fourth type of sentence might be termed as *interrogative*.

Indicative The indicative mood is used in factual statements. All intentions in speaking that a particular language does not put into another mood use the indicative. It is the most commonly used mood and is found in all languages. Example: "Paul is reading books." or "Paul reads books."

Imperative The imperative mood expresses commands, direct requests, and prohibitions. In many circumstances, directly using the imperative mood seems blunt or even rude, so it is often used with care. Example: "Read that book, Paul!"

---

1   http://en.wikibooks.org/wiki/Category%3ARhetoric%20and%20Composition

Subjunctive The subjunctive mood has several uses in independent clauses. Examples include discussing hypothetical or unlikely events, expressing opinions or emotions, or making polite requests (the exact scope is language-specific). Example: " God bless America."

37.12 Tag Question

```
A type of question where a pronoun is attached to the end of the
declarative clause, where the pronoun agrees with number and gender
of the subject in the declarative clause.
```

Tag questions are used for the purpose of emphasis.

When using tag questions there are four things to watch for:

1. What kind of verb is it?

2. What tense is the verb?

3. Is the sentence affirmative or negative?

4. Do you change the pronoun?

Some additional things to look for when using tag verbs are:

~Copy the auxiliary after the end of the declarative clause

~Insert a "do" support where the auxiliary is missing (Note that the "do" support agrees in number and tense.)

~If the declarative clause is negative, then the tag should be positive.

~If the declarative clause is positive, then the tag should be negative.

```
For Example:
    ~   We are meeting at 7 o'clock, aren't we?
        The tag question would be "aren't we" to make an emphasis on
the first part of the sentence.
    ~   He won't drive in the storm, will he?
        The tag question in this example is "will he"
```

37.13 Wh-Question

There can be nine types of Wh questions based on the sentence structure. The "Wh" words that forms the questions are:

Who (or Whom) ?Person

What?Object/Idea/Action

Whose?Possession

Which?Specific subject

When?Time

Where?Place

Why?Reason

How?Manner

The Wh word can function as the subject, object or possessive determiner of the interrogative clause.

```
For example:
  Who gave John permission to watch movies? (subject)
  From whom did John get permission to watch movies? (object)
  Whose book did John read yesterday? (possessive determiner)
```

There are few generalizations which can be noted here:

1. If the 'Wh' is the subject then the structure of the sentence remains intact
2. If the 'Wh' is not the subject then auxiliary inversion is required to form the question

To form questions with 'Wh' word?

1. Begin with the 'Wh' word
2. If the 'Wh' word is the subject then no change in the structure is required
3. If 'Wh' word is not the subject then subject-auxiliary inversion is required
4. If the auxiliary is missing, then appropriate "do" support is to be added to form the question
5. The "do" support should match in tense and number and it will change the verb to bare infinitive.

The grammar used with 'Wh' questions depends on if the topic being asked about is the *subject* or *predicate* of a sentence. When using the subject pattern, you will need to input the person or thing being asked about with the appropriate 'Wh' word for that sentence.

```
 For example:
Jack is playing with Jill
a. Who is playing with Jill? ('Wh' word is the subject -- somebody
is doing the action of playing)
b. To whom is Jack playing music? ('Wh' word is the object --
somebody is receiving the action of Jack's playing)
```

37.14 Clauses

A clause is a group of words with a subject and a predicate. A sentence containing a single clause is called **uniclausal** and a sentence with more than one clause is called **multiclausal.** Clauses having one finite verb, as in **uniclausal** or minimum of one finite verb construction in a **multiclausal** structure is called **finite clauses.** A clause having a non-finite verb is called a **non finite clause.**

An **independent clause** is part of sentence that can function as a stand-alone structure. A **dependent clause** on the other hand cannot function by itself and needs an independent clause to complete its meaning.

A third type of clause is known as **matrix clause**, which function as an independent clause but requires a complement clause to complete the meaning.

Subordinate Clause

Subordinate clauses are sometimes called dependent clauses. They begin with a subordinate conjunction or a relative pronoun and contain both a subject and a verb. Some common subordinate conjunctions are: although, since, before, because, after, if, whenever, which, and when. example: Although it was dark outside, Jill went to play basketball.

Relative Clause

A relative clause functions as a modifier and works as an adjective. It has four main features:

```
1. contains a subject and a verb
2. begins with a relative pronoun-who, whom, that,
   which, whose or a relative adverb-why, when, where
3. functions as an adjective
4. can be restrictive or non-restrictive
```

Example of a restrictive relative clause: Participants in this marathon who are high school students need to bring permission slips signed by their parents.

Example of non-restrictive relative clause: Participants in this marathon, who come from all over the city, must sign in by 8AM.

1.A restrictive relative clause would change the meaning if deleted, so commas aren't needed. (In the example above, the clause restricts the people who need to bring permission slips to only the high school students.)

2.A non-restrictive relative clause is just extra information about the subject and may be omitted without changing the meaning.

Complement Clause

A complement clause is a notional sentence or predication that's an argument of a predicate

example: I know that it is raining hard.

There are three types of complement clauses: ordinary, noun, and adjective

Noun Clauses

Noun clauses can function as a subject, subject complements, objects of prepositions, or direct objects. So a noun clause cannot stand apart but is always contained within a clause. A few examples of noun clauses that usually will begin with a relative pronoun are: that, whomever, whose, which, and whoever. Here the construction of the clause occurs directly after the noun phrase.

```
    For Example:
  He asked when she went to the library.
  The italicized section is an example of a direct object function.
```

> He was looking for *whichever car was the best find.*
> In this example, the section in italics is an object of a
> preposition.

For instance, in the first example for the independent clause isn't just *he asked* but *he asked when she went to the library.*

Adjective Clauses

Adjective clauses modify nouns and pronouns in other clauses.

A adjective clause always begins with a relative pronoun (that, who, whom, whose, which) or a relative adverb (where, when, why).

> For Example:
> The test, *which took an hour*, earned me an A for the class.
> Have you seen the desk *where Kelsi sat*?
> -The parts in italics are the adjective clauses for the nouns *test*
> and *desk*.

Adverb Clauses

Adverb clauses modify a verb, an adjective or an adverb.

Adverb clauses begin with subordinating conjunctions: when, because, than, where, before, after

> For Example:
> Hitchcock paved the way for directors *when he created a new filmmaking style.*
> (when... modifies the verb)
> Hitchcock was important *because he proved that horror doesn't need gore.*
> (because... modifies the adjective)

Ordinary Clauses

An ordinary clause functions like a complement clause using *that* as the most common word to form the structure. For example: *That the earth is flat* was a common misperception.

The italicized portion suggests an ordinary complement clause in the subject position.

37.15 Partitive

Partitive construction helps to modify count and non-count nouns.It denotes a part of a whole. The partitive noun phrase agrees in number and tense according to its appearance in the subject place.It takes the following structure:

NP (count)+of+ NP.

example: *A pair of shoes* is what I need. (the partitive is in italics)

> *A lot of work* is required before this project is over. (the partitive is in italics)

37.16 Collective

This is a usage which is based on the semantic and pragmatic use of the language. A variation could be noted in Standard American English (SAE) and British English (BE).

examples: The home team has routed the visitors. (SAE)

> The home team have routed the visitors. (BE)

37.16.1 Phrasal Verb

A *phrasal verb* is a phrase construction which is made up of a verb and an adverbial particle or a preposition. It is also understood as an idiomatic construction where the meaning is different from the sum of its parts. It can be either **prepositional** (non separable) or **particle verbs** (separable).

prepositional: The parents *called on* the teacher.

particle verb: He *looked* the number *up*.

38 Sentences

1. REDIRECT Rhetoric and Composition/Types of Sentences[1]

---

1   http://en.wikibooks.org/wiki/Rhetoric%20and%20Composition%2FTypes%20of%20Sentences

39 Active and Passive Voice

Disclaimer: In everyday writing, the active voice is used to concisely and forcibly describe people's actions. The passive voice also has important rhetoric uses in everyday writing. It is more common in formal writing that tries to be less personal. The terms "active" and "passive voice" and their significance to good writing are explained in the article below.

39.1 Voice in English Writing

Languages have different levels of formality that vary with the purpose, the audience, and the situation. Generally, written English is more formal than spoken English because the person has more time to think about what to say. Formal writing uses fewer personal pronouns and less colloquial language, or slang. Another important difference is the use of grammatical voice.

"Voice" has two meanings in writing. "Voice" can be defined as "how the writer's personality and attitude toward the topic are revealed to the audience." Voice, in this definition, is what makes one writer sound different from another. "Voice" is also a grammatical term; for clarity, it may be referred to as "grammatical voice." There are two voices discussed in this section: the active voice and the passive voice.

39.2 Active and Passive Voice Sentences

Most English sentences are written with active, passive, or neuter verbs, such as "to be" verbs. The active and passive voices are the two main voices in English, but some sentences may also be considered to be in the middle or mediopassive voice. Voice is the relationship between the subject and the verb in a clause or the transfer of action.

- In the active voice, the subject performs the action. The subject of an active-voice construction is known as an agent. A clause with an active, transitive verb will be in the form of subject-verb-object.

Example: The student **finished** the exercise.

- In the passive voice, the subject receives the action. The subject of a passive-voice construction is known as a patient. An active voice clause can be passivized, or recast in the passive voice (for example, to increase formality), by making the object of the active clause the subject of the passive clause. "The exercise" is the object in the sentence above. The verb will be "was finished." For a passive verb, the tense and subject-verb agreement are always shown through the auxiliary verb "to be." The main verb is always the past participle. The subject of the active voice sentence can be included in a prepositional phrase with "by."

Example: The exercise **was finished** by the student.

Active Voice	Passive Voice
The teacher **referred to** "voice" as a grammatical term.	"Voice" **was referred to** as a grammatical term by the teacher.
The man **yelled at** the waiter.	The waiter **was yelled at** by the man.
Millions of people **lived in** the houses.	The houses **were lived in** by millions of people.

Intransitive verbs can be used in the passive voice when a prepositional phrase is included.

Intransitive verbs without prepositional phrases cannot be passivized. There is no word to become the subject of the sentence.

Active voice: Millions of people lived.

Passive voice: ? was lived.

Linking verbs (such as being verbs) are intransitive verbs that can never be used in the passive voice. They do not show action and are thus neither active nor passive. They are called neuter verbs.

39.3 Use of the Passive Voice

Converting an active-voice clause to a passive-voice clause does not change meaning, but can be done for increased formality or emphasis. Linguistic studies have found high percentages of passive verbs in formal writing. The passive voice can emphasize an agent, a patient, or an adverb. It can be used for narrative flow and continuity in conversations.

Emphasizing the agent: *Hamlet* was written by Shakespeare.

The passive voice emphasizes Shakespeare by putting his name at the end, the most emphatic part of a sentence.

Emphasizing the patient: Jamey was fascinated by Language Arts.

The passive-voice construction emphasizes Jamey more effectively than the active-voice equivalent "Language Arts fascinated Jamey."

Emphasizing the adverb: That is strictly prohibited.

Because a passive verb consists of two words, an adverb becomes emphatic when placed between "to be" and the past participle.

The passive voice can be used to eliminate first- and second-pronouns in formal writing.

Active voice: I hope that....

Passive voice: It is hoped that....

In formal writing, the writer may want to alternate between sentences in the first person and passive sentences in which the pronoun is implied to prevent the monotony caused by starting too many sentences with "I."

Research studies are described in the passive voice. Research is intended to be objective, without the biases of the researchers conducting the experiments. An experiment should be the same no matter who performs it.

Active voice: I collected samples from the subjects.

Passive voice: Samples were collected from the subjects.

A sentence in the imperative mood can be rewritten in the passive voice to make it more formal or less harsh.

Active voice: Do not smoke.

Passive voice: Smoking is prohibited.

Active voice: Avoid contractions in formal writing.

Passive voice: Contractions should be avoided in formal writing.

The examples above for first- and second-person pronouns make use of the institutional passive, which omits the agent. In writing and speech, almost eighty-five percent of passive sentences are in the institutional passive.

39.4 The Structural Difference

The difference between active and passive is in how many noun phrases in the sentence that are not introduced with the use of a preposition. Compare the following sentences:

```
                    I dropped the ball.
                    The ball was dropped by me.
```

```
                    The man offered the butler a reward.
                    The Butler was offered a reward by the man.
```

- In the `active voice`, the sentence has between two and three noun phrases that do not require a prepositional phrase. These are called **the subject**, the **direct object** and the **indirect object**.
  - I dropped the ball. ("I" is the subject. "The ball" is the direct object.)
  - The man offered the butler a reward. ("The man" is the subject. "The butler" is the indirect object and "a reward" is the direct object.)
  - The man offered a reward to the butler. ("The man" is still the subject. "A reward" is still the direct object, but "the butler" is now part of a prepositional phrase and is no longer an indirect object.)

- In the `passive voice`, the sentence has one fewer noun phrase than the corresponding active. The subject is removed and can appear only in an optional prepositional phrase.

The object is promoted to subject. For ditransitive verbs, the direct or indirect object can become the subject.

- The ball was dropped by me. ("The ball" is now the subject. "Me" shows up in an optional "by"-phrase.)
- The Butler was offered a reward by the man. ("The butler" is now the subject. There is only one object: "a reward." "The man" shows up in an optional "by"-phrase.)
- A reward was offered to the butler by the man. ("A reward" is now the subject. "The butler" is not considered an indirect object because it is part of a prepositional phrase. "The man" shows up in an optional "by"-phrase.)

Without a change in meaning, using the active or passive voice can emphasize different noun phrases in the examples above.

40 *Understanding Mechanics*

41 Mechanics

41.1 What is Mechanics?

The word "mechanics" refers primarily to spelling and punctuation; in short, aspects of writing that are not shared by speaking. When and where should you use a comma? What are the rules for semicolons? Questions like this..

- Punctuation[1]

Periods, colons, semi-colons, commas, question marks, apostrophes, hyphens, parentheses, brackets, and dashes.

Category:Rhetoric and Composition[2]

---

1   Chapter 42 on page 233
2   http://en.wikibooks.org/wiki/Category%3ARhetoric%20and%20Composition

42 Punctuation

42.1 What Is Punctuation For?

"Proper punctuation" shows up repeatedly in discussions about expectations and criteria for what constitutes good academic writing — whether it's administrators, teachers, students, or legislators talking about what should be taught in the first-year writing classroom. But the word "proper" might limit or even mislead our thinking of punctuation. Used knowledgeably and deliberately, punctuation is more than proper; it's essential to making meaning. Also, there's a faint connotation of "arbitrary" with the word "proper" — and effective punctuation is anything but arbitrary.

Nor is punctuation merely a reflection of oral behavior, as suggested by the familiar injunctions "Use a comma for a pause" or "Where your voice drops, use a period." Instead, punctuation functions as a rich set of clues that have emerged specifically for readers working through text on a page or screen, visually and two-dimensionally.

The nature of reading demands such clues precisely because text is not speech. Speakers have pitch, pace, hand gestures, facial expressions, and other means to let a listener know such things as which points to link to each other and which points should stand on their own, or whether information is necessary in that it restricts meaning or whether it is extraneous. Moreover, ordinary speech usually accommodates a listener's questions, allowing for a more rapid arrival at a joint understanding between speaker and listener. The greater temporal and spatial distance between writer and reader, however, calls for a code that can work to give clues about the writer's intended meaning in the absence of such direct two-way communication.

42.2 Is It Worth the Work?

While punctuation does function as a vital part of making meaning within a text, it can't be denied that it serves another function as well: that of credibility marker. Using punctuation according to the conventions of the academic community does serve as a sort of license into, and within, that community. To take the time and effort to learn and use punctuation conventionally sends the message to readers that "I'm part of your community; I can speak your language (use your code). So, listen to me." It signals a sort of collegial willingness to hear and to be heard: to use a common code that enhances and expands understandability instead of restricting it to yourself. Codes can exclude and include; by using the code of "correct" punctuation, you're signaling a willingness to be included in a group of people who've agreed on how to use certain dots and squiggles on the page to indicate certain relationships among ideas. For whatever reason you value inclusion in the academic community, subscribing to (buying into) conventional punctuation is one among many certificates of authenticity you can carry.

Why is that? Why should conventional punctuation exert such influence? Part of the answer can be found in the way different punctuation marks support characteristics that the academic community values in its overall discourse. This is another way in which conventional punctuation operates on more than a merely arbitrary level: It serves to indicate relationships among ideas in a sentence or paragraph that echo the very ways in which the academic community organizes and develops its lines of thought. Those ways include segmentation, coordination, subordination, modification, and supplementation -- concepts discussed later in this section.

42.3 What's With All the Jargon?

Have you ever tried to complete a task with someone who doesn't know the names of the objects you're working with? Think of changing your oil with a person who doesn't know the terms "dipstick," "oil pan," "drain plug," or "filter wrench." Or imagine trying to show someone how to make an omelet, and they don't know what a "whisk" is or what it means to "dice" onions. Chances are, it will take longer than usual for you to get the task done; perhaps you may even decide to start off with a brief vocabulary review before focusing on the task itself. Let's face it, "that thingy there" takes you only so far.

Like other specialized subjects, punctuation has a specialized vocabulary that allows us to talk about it: a set of terms we use to name parts, describe purposes, explain activities, and identify errors. The attractive thing about a lexicon is that it saves time by eliminating a lot of guesswork and reinvention. While punctuation jargon can sometimes sound unnecessarily inflated (the word "and," for example, is a "coordinating conjunction") or even faintly accusatory (an unnecessary comma is called "disruptive"), having a consistent set of terms makes it easier to use punctuation correctly.

In short: Yes, it does help to know some of the jargon when learning punctuation. The good news is, once you learn a few terms, you can plug them into formulas that you can use to quickly get a solid grasp on correct punctuation.

42.3.1 OK, which terms do I need to know?

The sections below about specific punctuation marks introduce terms as you'll need them. But there are a few terms it helps to know beforehand.

Independent clause

This is a group of words that could stand on its own as a complete sentence because it expresses a complete thought.

How can you tell if a thought or sentence is "complete"? While there are more complicated tests involving more jargon, one simple test that usually works is to read the group of words out loud with extra expressiveness. We almost always can "hear" completeness or incompleteness. Every independent clause must have a subject (even if it is only implied as in a command) and a verb (even if it is only the verb to be).

When you read an independent clause aloud, it has a sound of being finished. You and any other listener are not waiting for more information. Your voice usually drops with an air of finality when you are done reading an independent clause aloud.

Examples:

- *Conflict resolution requires looking first at involved parties collectively.*
- *One challenge is determining whether all parties truly want to resolve the conflict.*
- *The conflict may be serving another purpose.*

Dependent clause

In contrast, when you read a dependent clause aloud, you or your listener has the feeling of "Well...? What's next? Finish it up!" A dependent clause is a group of words that can't stand on its own as a sentence because it does not express a complete thought. It leaves the listener (and reader) hanging.

In addition, there are certain words that make a clause dependent. When the following words appear at the beginning of a clause, that clause is dependent:

after, although, as, as if, as long as, as soon as, as though, because, before, during, even if, even though, ever since, if, in case, in order that, once, on condition that, provided that, since, so that, then, though, unless, until, what, whatever, when, whenever, whether, which, whichever, while, whomever, whose, why

Examples:

- *Until all parties agree that resolution is a shared priority*
- *Which allows the process to move forward*
- *An example being one person who retains power as long as the conflict goes unsolved*

Independent clause and **dependent clause** refer to groups of words. Two more terms it helps to know beforehand are labels for certain individual words.

Coordinating conjunctions

When these seven short words words link two independent clauses together within one sentence, they are called coordinating conjunctions:

and, but, for, nor, or, so, yet

Each coordinating conjunction signals a specific relationship between the independent clauses it joins.

- **And** signals addition and extension. Used with a comma between two independent clauses, it tells the reader that the thoughts expressed in those clauses should be considered together and with equal weight.
  Each workplace conflict is unique, and each requires its own assessment.

- **But** expresses contrast. It tells readers that the thought expressed in the second independent clause is in opposition to, or otherwise different from, the thought expressed in the first independent clause.

  Each workplace conflict is unique, but several general principles apply to finding solutions.

- **For** signals that the second thought is a statement of causation relative to the first thought or that the second thought should be considered as significantly informing the first thought.

  Each workplace conflict is unique, for each context is unique.

- **Nor** links two complete thoughts expressed as negatives, indicating that neither is an option.

  Serious conflicts cannot be solved by ignoring them, nor can they be solved by attempting to legislate past them.

- **Or** conveys option/choice or consequence (as in the sense of "or else") between the two thoughts.

  Conflicts may be resolved with one mediated discussion, or extended negotiation may be required to bring about consensus.

- **So** signals that the second thought is a statement of effect or consequence relative to the first thought.

  Workplace conflicts can ultimately be opportunities for growth, so managers should approach them confidently.

- **Yet** tells the reader that the thought expressed in the second independent clause is in opposition or contrast to the first. It also can indicate simultaneity, in effect saying to the reader, "At the same time, after you've read the first thought, you should also consider this thought."

  Workplace conflicts can ultimately be opportunities for growth, yet most managers approach them with dread and apprehension.

Conjunctive adverbs

These are words expressing a relationship or transition between two independent clauses. Common conjunctive adverbs are:

so, otherwise, also, consequently, for example, furthermore, however, in addition, in contrast, in fact, instead, likewise, moreover, nevertheless, otherwise, still, then, therefore

Conjunctive adverbs other than SO or OTHERWISE require either a period or semicolon preceding them and a comma following them. Once you understand these terms, you're ready to look at punctuation formulas for using commas, semicolons, and colons.

Example #1 The CEO will be attending the lecture; accordingly, the vice president will be available for the luncheon at noon.

The two clauses are independent. The semicolon replaces a coordinating conjunction and indicates that the two clauses are independent.

Example #2 Jaime wanted to see "Billy Madison"; however, Nick wanted to see "Happy Gilmore."

The two clauses are independent. The semicolon replaces a coordinating conjunction and indicates that the two clauses are independent.

Category:Rhetoric and Composition[1]

42.3.2 Uses of "That"

That in the English language serves five different syntactic functions. They are:

> 1. Demonstrative determiner
>   example: *That* house

> 2. Demonstrative pronoun
>   example: *That* is my car

> 3. Functions as a noun
>   example: *That* works for me.

> 4. Complementizer
>   example: I know *that* she was waiting for me

> 5. Relative pronoun
>   example: The book *that* I read was interesting

---

1   http://en.wikibooks.org/wiki/Category%3ARhetoric%20and%20Composition

43 Commas

43.1 What Do Commas Do?

As you can see in the list below, commas serve several different purposes. For now, don't worry about any unfamiliar terms; simply observe the main actions commas do: *join, emphasize, contain,* and *separate.*

1. They work with a coordinating conjunction to **join two independent clauses** within a sentence.
2. They **emphasize introductory elements** at the beginning of a sentence or clause.
3. They **set off cumulative elements** at the end of a sentence or clause.
4. They **separate a dependent clause at the beginning of a sentence** from the independent clause following it.
5. They work in pairs to **contain restrictive modifiers** within a sentence.
6. They work in pairs to **contain parenthetical expressions** within a sentence.
7. They **separate two or more adjectives** that independently describe the same noun.
8. They **separate quotations** from their attributions.
9. They **separate items in a list.**
10. They **separate elements in dates, numbers, personal titles, and addresses.**

While there are many different ways to use commas in writing, most comma usages fall into three situations. If you know the basic rule for these three cases, you should be set for comma usage.

1. Put a comma before a coordinating conjunction (**for, and, nor, but, or, yet, so**) that separates two independent clauses. *Example: I wanted to drive to the mall,* **but** *my car wouldn't start.*
2. Put a comma after introductory words, phrases, or clauses in a sentence. *Example:* **Although** *it was a good offer, I felt that I needed to explore other options.*
3. Use commas to set off elements that interrupt or add information in a sentence. *Example: Tommy,* **my older brother,** *loved to punch me for telling his secrets.*

43.2 Commas with two independent clauses

Used with coordinating conjunctions, commas allow writers to let readers know how their complete thoughts (as expressed in independent clauses) relate to one another. After all, our thoughts build on each other and interact with each other. Unless we're merely listing things or free-associating, our thoughts rarely develop in separate "boxes," but rather tend more to develop in relationship with one another.

When it's time to put those thoughts into written text, commas used with coordinating conjunctions help us indicate the relationships among our thoughts. They help us avoid the choppy, flat style that comes from every thought becoming a separate separate sentence, walled off from other sentences with the finality of a period:

Example of periodic text: *Building consensus ends with synthesis. It begins with analysis. Of course, the ultimate goal is finding commonality. The final product is a single course of action. However, a consensus derives validity only from agreement among the many. The first step in reaching consensus is to survey the different viewpoints involved.*

If we add commas with coordinating conjunctions to this group of sentences, our reader will be able to see more clearly the relationships that exist among the complete thoughts:

The same text with commas and coordinating conjunctions: *Building consensus ends with synthesis,* **but** *it begins with analysis. Of course, the ultimate goal is finding commonality,* **and** *the final product is a single course of action. However, a consensus derives validity only from agreement among the many,* **so** *the first step in reaching consensus is to survey the different viewpoints involved.*

43.2.1 The formula

Use a comma to join two independent clauses (IC) with a coordinating conjunction (CC). Place the comma before the coordinating conjunction.

IC, CC IC.

Coordinating Conjunctions--For, And, Nor, But, Or, Yet and So--are often referred to by the mnemonic device used to memorize them: FANBOYS

43.2.2 Errors

A comma and a coordinating conjunction must appear together in order to have enough "strength" to join two independent clauses. These errors happen when one or the other is missing:

Two independent clauses joined by just a coordinating conjunction (no comma) or joined by nothing at all -- they just collide -- is called a **run-on sentence** or sometimes a **fused sentence**.

Examples of run-on or fused sentences:

- *Several environmental organizations recognized the treaty but few endorsed it.*
- *Internet communities redefine the notion of space they take the concept beyond physical dimensions.*

Two independent clauses joined by just a comma (no coordinating conjunction) is called a **comma splice.**

Example of a comma splice: *Economists predicted lower personal debt loads resulting from tax cuts, this did not happen.*

43.3 Commas with introductory words and phrases

Another relationship between thoughts we signal to our readers is that of **introduction**. We often want to give our readers some background before laying out our main thought, or we want to give some information first that limits or otherwise modifies the information in our main thought. Introductory elements can be one word or several so long as they do not contain a finite verb. An introductory element that includes a finite verb is likely to be a clause instead. Common ones are **transition words** and **statements about time, place, manner, or condition**.

Using a comma after an introductory element requires your reader to pause, and so should only be done with good reason.

43.3.1 Introductory Words

Introductory words are set off with a comma when the introductory word is a participle, modifies the entire clause following it, or when not including it might lead to misreading.

Examples of sentences with introductory words:

- *Humiliated, she fled from the diner.* (participle)
- *Moreover, several groups actively opposed the treaty.* (modifies entire clause)
- *Inside, traders shouted orders out.* (*Inside Traders* would be ambiguous)
- *Quickly tie your shoe* (*Quickly* is a simple adverb, it only modifies *tie*.)

43.3.2 Introductory Phrases

Introductory phrases are not set off with a comma without good reason. Phrases that contain verbals, absolute phrases, long prepositional phrases, or compound prepositional phrase are set off. Short prepositional phrases are only set off for purposes of emphasis. Phrases that show inversion in sentence structure can also be followed by a comma.

Examples of sentences with introductory phrases:

- *Calling in sick for work, Beth hoped her boss would not suspect anything.* (Phrase contains a verbal)
- *The stock market falling in Tokyo, Alex called his stock broker.* (Absolute phrase)
- *Beneath the antique wooden fishing boat, barnacles had grown for years.* (Long introductory phrase, but even here the comma is optional.)
- *Underneath the noses of her parents, Ruth had hoarded three kilograms of cocaine.* (Compound prepositional phrase)
- *In a cold sweat, Henry read the letter addressed to his wife.* (emphasis)
- *Drunk and angry, Joel burst into the room.* (inverted structure)
- *After school I went to my uncle's house.* (short prepositional phrase)
- *Before the parade I want to eat pizza.* (short prepositional phrase)
- *By the earthen hearth my mother read to me from the book of Acts.* (short prepositional phrase)

43.4 Commas with cumulative clauses

Another type of relationship between ideas that we signal to readers with a comma is that of **accumulation**. Occurring at the end of a sentence, **cumulative clauses** hook up to a main clause and add further information. Using cumulative clauses is a good way to avoid having to use two sentences when one will do.

Examples of sentences with cumulative clauses:

- *Nine senators changed their vote, passing the bill into law.*
- *Three years of above-average rainfall raised the water table, turning formerly usable fields into wetlands.*
- *Peers frequently reinforce the behavior, leading it to become an ingrained habit.*

43.5 Commas and dependent clauses

Remember, when you read a **dependent clause** aloud, you or your listener has the feeling of "Well...? What's next? Finish it up!" A dependent clause is a group of words that can't stand on its own as a sentence because it does not express a complete thought. It leaves the listener (and reader) hanging.

Examples of dependent clauses:

- *although psychology and applied psychology are separate disciplines*
- *when sanctions proved too difficult to enforce*
- *because it was undated*

Dependent clauses, as their name implies, "depend" on another clause to form a complete sentence. Dependent clauses must be paired with independent clauses.

43.5.1 The formula

When the dependent clause comes before the independent clause, use a comma after the dependent clause.

DC, IC.

When the dependent clause comes after the independent clause, just run right through without a comma.

IC DC.

Examples:

- *Although psychology and applied psychology are separate disciplines, they both are relatively recent additions to the university.*
- *The U.N. approved military action when sanctions proved too difficult to enforce.*
- *Archaeologists used contextual clues to date the manuscript because it was undated.*

43.5.2 Errors

A **disruptive comma** is one used before a dependent clause that comes after the independent clause. Writers often make this mistake when the dependent clause begins with because.

Examples of disruptive commas:

- *The future of print newspapers appears uncertain, due to rising production costs and the increasing popularity of online news sources.*
- *Some argue that print newspapers will never disappear, because of their many readers.*

43.6 Commas and restrictive modifiers

You know what it's like to talk to someone and add explanations as you go, even right in the middle of your thoughts, to make sure your listener knows exactly which things you are talking about? When those explanantions show up in a written sentence, they are called **modifiers**. Modifiers can be **nonrestrictive** -- meaning that you can drop them out of a sentence and you won't change the meaning. **Restrictive** modifiers are ones whose meaning is essential to the overall meaning of the sentence; if you dropped a restrictive modifier, the meaning of the sentence would change.

Use a pair of commas to set off a nonrestrictive clause. Don't use commas around restrictive clauses.

Examples:

- *The committee, headed by Dr. Suarez, met weekly to develop a budget.*
  In this sentence, the phrase "headed by Dr. Suarez" is nonessential to the meaning of the main clause, which is that the committee met weekly. Presumably only one committee has been under discussion in previous sentences. However, if the discussion is of several committees, and the writer wants to point out that it was that one specific committee headed by Dr. Suarez that met weekly, the commas would be removed:
- *The committee headed by Dr. Suarez met weekly to develop a budget.*
- *Employees who participate in the company's fitness classes pay a lower health insurance premium.*
  Here, no commas are used, since it is not just any and all employees who pay a lower health premium, but only those who participate in the company's fitness program. Notice the difference in the next sentence, in which the nonrestrictive modifier adds information but wouldn't change the meaning if it was taken out:
- *Employees, who have access to the company's gym and fitness classes, are encouraged to practice preventive healthcare.*

43.7 Commas and parenthetical elements

Much like a nonrestrictive modifier, a parenthetical expression provides extra information or commentary in the middle of a sentence. A parenthetical element, however, often sounds more obviously "speech-like" and interjectory. Use a pair of commas to set off a parenthetical element.

Examples:

- *The candidate, much to the committee's surprise, voluntarily revealed her positions on several key controversies.*
- *The question has, incidentally, since become moot.*

43.8 Commas with multiple adjectives

When you use more than one descriptive word (adjective) to describe something (a noun), ask yourself whether the adjectives work independently to describe the noun, or if they build on each other and work together to describe the noun.

One way to tell is to reverse the order of the adjectives. If you can reverse the order and the meaning stays the same, the adjectives are working independently and should be separated by a comma. If you reverse the order and it doesn't make sense, the adjectives are working together and should not be separated by a comma.

Another test is to put "and" between the adjectives. If you can do that and retain the meaning, the adjectives are working independently and need a comma between them. If inserting "and" between the adjectives changes the meaning, the adjectives are working together and shouldn't be separated from each other by a comma.

If multiple adjectives before a noun work independently, use a comma between them. If they work together, don't.

Examples of adjectives working independently:

- *An open, exploratory, and inclusive spirit marked the meeting.*
  Test: *An open **and** exploratory **and** inclusive spirit marked the meeting.*
- *A direct, conversational tone made the instructions easy to understand.*
  Test: *A conversational, direct tone made the instructions easy to understand.*

Examples of adjectives working together:

- *Local health officials recently released guidelines for dealing with avian flu outbreaks.*
  Test: *Health local officials recently released guidelines for dealing with flu avian outbreaks.* **Do not use commas.**
- *An extruded plastic stem keeps the component stable.*
  Test: *An extruded **and** plastic stem keeps the component stable.* **Do not use a comma.**

43.9 Commas with quotations

Use a comma to set off the **attribution** -- the phrase that says who said or wrote a quotation -- from the quotation itself. Notice that the comma goes inside the quotation marks, even if the quotation is a complete sentence and would, if appearing on its own, take a period at the end.

Examples:

- *"The ballot is stronger than the bullet," writes Abraham Lincoln.*
- *"Politics is the art of looking for trouble, finding it everywhere, diagnosing it incorrectly, and applying the wrong remedies," said Groucho Marx.*

Use a pair of commas to set off the attribution when it appears in the middle of the quotation.

Example: *"In a time of universal deceit," writes George Orwell, "telling the truth becomes a revolutionary act."*

Do not replace a question mark or exclamation point in a quotation with a comma.

Example: *"When will our consciences grow so tender that we will act to prevent human misery rather than avenge it?" writes Eleanor Roosevelt.*

Do not use a comma to set off quotations that occupy a subordinate position in a sentence, often signaled by the words **that**, **which**, or **because**.

Examples:

- *Emphasizing the importance of staying in touch with the populace, James Madison wrote that "a popular government without popular information, or the means of acquiring it, is but a prologue to a farce or a tragedy, or both."*
- *Participating in a democracy takes a strong stomach because "it requires a certain relish for confusion," writes Molly Ivins.*

43.10 Commas in a list

Use commas between items in a list when there are three or more.

The final comma, the one before "and" or "or", is known as the Oxford comma, Harvard comma or serial comma. The Oxford comma should always be used where it is needed to avoid confusion (for example where one or more items in the list already include the word "and"). Otherwise it is optional. The Oxford comma is relatively uncommon in British English, except where used to avoid confusion. Not using the Oxford comma is relatively uncommon in American English, except in newspapers and magazines.

Examples:

- *Additional supplies required are a burner, beaker(,) and safety goggles.*
- *The position requires expertise in building consensus, formulating policy(,) and developing long-range goals.*
- *The English-speaking countries include Dominica, Trinidad and Tobago, and Jamaica.*

43.11 Commas in dates, numbers, personal titles, and addresses

Use commas to separate the day of the week from month and to set off a year from the rest of the sentence.

Examples:

- *On December 12, 1890, orders for the arrest of Sitting Bull were sent.*
- *Graduation is set for May 20, 2006.*

You do not need to use a comma when giving only the month and the year.

Example: *The next presidential election will take place in November 2008.*

Use commas to separate number into groups of three when they are more than four digits long. The comma is optional when the number is four digits long.

Examples:

- *2,400 (or 2400)*
- *50,000*
- *340,000*

Do not use a comma in street addresses or page numbers.

Examples:

- *The table appears on page 1397.*
- *The fire occurred at 5509 Avenida Valencia.*

When following a name with a title, use a comma (if the title is at the end of the sentence) or two (if the title is in the middle of the sentence) to separate the title from the rest of the sentence.

Examples:

- *Paul Hjort, D.C., practices chiropractic medicine in central Minnesota.*
- *Earnings far exceeded projections last quarter, according to Hitomi Masamura, Vice President for Operations.*

Separate each element of an address is with commas. However, do not use a comma before a ZIP or other postal code.

Examples:

- *Bob Dole grew up in Hope, Kansas.*
- *Write to the program advisor at 645 5th Street, Minerton, Indiana 55555.*

Commas[1]

---

1   http://en.wikibooks.org/wiki/Category%3ARhetoric%20and%20Composition

44 Semicolons

44.1 Use

A semicolon introduces a pause greater than that of a comma but less than that of a period.

To Clarify a Series

Semicolons separate elements of a series when the items are long or when individual segments contain material that also must be set off by commas.

- Example: She leaves a son, Mike Nach, of Arizona; a daughter, Emily Rosa, of Colorado; and a sister, Sara Evans, of Minnesota.

To Link Independent Clauses

A semicolon joins two independent clauses[1] within one a sentence without the use of a coordinating conjunction.

- Example: The horse was due for an immunization; the veterinarian administered one today.

To Set Off a Conjunctive Adverb

Semicolons are used, along with a comma, to set off conjunctive adverbs. A conjunctive adverb is a modifier[2] that describes a relationship between ideas in two clauses. Some common conjunctive adverbs are "however," "indeed," "consequently," etc.

- Example: I like pepperoni; however, today I ordered Canadian bacon on my pizza.

Placement with Quotes

Semicolons should always appear outside quotation marks.

- Example: Marcus often says that "people should remain true to their faith"; however, he is not a man of faith.

44.2 Common Misuses

Some examples of improper use of the semicolon:

- Between a subordinate clause and the rest of the sentence. Example: Unless you are coming home before your curfew; don't bother coming home.

---

1   http://en.wikibooks.org/wiki/Rhetoric%20and%20Composition%2FTypes%20of%20Sentences
2   http://en.wikibooks.org/wiki/Rhetoric%20and%20Composition%2FParts%20of%20the%20Sentence

- Between an appositive[3] and the word to which it refers. Example: My favorite animal is a parakeet; a type of bird.
- To introduce a list. Example: I own these cars; a Dodge Stealth, an Acura RSX, and a Geo Storm.

---

3   http://en.wikibooks.org/wiki/English%20in%20Use%2FCommas

45 Colons

Colons are used to draw attention to certain words. They are used after an independent clause to direct attention to a list, appositive or quotation, between independent clauses when the second clause summarizes or emphasizes the first clause, or after the greeting in a formal letter. Some examples follow.

Use of Colons		
Case	**Example**	**Note**
List	• I have three sisters: Catherine, Sarah and Mary. • Sandwich requires several ingredients: bread, butter, cheese, ham and tomatoes.	
Appositive	• My mom has three pets: two cats and a dog.	
?	There was only one possible explanation: The train had never arrived.	
Quotation	In the words of Homer: "Doh!"	
Between independent clauses	Life is like a box of chocolates: you never know what you're going to get.	
Introduction of a definition	Hypernym of a word: a word having a wider meaning than the given one.	Is a special case of appositive.
After salutation	Dear Sir or Madam:	
In a dialogue	Patient: Doctor, I feel like a pair of curtains. Doctor: Pull yourself together!	

Use of Colons		
Case	**Example**	**Note**
Separation of title from subtitle	Star Wars Episode IV: A New Hope	
Separation of the chapter and the verse numbers of religious scriptures	• John 3:14–16 (or John III:14–16) • The Qur'an, Sura 5:18	
Separation within time of the day	• The concert finished at 23:45. • This file was last modified today at 11:15:05.	

Common Misuse of Colons		
Case	**Example**	**Note**
Between a verb and its object	• Some important computer programs are: Word, Excel and Publisher. • Sandwich requires: bread, butter, cheese, ham and tomatoes.	By omitting the colon, the example becomes correct.
Between a preposition and its object	My cars of choice consist of: Honda Accord and Ford GT.	By omitting the colon, the example becomes correct.
After "such as", "including" or "for example"		

Colons[1]

---

1   http://en.wikibooks.org/wiki/Category%3ARhetoric%20and%20Composition

46 Apostrophes

46.1 Use

Apostrophes are used to indicate possession and in contractions.

Add an 's when the noun does not end in an "s" (driver's) or when the noun is singular and ends in an "s" (Lois's).

However, if the pronunciation of a word would be awkward with the "s" added, it is acceptable not to use the extra "s".

If the noun is plural and ends in "s", you don't need to add an apostrophe (diplomas' instead of diploma's).

Joint Possession

If there is a compound noun, add the possessive apostrophe to the last noun.

Example: *I went to see Anthony and George's new apartment.* (The apartment belongs to both Anthony and George.)

If the compound noun indicates individual possession, add the apostrophe to both nouns.

Example: *Mary's and Brian's sense of style was quite different.* (Mary and Brian have individual senses of style.)

Compound Nouns

If a compound noun uses dashes, place the apostrophe after the last nouns.

Example: *My brother-in-law's house*

46.2 Common Misuses

- Do not use apostrophes in nouns that are not possessive. Example: Some parent's are more strict than mine. (Apostrophe is not necessary)
- Do not use an apostrophe in possessive pronouns such as its, whose, his, hers, ours, yours, and theirs.

Category:Rhetoric and Composition[1]

---

1   http://en.wikibooks.org/wiki/Category%3ARhetoric%20and%20Composition

47 Quotation Marks

47.1 Use

Quotation marks are used to mark direct quotations. This is to give the original writer or speaker credit for their work. If you are paraphrasing, you do not need quotation marks.

- If you are using a long quotation (long is constituted by 4 or more typed lines), instead of quotation marks, you should indent the quotation. If the quote is two or more paragraphs, indent the first line of the paragraphs an additional five spaces (plus the indent of the rest of the quote). When indenting to quote, you do not need to use quotation marks.
- If your quote has a quote within it, the inner quote needs one quotation mark and the outer quote needs two quotation marks.
- Use quotation marks around the titles of short works such as newspapers and magazine articles, poems, short stories, songs and chapters.
- Periods and commas should be placed inside the quotation marks. Colons and semicolons should be placed outside the quotation marks. Question marks and exclamation points should be placed inside the quotation marks, unless the punctuation applies to the whole sentence (not just the quote).
- You can set off words by using quotation marks instead of italicizing or underlining them.

47.2 Using quoted material within your own writing

- If a quotation is introduced formally, use a colon.
- If a quotation is being used with "he said" or "she said," use a comma.
- If a quotation is blended into the writer's sentence, you can use a comma, although no punctuation may be more appropriate.
- If a quotation is used at the beginning of a sentence, use a comma after the quote unless the quote ends in a question mark or exclamation point.
- If you choose to break up the quotation with your own words, use commas to offset the quotation from your explanation.

Category:Rhetoric and Composition[1]

---

1   http://en.wikibooks.org/wiki/Category%3ARhetoric%20and%20Composition

48 Hyphens and Dashes

Dashes ("—", "–") are used to mark an interruption within a sentence, while **hyphens** ("-")
are used to join two parts of a compound word, or to indicate that a word has been split at
the end of a line. A dash is approximately as long as two hyphens.

48.1 Dash

Dashes are minus-shaped characters used to mark an interruption within a sentence. They
are used in much the same way as parentheses.

There are two kinds of dashes: *em dashes* looking like "—", and shorter *en dashes* looking
like "–". It is usual to either use em dashes without spacing, or en dashes with spacing, but
not em dashes with spacing, as shown in the following two examples:

Example: Three unlikely companions—a canary, an eagle, and a parrot—flew by my window
in an odd flock.

Example: Three unlikely companions – a canary, an eagle, and a parrot – flew by my
window in an odd flock.

In most word processors, there is a keystroke combination that will produce an em-dash:

- Windows: em-dash: Alt-0151.
- Windows: en-dash: Alt-0150.
- Mac: em-dash: shift-option-dash.

48.2 Hyphen

A hyphen joins two parts of a compound word.

Example: governor-elect, twenty-five, half-baked.

Hyphens can also be used to make compound words more understandable. Consider these
words:

- Man-eating dog
- Man eating dog

The first example describes a particular type of dog (man-eating). The second example,
alas, suggests that a man is eating a dog.

Or consider the case of the flaming-red pickup truck, as opposed to its more alarming cousin,
the flaming red pickup truck.

In general, if the first of two adjectives is describing the second, and not the noun following, you should use a hyphen: deep-blue water, good-tasting hamburger, happy-faced child.

48.3 Width Difference

The em dash is roughly as wide as two hyphens. In the days of typewriters, it was actually written as two hyphens. An en dash is shorter than em dash while wider than a hyphen.

Category:Rhetoric and Composition[1]

---

1   http://en.wikibooks.org/wiki/Category%3ARhetoric%20and%20Composition

49 Parentheses

49.1 What Do Parentheses Do?

Parentheses can be used to enclose an interjected, explanatory, or qualifying remark, mathematical quantities, etc. The words placed inside the brackets are not necessary for the interrupted sentence to be complete.

Setting off incidental/accompanying information

Examples:

1. Be sure to call me (extension 2104) when you get this message.
2. Copyright affects how much regulation is enforced (Lessig 2004).

Enclose numbers and letters that label items listed in a sentence

Category:Rhetoric and Composition[1]

---

1   http://en.wikibooks.org/wiki/Category%3ARhetoric%20and%20Composition

50 Capitalization

Capitalize means to use uppercase for the first letter of a word.

50.1 Basic Principles

- **Proper nouns**: Capitalize nouns that are the unique identification for a particular person, place or thing.
  Example: Michael, Minnesota, North America.
- **Proper names**: Capitalize common nouns like party only when they are part of the full name for the person, place or thing.
  Example: I am a member of the Democratic Party.
  Example: Are you going to the party?

They are also lowercased when being used in a plural setting:

- Example: The Democratic and Republican parties.
- **Sentences**: Capitalize the first word of every sentence including quoted statements and direct questions.
- **Composition**: Capitalize the main words in the names of books, movies, plays, poems, operas, songs, radio and television programs, etc.
  Example: Family Guy.
- **Titles**: Capitalize formal titles only when used in front of a name, not when used after the name.
  Example: Associate Professor John Doe / John Doe, associate professor.
- **Academic titles**: Capitalize and spell out formal titles only when they precede a name.
  Example: Chancellor David Nachriener.

Category:Rhetoric and Composition[1]

---

1   http://en.wikibooks.org/wiki/Category%3ARhetoric%20and%20Composition

51 *Common Errors*

52 Know your patterns

Getting your grammar and punctuation right in your writing is easier than you think. That's because, for the most part, writers don't make every mistake. Instead, we tend to make a few of the same mistakes multiple times, such as always missing the comma after an introductory clause, or forgetting to match up our nouns and pronouns in the right way. This means that you don't have to worry about learning every grammar and punctuation rule; chances are, you follow most of them already.

Following patterns allows you then to focus only on the mistakes you make habitually — and often a writing instructor or writing center tutor can help you identify what those are. Once you know what they are, it's a matter of making sure you understand how to find those errors when editing your own writing and how to correct them.

"It is perfectly okay to write garbage — as long as you edit brilliantly."
C.J. Cherryh, science fiction and fantasy writer

Don't worry about having to memorize the grammar and punctuation rules you need to implement or learning them so deeply that you'll never again make certain errors. Both of these things usually come in time, but what's most important when you're first diving into the world of punctuation and grammar are these two habits:

- **leaving time to edit at the sentence level after you've finished drafting.** The best writers don't write error-free; rather, the best writers edit their work.
- **having and consulting resources when correcting your mistakes.** Why do you think there are hundreds of writer's handbooks online and at the bookstore?! It's precisely because writers of every stripe make mistakes in grammar and punctuation and need to frequently (and repeatedly) look up the answers. You may internalize the rules for using a colon after you've looked them up twenty-nine times — or you may not, so your handbook might just start falling open to that page. That's just fine; the important thing is having a handy place to look up rules when you're editing.

Category:Rhetoric and Composition[1]

---

1   http://en.wikibooks.org/wiki/Category%3ARhetoric%20and%20Composition

53 Homonyms

Homonyms can be tricky to figure out! The following examples of common homonym mistakes prove that spell-check can only go so far in helping to error proof your document.

Remember that two words that sound the same don't always have the same meaning. If you are ever in doubt which one to use, check your dictionary.

53.0.1 Affect, Effect

- **Affect** is most commonly a verb, usually meaning 'influence'. (An easy way to remember this is that 'affect' starts with an "a", as does 'action'.) As a noun, it is a psychological term for emotion.
- **Effect** is most common as a noun meaning 'result'. 'Effect' used as a verb means 'bring about' some kind of change.
  - Example: The game **affected** the standings. Its **effect** was overwhelming. It **effected** a change in the **affect** of the winning team's captain.

53.0.2 Afterward, Afterwards, Afterword

- **Afterward** and **afterwards** are synonymous adverbs meaning that an event occurs later than another.
- An **afterword** is an epilogue.

53.0.3 Aid, Aide

- **Aid** is a noun meaning 'assistance' or a verb meaning 'assist'.
- An **aide** is a person who serves or offers assistance.
  - Example: "The **aide** will **aid** the victim."

53.0.4 It's, Its

- **It's** is a contraction, short for either **It is** or **It has**.
- **Its** is the possessive form of **it**. This usually means that the following noun phrase belongs to 'it'. It is important to recognise that 'its' the possessive form does not have an apostrophe - it is in the same category as 'his'.
  - Example: **"It's** (It is) my dog." "The computer crashed a few minutes ago, and **it's** (it has) done it again!" "What is **its** name?"

53.0.5 Lay, Lie

- **Lay** is the action word.
- **Lie** is the state of being or a telling someone something untruthful on purpose.
  - Example: "I will **lay** the book on the desk."
  - Example: "I plan to **lie** in bed most of Saturday."
  - Example: "Jim will probably **lie** to get out of being punished for breaking the window."

53.0.6 To, Too, Two

Figuring out which of these three forms have stumped more than one person! You can find a quick way to tell them apart below:

- **To** is generally used to describe a relationship between things. It is also used as an infinitive verb, as in "I love **to** eat."
  - Example: "Matt is going **to** the doctor." "This gift is **to** you." "It is ten minutes **to** seven."
- **Too** is usually used when you are describing an excess or is used when noting something is *in addition*
  - Example: "I usually eat **too** much on Thanksgiving." or "Joe cleaned the house, washed the car, and mowed the lawn, **too**.
- **Two** is the word you use for the number **2**.
  - Example: "You have **two** minutes left before class starts."

53.0.7 Then, Than

- **Then** indicates time.
  - Example: "First we went to dinner, and **then** we went to the show."
- **Than** is comparative.
  - Example: "I would rather see the comedy **than** see the horror movie."

53.0.8 Versus, Verses

- **Versus** indicates opposition.
- **Verses** is the plural of verse, as related to poetry.

Category:Rhetoric and Composition[1]

---

1   http://en.wikibooks.org/wiki/Category%3ARhetoric%20and%20Composition

54 Lack of agreement between subject and verb

Subject agreement is that the agreement of subjects and verbs

54.1 Examples

- **Singular**: *The **whale**, which doesn't mature sexually until six or seven years old and which has only one calf per year, **is** at risk for extinction because **it reproduces** so slowly.*
- **Plural**: ***During election season, several civic** groups sponsor**public debates in which** candidates present**their views and audience** members ask**questions.***
- **Singular**: ***Digging**a few inches into the dunes, even at 750 feet above the valley floor, **reveals** wet sand.*
- **Plural**: *The **dunes comprise** small **rocks** and dry, sandy **soil** that constantly **form** strange designs under the ever-present wind.*

54.2 What is subject-verb agreement?

Subject-verb agreement is something most native speakers know pretty automatically, but we can make mistakes when writing, especially when several words separate a particular subject and verb. As you can see in the following examples, "of" phrases can be misleading, too. The trick is to find the "root" noun: the one actually performing the action of the verb. There are two easy ways to spot the subject of a sentence: 1) Find the verb and ask the question, "Who or what is performing this act?" 2) Cross out all prepositional phrases. These simply tasks should lead you right to the subject of the sentence.

54.3 Examples

- ***Characteristics**of the middle child often **include** an equitable temperament and high feelings of security and self-esteem.*
- *The opportunity **cost** of loaning out the funds **is** usually reflected in the interest rate.*
- *A certain **percentage** of the cars produced by major manufacturers **meets** stricter emission standards in order for the company to sell their products in regulated regions.*

54.4 Other guidelines

Other guidelines for making subjects and verbs agree include:

- Noncount nouns — those that don't have a singular or plural form, such as *furniture, baggage, poetry, melancholy* — take a singular verb.
- Two or more singular nouns joined by an "and" take a plural verb: *A timely, relevant **topic** and an **environment** of trust **produce** a good class discussion.*
- When two nouns differing in number are joined by "or," the verb should take the form of the noun closest to it: *Most viewers of the painting assume that either the monkey's **antics** or the handler's **chagrin** causes the young men's laughter.*

If you struggle with problems in subject-verb agreement, leave time to edit your paper once through just for that error: go through each sentence, underlining each subject and verb pair and checking that they agree.

Category:Rhetoric and Composition[1]

---

1   http://en.wikibooks.org/wiki/Category%3ARhetoric%20and%20Composition

55 Lack of agreement between noun and pronoun

55.1 Rules

Pronouns (words such as *it, her, them, this, someone, who, him, they, themselves, herself,* etc.) replace specific nouns (persons, places, or things) so you don't have to keep repeating them. Like subjects and verbs, pronouns and nouns need to agree in "**number**": in whether they are singular or plural. They also need to agree in **gender**: masculine, feminine, or inclusive (both).

Errors in noun-pronoun agreement usually simply result from writing quickly and not editing closely enough. Three specific instances, though, can cause problems:

1. The nouns *each*, and *one* are all singular and take singular pronouns; *either* or *neither* is singular unless it specifically refers to plural alternatives.
2. When using singular nouns that refer to both sexes or for which the gender is not known, use both masculine and feminine pronouns together (*him or her, he or she, himself or herself, his or her*) or rewrite the sentence to make the noun and the pronoun both plural. (If all of the members of a group are of one gender, it is acceptable to use the male or female pronoun, as in "Each member of the football team will take **his** gear onto the bus.")
3. Some nouns can be either singular or plural: *audience, group, team, unit, class,* and others. Use a singular pronoun if the group is acting as a unit, as in "The audience expressed its appreciation with loud applause." Use a plural pronoun if the group is acting as individual members, as in "The team went their separate ways, some showering, some leaving the stadium, some drinking champagne, and some going home to sleep." [In the second example, it's a good idea to write "team members" to be clear.]
4. The words "They" and "Their" are third-person plural personal pronouns in Modern English. The "singular" they and their is used as a gender-neutral singular rather than as a plural pronoun, but the correctness of this usage is disputed.

55.2 Examples

- Every one of the studies indicated ~~their~~ **its** methodology.
- Neither Jackson nor Juarez believed ~~they~~ **he** had been represented unfairly.
- Each researcher included a control group with ~~their his~~ **his or her** test group.
- By 1999, the lacrosse team had outgrown ~~their~~ **its** space.
- Neither a crocodile nor a lion ~~are~~ **is** a suitable pet.

- Either Ed or Bill ~~are~~ **is** a plumber.

But --

- Neither crocodiles nor lions ~~is~~ **are** suitable pets.
- Either Ed and Bill or Ted and Jeff ~~is~~ **are** plumbers.

Category:Rhetoric and Composition[1]

---

1   http://en.wikibooks.org/wiki/Category%3ARhetoric%20and%20Composition

56 Missing comma after introductory element

When you begin a sentence with a word or group of words that provides some background, introductory, or otherwise preliminary information, put a comma between this word or phrase and the rest of your sentence. The comma here tells your reader to pause, take the background information into consideration, and get ready to move on to the main part of the sentence.

To help you recognize places in your sentences where you are missing commas after introductory clauses, read your writing out loud. Chances are good you'll naturally pause after introductory phrases. You can also check the beginning of each sentence to look for words or phrases that add information about time, place, or manner or for words that serve as transitions; these are all common introductory elements.

EXAMPLES

Incorrect: Before the budget passed several lawmakers filibustered to stop it.

Correct: Before the budget passed, several lawmakers filibustered to stop it.

Incorrect: However supporters saw the legislation through.

Correct: However, supporters saw the legislation through.

Learn more under "Commas after introductory elements" here.[1]

Category:Rhetoric and Composition[2]

---

1   Chapter 43 on page 239
2   http://en.wikibooks.org/wiki/Category%3ARhetoric%20and%20Composition

57 Sentence fragment

Sentence fragments. Might sound good at first! More trustworthy. Because they're simple. Not trying to complicate things. Like when a sentenc goes on and on. Making you lose track of the ideas. Not like straight talk.

We use fragments constantly when talking, emailing, IMing: They save time and space and sound "natural." Advertisements frequently use them to draw attention to key concepts. In academic writing, however, all but the most occasional use of fragments is considered inappropriate: too folksy, too speech-like and colloquial.

There are a number of grammar-technical ways to recognize fragments, but **the best way to find them in your writing is to read your work out loud.** Listen for any sentences that may end in a period or other end punctuation but seem to leave you hanging, as if you want to say, "Well ... ? Now what? Go on, finish it up!" The end punctuation may tell you to express "ending" (our voice usually falls when we're reading out loud and get to a period), but the thought won't be finished.

Try reading the following paragraph out loud and seeing if you can pick out the fragments -- that is, the sentences that seem to leave you hanging.

Getting published is simultaneously one of the most exhilarating and taxing goals writers writers can set for themselves. Calling for equal parts patience and persistence. It is often a team effort among several players. Such as, the writer, perhaps an agent, friends and peers who will edit and respond to the work, and previously published writers who can provide advice. Another tension writers must negotiate when pursuing publication is audience appeal and personal integrity to one's work. What is often called "being true to oneself." Because getting published calls on writers to be flexible yet unique at the same time.

As you can see in the revised version below, **fixing fragments** is usually a matter of

- hooking up the fragment to the sentence before or after it (whichever one it seems to relate to), often using a comma, colon, or em dash;
- adding the missing actor (noun) or action (verb); or
- fleshing out the thought to express what was previously not "spelled out."

*Getting published is simultaneously one of the most exhilarating and taxing goals writers writers can set for **themselves, calling** for equal parts patience and persistence. It is often a team effort among several **players, such as** the writer, perhaps an agent, friends and peers who will edit and respond to the work, and previously published writers who can provide advice. Another tension writers must negotiate when pursuing publication is audience appeal and personal integrity to one's **work: what** is often called "being true to oneself." Because getting published calls on writers to be flexible yet unique at* *the same **time, it can be the most challenging yet most rewarding experience writers undertake.***

Category:Rhetoric and Composition[1]

---

1   http://en.wikibooks.org/wiki/Category%3ARhetoric%20and%20Composition

58 Missing or misplaced apostrophe

For such a little piece of punctuation, the apostrophe is really noticeable when it's used wrong. And, there seems to be a lot of confusion about how it's used: a casual look at ads, signs, and other everyday writing reveals a wildly exotic sprinkling of apostrophes in all kinds of places. That's why mastering the apostrophes' uses can really bolster your credibility in writing: so many people get them wrong!

The main thing to know is that **apostrophes' primary jobs are to form possessives and to stand in for missing letters in a contraction.** Apostrophes are only *very* rarely used to form plurals.

You use possessive forms when you want to indicate ownership, or "belonging to." **Possessives are almost always formed by adding an apostrophe and an "s" to the end of a noun (a person, place, or thing).** In contrast, **plurals** are usually formed by adding an "s" or "es" to the end of a noun *without* an apostrophe.

EXAMPLES

Possessives use apostrophes.

The amendment's language clarifies the terms left undefined in the original law. **"language" belongs to "amendment"; "terms" is plural**

A review of the month's headlines reveals nine front-page pieces about the local school board election. **"headlines" belongs to "month"; "headlines" and "pieces" are plural**

Sara Jones' study of language use and class is considered a classic in the field. **"study" belongs to "Jones"; the apostrophe moves to the end because the noun ends in "s"**

Plurals do not take apostrophes.

*Three key **ideas** emerged in the introduction.*

*The organization was restructured after **decades** of poor performance.*

*All **animals** have an innate evolutionary drive to pass along **genes** to offspring.*

But plurals that are also possessive do use apostrophes. Notice how the position of the apostrophe moves depending on whether the plural ends with "s" or not.

*The book traces the **Kennedys'** influence on national politics.*

*The library science degree offers a special emphasis in **children's** literature.*

*The board changes the policy after the **stakeholders'** objections.*

Apostrophes are also used to stand in for missing letters in a contraction.

EXAMPLES

*The conclusion **doesn't [does not]** follow from the evidence.*

*Remove the test tubes from the sterilizer when the **cycle's [cycle is]** finished.*

*This committee will file a final report when **we're [we are]** done with the applications.*

Do not use an apostrophe to form the plurals of numbers or acronyms.

EXAMPLES

1980s

eights

three CEOs

these JPEGs

Category:Rhetoric and Composition[1]

---

1   http://en.wikibooks.org/wiki/Category%3ARhetoric%20and%20Composition

59 Unnecessary tense shift

59.1 What is a tense shift?

Verbs are action words. "Tense" refers to the time when an action takes place: past, present, or future. Necessary tense shifts simply make it clear to your reader when actions have taken, are taking, or will take place. When you "shift tense unnecessarily," however, it means you change the times when actions are taking place within a chunk of text in a way that doesn't seem to make sense. Notice how the tense changes cause confusion in the following examples.

59.2 Examples of confusing tense shifts

- *In February 2003, the Sefton City Council **passed** an ordinance that **limited** the number of dogs city residents **could keep** on their property to three. Several residents **objected** and formally **petitioned** the council to repeal the ordinance, but the council **upheld** it. Their reasoning **is** that having more than three dogs **creates** potentially dangerous situations. In November 2004, however, changes in the Council's membership **resulted** in the ordinance being repealed.*
- *While St. Cloud **struggles** with keeping rental housing from dominating the housing market, other communities in central Minnesota **undertook** several initiatives to build more apartments and condominiums.*

The best way to find unnecessary tense shifts is to read a piece of writing through one time just looking for tense and asking yourself whether each verb tense accurately reflects the time period it took place, takes place, or will take place in. Start by using a highlighter to mark each verb, and then ask yourself if the "time" is correct for each one.

The correction:

- *In February 2003, the Sefton City Council **passed** an ordinance that **limited** the number of dogs city residents **could keep** on their property to three. Several residents **objected** and formally **petitioned** the council to repeal the ordinance, but the council **upheld** it. Their reasoning **was** that having more than three dogs **creates** potentially dangerous situations. In November 2004, however, changes in the Council's membership **resulted** in the ordinance being repealed.*

(No reason exists to believe that those who then thought that three or more dogs in a household created a dangerous situation have changed their minds or that dogs' behavior in a group of three or more has changed. The composition of the council had changed, and the composition of the city council having changed, the city council voted differently).

- *While St. Cloud **struggled** with keeping rental housing from dominating the housing market, other communities in central Minnesota **undertook** several initiatives to build more apartments and condominiums.*

if referring to a situation in the past -- or --

- *While St. Cloud **struggles** with keeping rental housing from dominating the housing market, other communities in central Minnesota **undertake** several initiatives to build more apartments and condominiums.*

if referring to a current situation.

Category:Rhetoric and Composition[1]

---

1   http://en.wikibooks.org/wiki/Category%3ARhetoric%20and%20Composition

60 Run-on sentence

60.1 What is a run-on sentence?

While a run-on sentence, also known as a fused sentence, might just seem to be the type of sentence that goes on and on without a clear point, the technical grammatical definition of a run-on sentence is one that fuses, or "runs together," two or more independent clauses (basically, clauses that express a complete thought and could stand on their own as full sentences) without punctuation to separate them. They may have nothing between them, or they may have a coordinating conjunction (and, or, nor, but, for, so yet) between them but not the comma that needs to accompany the coordinating conjunction when separating two independent clauses.

You can often find run-on sentences in your work by reading it aloud. The run-on sentences will trip you up: you'll want to pause or otherwise come to some sort of end when you hit the end of an independent clause, but a run-on, with its lack of punctuation, doesn't signal you to do that. Try reading the following examples of run-on sentences out loud, and notice where two clauses seem to collide:

60.2 Examples of run-on sentences

- *Every day, millions of children go to daycare with millions of other kids there is no guarantee that none of them are harboring infectious conditions.*
- *Many daycare centers have strict rules about sick children needing to stay away until they are no longer infectious but enforcing those rules can be very difficult.*
- *Daycare providers often undergo extreme pressure to accept a sick child "just this once" the parent has no other care options and cannot miss work.*

60.3 Fixing run-on sentences

Once you find a run-on sentence and notice where the two independent clauses "collide," you can then decide on how best to separate the clauses:

- You can make two complete sentences by inserting a period; this is the strongest level of separation.
- You can use a semicolon between the two clauses if they are of equal importance, and you want your reader to consider the points together.
- You can use a semicolon with a transition word to indicate a specific relation between the two clauses.

- You can use a coordinating conjunction and a comma, also to indicate a relationship.
- Or, you can add a word to one clause to make it dependent.

60.4 Examples of fixed run-on sentences

Notice how the sentences above have been punctuated in the following examples.

- *Every day, millions of children go to daycare with millions of other **kids**. **There** is no guarantee that none of them are harboring infectious conditions.*
- *Many daycare centers have strict rules about sick children needing to stay away until they are no longer **infectious; however**, enforcing those rules can be very difficult.*
- *Many daycare centers have strict rules about sick children needing to stay away until they are no longer **infectious, but** enforcing those rules can be very difficult.*
- *Daycare providers often undergo extreme pressure to accept a sick child "just this once" **because** the parent has no other care options and cannot miss work.*

Learn more under "commas with two independent clauses" here.[1]

Category:Rhetoric and Composition[2]

---

1   Chapter 43 on page 239
2   http://en.wikibooks.org/wiki/Category%3ARhetoric%20and%20Composition

61 Disruptive comma

Disruptive commas are simply those that aren't needed -- those that "disrupt" the flow of the sentence. Here are some guidelines about places where you *don't* need to use commas.

Don't put a comma between a noun and the action it's doing, even when several words come between them.

*Most organic **compounds** ₋ **contain** oxygen, nitrogen, and halogens.*

*In the Islamic bayaa ceremony, prominent **citizens** ₋ **pledge** allegiance to a newly elected leader.*

*A **visit** to The City Museum's exhibit on the origins of photography ₋ **provided** an inspiring start to the class.*

Don't put a comma before these words unless there is an independent clause on each side

and, or, but, for, so, nor, yet.

The town was first settled in 1865 ₋ and incorporated in 1868.

The study sample was the correct size ₋ but insufficiently diversified.

The Australian conductor Richard Bonynge was born in Sydney ₋ and returned there after studying in London.

Don't put a comma before a list.

The neighborhood contains several examples of classic mid-century architecture, including ₋ the Dean Martin, Frank Sinatra, and Kennedy homes.

The recommended treatment focuses on changes in diet, such as ₋ increased fiber, less fat, and fewer processed foods.

The group of benefits considered standard is made up of ₋ health insurance, disability insurance, and a retirement account.

Category:Rhetoric and Composition[1]

---

1   http://en.wikibooks.org/wiki/Category%3ARhetoric%20and%20Composition

62 Dangling modifier

62.1 What Is a Dangling Modifier?

A common way to save words and combine ideas is by starting a sentence with a phrase that provides additional information about an element in the sentence without having to make a whole separate sentence to say it. In the following example, notice how three choppy sentences condense into one smoother sentence with the use of such an opening phrase, which is called a modifier:

- **Original**: *The Student Council exists to represent students to the faculty and administration. It also oversees student organizations. The Student Council plays an important role in campus life.*
- **Rewrite**: *Responsible for representing students to the faculty and administration and overseeing student organizations, the Student Council plays an important role in campus life.*

Here are some other examples of sentences that begin with a phrase providing this sort of additional information:

- *An example of bottom of the pyramid targeting, microcredit ventures lend small amounts of money to those with minimal assets.*
- *Found in tropical southern Asia, the Asian Koel belongs to the cuckoo order of birds.*
- *After completing the experiment, the most bacteria appeared in the scraping taken from the drinking fountain.*

Notice something odd about the last one? The modifier -- "After completing the experiment" -- doesn't match what follows it: The *bacteria* didn't complete the experiment (presumably, a researcher did)! The rule for using modifiers at the beginning of a sentence is that **the thing being modified must immediately follow the modifier.** Sometimes this requires you to rearrange the sentence; other times you have to "spell out" what is being modified if you didn't include it.

62.1.1 Examples

- **Dangling modifier**: *Covering most of Minnesota, the illustration showed the glacier that left the state with its thousands of lakes.*
- **Corrected**: *Covering most of Minnesota, the glacier left the state with its thousands of lakes, as depicted on the illustration.*
- **Dangling modifier**: *Trekking across the desert, fierce winds swirled around the riders.*
- **Corrected**: *Trekking across the desert, the riders were assaulted by fierce winds.*
- **Dangling modifier**: *First coined in 1980, historian Linda Kerber used the term "republican motherhood" to describe a phenomenon occurring after the Revolutionary War in*

which women were encouraged to promote the ideals of liberty and democracy to their children.

- **Corrected**: *First coined in 1980, the term "republican motherhood" was used by historian Linda Kerber to describe a phenomenon occurring after the Revolutionary War in which women were encouraged to promote the ideals of liberty and democracy to their children.*

62.2 What Is a Misplaced Modifier?

Whereas a dangling modifier is "left hanging," so to speak, with its referent missing in action, a misplaced modifier's referent is present and accounted for, but as its name implies, the modifier itself is out of place within the sentence, such that it seems to modify another referent in the sentence, resulting in ambiguity or confusion.

62.2.1 Examples

- **Misplaced**: Erik couldn't ride his bicycle *with a broken leg.*
- **Misplaced**: The little girl walked the dog *wearing a tutu.*
- **Misplaced**: *Just* don't stand there.

- **Correct**: *With his broken leg,* Erik couldn't ride his bicycle
- **Correct**: *Still wearing a tutu,* the little girl walked the dog.
- **Correct**: Don't *just* stand there.

62.3 What Is a Squinting Modifier?

Unlike a dangling modifier or a misplaced modifier, a squinting modifier is placed right next to the word it refers to, but it is also near another word that it might be modifying, which can cause confusion.

62.3.1 Examples

- **Squinting**: Cycling uphill *quickly* strengthens the leg muscles.

- **Correct**: *Quickly* cycling uphill strengthens the leg muscles.

Or

- **Correct**: Cycling uphill can *quickly* strengthen the leg muscles.

- **Squinting**: Using modifiers *clearly* will improve your writing.

- **Correct**: *Clearly* using modifiers will improve your writing.

Or

- **Correct**: Using modifiers will *clearly* improve your writing.

Category:Rhetoric and Composition[1]

1   http://en.wikibooks.org/wiki/Category%3ARhetoric%20and%20Composition

63 *Citing Sources*

64 Citation

64.1 Overview

Citations

- Purpose
  - Avoid plagiarism
  - Enable verification
- Location
  - In-text or parenthetical
  - Bibliography
- Style
  - MLA
    - Title for bibliography: Works Cited
    - In-text – example: (Goodview 98)
  - APA
    - Title for bibliography: References
    - In-text – example: (Goodview, 1998, p. 98)

Any time you use in your paper information that you paraphrase, summarize, or quote from another source, you must give the author or the publication proper credit. Failure to do so is considered plagiarism[1].

Plagiarism can be avoided by using **parenthetical citations** alias **in-text citations** within the text of your paper or essay and by using a **bibliography** (a list of your sources) at the end of your paper or essay.

The specific details of how to cite sources are prescribed in various citation styles. One of the most common writing systems in the educational systems is The Modern Language Association (MLA) style of writing. Most students learn first how to write using the MLA format in elementary school. Another very common writing system frequently used by the social sciences is the American Psychological Association (APA) format.

In MLA the bibliography is titled "Works Cited," and in APA the list is titled "References."

---

1   Chapter 65 on page 301

64.2 Citing Outside Sources In-Text

Your in-text citations should correspond to the first item listed in your bibliographic citations, which is usually the author's last name. For example, if the in-text citation looks like this:

In a 1949 visit to members of Congress, Hemingway repeatedly reported of the natural beauty that would be destroyed by exploring for oil in Alaska (Booth 216).
Example of an MLA parenthetical citation.

Then by going to the bibliography page and looking down the list of sources, the name "Booth" should start the citation. For example,

Works Cited   Booth, Fredrick. The Effect of Hemingway on Alaska. Hartford: ---. Wilmington UP, 1998.
Example from MLA Works Cited page.

64.2.1 Parenthetical Citations

Parenthetical Citations serve to inform your reader of where you found the data or quotation you are providing to them. Generally, in MLA, if you are citing more than one source, you should include the author's or editor's name and the page number in your parenthetical citation. For example: (Jones 127). If you are only using a single source which is already identified elsewhere in the text, simply use the page number.

MLA Examples

MLA Parenthetical (or In-Text) Citation Examples:

Hemingway's arguments against oil drilling in Alaska continued to intensify in his later life. In a 1949 visit to members of Congress, Hemingway repeatedly reported of the natural beauty that would be destroyed by exploring for oil in Alaska (Booth 216). Later that year, Hemingway went on to request, and to be granted, an audience with the President where he shared a multitude of research against drilling (Goodview 98). Hemingway, along with countless other supporters, continued to call upon legislators from both sides of the aisle until the idea of Alaskan oil exploration was naught, or so they thought. "It is a victory for all the inhabitants of the earth that the State of Alaska's natural beauty, wonder, and habitat will remain unharmed by human greed so that our children and grandchildren and generations after them will be able to catch a glimpse of an unspoiled planet" (Chandler 143). The idea of an unspoiled planet was, unfortunately, relatively short lived.
An example of MLA parenthetical citations.

You may also mention the author's name within the text rather than in a parenthetical citation.

> Hemingway's arguments against oil drilling in Alaska continued to intensify in his later life. According to Booth, in a 1949 visit to members of Congress, Hemingway repeatedly reported of the natural beauty that would be destroyed by exploring for oil in Alaska (216). Goodview reports that later that year Hemingway went on to request, and to be granted, an audience with the President where he shared a multitude of research against drilling (98).
>
> An example of MLA parenthetical citations.

If a source has two to three authors, mention all the names within the text, or in a parenthetical citation, separated by "and."

> Hemingway's arguments against oil drilling in Alaska continued to intensify in his later life. According to Booth and Goodview, in a 1949 visit to members of Congress, Hemingway repeatedly reported of the natural beauty that would be destroyed by exploring for oil in Alaska (216). Later that year Hemingway went on to request, and to be granted, an audience with the President where he shared a multitude of research against drilling (Goodview, Chandler, and Smith 98).
>
> An example of MLA parenthetical citations.

If your source has four or more authors, you may mention only the first author's last name followed by "et al.," or you may use all the author's last names.

> Hemingway's arguments against oil drilling in Alaska continued to intensify in his later life. According to Booth et al., in a 1949 visit to members of Congress, Hemingway repeatedly reported of the natural beauty that would be destroyed by exploring for oil in Alaska (216). Later that year Hemingway went on to request, and to be granted, an audience with the President where he shared a multitude of research against drilling (Goodview et al., 98).
>
> An example of MLA parenthetical citations.

More detailed information regarding MLA in-text citations can be found at *The Owl*,[2] Purdue's online writing guide, and at Literacy Education Online (LEO)[3], St. Cloud State University's online writing guide.

APA Examples

APA Parenthetical (or In-Text) Citation Examples:

In APA format, you also include the author's name in parenthetical citations; however, whenever you use the author's name in APA, you **must** also include the **date** of the publication.

---

2   http://owl.english.purdue.edu/owl/resource/557/02/

3   http://leo.stcloudstate.edu/research/mla.html

> Hemingway's arguments against oil drilling in Alaska continued to intensify in his later life. In a 1949 visit to members of Congress, Hemingway repeatedly reported of the natural beauty that would be destroyed by exploring for oil in Alaska (Booth, 2000, p. 216). Later that year, Hemingway went on to request, and to be granted, an audience with the President where he shared a multitude of research against drilling (Goodview, 1998, p. 98). Hemingway, along with countless other supporters, continued to call upon legislators from both sides of the aisle until the idea of Alaskan oil exploration was naught, or so they thought. "It is a victory for all the inhabitants of the earth that the State of Alaska's natural beauty, wonder, and habitat will remain unharmed by human greed so that our children and grandchildren and generations after them will be able to catch a glimpse of an unspoiled planet" (Chandler, 1985, p. 143). The idea of an unspoiled planet was, unfortunately, relatively short lived.
>
> An example of APA parenthetical citations.

You may also mention the author's name within the text.

> According to Booth (2000), Hemingway's arguments against oil drilling in Alaska continued to intensify in his later life. In a 1949 visit to members of Congress, Hemingway repeatedly reported of the natural beauty that would be destroyed by exploring for oil in Alaska (p. 216). Goodview (1998) notes that Later that year Hemingway went on to request, and to be granted, an audience with the President where he shared a multitude of research against drilling (p. 98). Hemingway, along with countless other supporters, continued to call upon legislators from both sides of the aisle until the idea of Alaskan oil exploration was naught, or so they thought. One of these members is quoted by Chandler (1998) as saying of this time, "It is a victory for all the inhabitants of the earth that the State of Alaska's natural beauty, wonder, and habitat will remain unharmed by human greed so that our children and grandchildren and generations after them will be able to catch a glimpse of an unspoiled planet" (p. 143). The idea of an unspoiled planet was, unfortunately, relatively short lived.
>
> An example of APA parenthetical citations.

If you need to cite two authors of the same work who are mentioned within the text, use both their last names and separate it with "and."

> According to Chandler and Goodview (2004), Hemingway's arguments against oil drilling in Alaska continued to intensify in his later life. In a 1949 visit to members of Congress, Hemingway repeatedly reported of the natural beauty that would be destroyed by exploring for oil in Alaska (p. 216).
>
> An example of APA parenthetical citations.

If you do not mention the two author's names within the text, you do so in parenthesis using an ampersand instead of the word "and."

> Hemingway's arguments against oil drilling in Alaska continued to intensify in his later life. In a 1949 visit to members of Congress, Hemingway repeatedly reported of the natural beauty that would be destroyed by exploring for oil in Alaska (Chandler & Goodview, 2004, p. 216).
>
> An example of APA parenthetical citations.

If you have three to five authors, list them all by last name the **first** time you mention them in the text. Thereafter, only use the first author's last name followed by "et al."

According to Chandler, Goodview, and Petty (2004), Hemingway's arguments against oil drilling in Alaska continued to intensify in his later life. In a 1949 visit to members of Congress, Hemingway repeatedly reported of the natural beauty that would be destroyed by exploring for oil in Alaska (p. 216). Chandler et al. (2004) also noted that...
An example of APA parenthetical citations.

If you mention the authors in parenthetical citations instead of within the text, follow the same guidelines as noted above.

Hemingway's arguments against oil drilling in Alaska continued to intensify in his later life. In a 1949 visit to members of Congress, Hemingway repeatedly reported of the natural beauty that would be destroyed by exploring for oil in Alaska (Chandler, Goodview & Petty, 2004, p. 216). Later that year Hemingway went on to request, and to be granted, an audience with the President where he shared a multitude of research against drilling (Goodview, 1998, p. 98). Hemingway, along with countless other supporters, continued to call upon legislators from both sides of the aisle until the idea of Alaskan oil exploration was naught, or so they thought. "It is a victory for all the inhabitants of the earth that the State of Alaska's natural beauty, wonder, and habitat will remain unharmed by human greed so that our children and grandchildren and generations after them will be able to catch a glimpse of an unspoiled planet" (Chandler et al., 2004, p. 143). The idea of an unspoiled planet was, unfortunately, relatively short lived.
An example of APA parenthetical citations.

If you have six or more authors, list only the first author's last name followed by "et al."

According to Chandler et al. (2007), Hemingway's arguments against oil drilling in Alaska continued to intensify in his later life.
An example of APA parenthetical citations.

If you do not know the author's name, use a portion of the article or book title instead. Titles of articles are placed within quotes. Book and report titles are italicized or underlined. (Note that in APA only the first word of an article title is capitalized.)

Hemingway's arguments against oil drilling in Alaska continued to intensify in his later life ("Hemingway's battle for Alaska," 2001).
An example of APA parenthetical citations.

For more information on APA in-text citations, see *The Owl* Purdue's online writing guide for APA citations[4] or *LEO* St. Cloud State University's online writing guide for APA citations[5]

---

4   http://owl.english.purdue.edu/owl/resource/560/03/
5   http://leo.stcloudstate.edu/research/apadocument.html

64.3 Citing Outside Sources in a Bibliography

While parenthetical in-text citations already indicate the sources of the information, a full identification of the cited sources is required to make it possible for the reader to unambiguously locate the source in a library or on the internet. The list of fully identified sources usually goes at the end of your paper, into a bibliography section. A full identification of a source usually includes the year of publication, the authors, the title of the work, the publishing organization, and more. The information included in the full identification of a source varies with the publication style such as MLA style and APA style.

MLA Works Cited

In MLA, you do this on your **Works Cited** page. To write your MLA works cited list, follow the steps below.

1. Start a new page for your list, and center the words "Works Cited" at the top of the page. There is no need to format the words any different than the rest of your text, so don't waste your time by underlining, italicizing, or making them bold.

2. Number this page in continuation of the pages in your essay or research work.

3. Start each entry flush with the left margin. Indent any subsequent lines five (5) spaces.

4. Alphabetize your sources by the author's last name or by using the information provided below.

Books - one author

a. Author - List author by last name, (comma) first name.

b. Title - Underline title and subtitle. Capitalize any major words even if not officially capitalized in the book's title.

c. Publication Information - Provide the city of publication and the state code if the city is unfamiliar, followed by a : (colon)- a space and the shortened version of the publisher's name (Penguin for The Penguin Press - a , (comma) and the year of publication.

Johnson, Steven. <u>Everything Bad is Good for You</u>. New York: Penguin, 2005.

Books - two or three authors

a. Authors - List the first author last name first. Then list the name (s) of the subsequent author(s) in normal order, with a , (comma) between the names and a ,and (comma and) before the last author.

b. Follow the remaining steps as you would with one author.

Caldwell, Ian, and Dustin Thomason. <u>The Rule of Four</u>. New York: The Dial Press, 2004.

Books - four or more authors

a. Authors - Give the first author listed on the title page, followed by a , (comma) and "et al."

b. Follow the remaining steps as you would with one author.

Pilot, John, et al. <u>A Lifetime of Success</u>. Minneapolis: Grey Wolf, 2005.

Books - corporate author a. Give the name of the group listed on the title page as the author even if the same group published the book.

b. Follow the remaining steps as you would with one author.

National Multiple Sclerosis Society. <u>Dealing with MS: a Guide for the Newly Diagnosed</u>. Los Angeles: National Multiple Sclerosis Soc., 2000.

Books - unknown author

a. Start the entry with the title, and list alphabetically by the first major word of the title.

b. Follow the remaining steps as you would with one author.

<u>Time Life Treasury of Letters</u>. New York: Harvard UP, 1976.

Books - two or more by the same author(s)

a. Arrange entries alphabetically by title.

b. List the name(s) of the author in the first entry, but in subsequent entries, us three hyphens followed by a period.

Tims, James. <u>What Went Right for Republicans in 2004</u>. New Orleans: Wave, 2004.

---. <u>What Went Wrong for Democrats in 2004</u>. New Orleans: Wave, 2004.

Books - editor or editors

a. Treat as you would an author, but add a comma "ed." for (or "eds." for more than one) editor.

b. Follow the remaining steps as you would with one author.

Pemberton, Michael A., and Joyce Kinkead. The Center Will Hold: Critical Perspectives on Writing Center Scholarship. Logan, UT: Utah State UP, 2003.

Website

a. Give the authors name (if known) last name followed by first name.

b. List the full title of the work in quotation marks.

c. List the complete works title (if applicable)in italics.

d. Give any version or file number.

e. Give the date of the document's last revision.

f. Finally, list http: and give the full URL address

Schanaansberg, Arthur. "Hurricane Katrina 2005". *What is Happening as a Result of the Greenhouse Effect.* November 6, 2005. `http://en.geowarming.org/recent_disasters`

Works Cited Example

Works Cited

Allyn, Fredrick. The Effect of Monopolies on Economies Throughout the World. Hartford: ---. Wilmington UP, 1998.

Collier, Sally, Sharon Pat, and Stephanie Quake. Capitalism: the Good and the Bad.

---. New York: Barton, 2003.

Fey, C. Jean, ed. The New Deal Today. Milwaukee: Wisconsin UP, 2004.

Rogers, Kent. "Do We Really Want to Raise the Minimum Wage." *Economic Realities in*

---. *Today's Global Economy*. 2005. `http://warathome.org/soundpolicies/review` Tift, Mary. How Did We Get Here: Economic Analysis of Carter through G.W..

---. Minneapolis: Dunkday, 2005.

Urbanski, Jenny and Helen Carter. How We Continue Competing. Chicago: Tribune, 2003.

Works Cited page example.

APA References Page

To cite your sources in APA format, you do this on your **References** page. To write your References page, follow the steps below.

1. Start a new page for your list, and center the word "References" at the top of the page. There is no need to format the words any different than the rest of your text, so don't waste your time by underlining, italicizing, or making them bold.

2. Number this page in continuation of the pages in your essay or research work.

3. Start each entry flush with the left margin. Indent any subsequent lines 1/2 inch, and double space the entries like the rest of your paper.

4. Alphabetize your sources by the author's last name and first initial, or by using the information provided below. If there is more than one author, list the first author by the last name first, followed by the first name initial, then for all others list the first initial first, followed by the last name, and separate by commas.

5. In dealing with the titles of all books, articles, or webpages, capitalize only the first letter of the first word of a title and subtitle, the first word after a colon or a dash in the title,

and all proper nouns.

6. Capitalize all major words in journal titles.

7. Italicize or underline book and journal titles. (Be consistent, always italicize, or always underline, but never use both.)

8. **Do not** italicize, underline, or put quotes around the titles of shorter works such as journal articles or essays in edited collections.

Books

a. Author - List author by last name, (comma) first name initial. If there are more than six authors, list the first author and first initial followed by "et al."

b. Year of publication in parenthesis.

c. Title - Underline or italicize the title and subtitle. Capitalize **only** the first letter of the first word of a title and subtitle, the first word after a colon or a dash in the title, and proper nouns.

d. Publication Information - Provide the city of publication and the state code if the city is unfamiliar, followed by a : (colon)- a space and the shortened version of the publisher's name.

Creakly, P. (2008). *Whatever you said is true: Unless you are lying.* New York: Penguin.

Journal article - by issue

a. Author - List author by last name, (comma) first name initial. If there are more than six authors, list the first author and first initial followed by "et al."

b. Year of publication in parenthesis. c. Title of the article - No underling, italics, or quotes are used. Capitalize **only** the first letter of the first word of a title and subtitle, the first word after a colon or a dash in the title, and proper nouns.

d. Title of the journal/periodical- Italicized or underlined. Capitalize the first letter of all words. e. Volume number(issue number), pages- The volume number and issue number are italicized.

Treasure, J. C., S. Kuepers, & J. Edward. (2000). How to determine whether people are lying to you by watching their eyes. *Human Behavior, 22(16),* 24-64.

Website

a. Authors name (if known) last name followed by first initial.

b. Year of publication in parenthesis.

c. Title of webpage document. Only capitalize the first letter of the first word.

d. Provide the date your retrieved it, listed in order by the month and day followed by a comma, then year followed by a comma.

e. Include the web address you retrieved if from. Do not end with a period.

Wertjes, A. (2007). Facts on finding truth. Retrieved January 21, 2008, from http://freedinformationforall.com

References Page Example

References

Creakly, P. (2008). *Whatever you said is true: Unless you are lying.* New York:Penguin.

Tresure, J. C., S. Kuepers, & J. Edward. (2000). How to determine whether people are

---. lying to you by watching their eyes. *Human Behavior, 22(16),* 24-64.

Wertjes, A. (2007). Facts on finding truth. Retrieved January 21, 2008, from

---. http://freedinformationforall.com

References page example.

More Examples on Formatting Bibliographies

See The Owl[6] or LEO[7]. n

64.4 See also

- The chapter Annotated Bibliography[8]
- The chapter Plagiarism[9]

10

---

6   http://owl.english.purdue.edu/owl/
7   http://leo.stcloudstate.edu/research/apadocument.html
8   http://en.wikibooks.org/wiki/..%2FAnnotated%20Bibliography
9   Chapter 65 on page 301
10   http://en.wikibooks.org/wiki/Category%3ARhetoric%20and%20Composition

65 Plagiarism

65.1 Overview of Plagiarism

According to *dictionary.com*, plagiarism is defined as the act of passing off as one's own the ideas or writings of another.

The Council of Writing Program Administrators' definition for plagiarism: In an instructional setting, plagiarism occurs when a writer deliberately uses someone else's language, ideas, or other original (not commonly-knowledge) material without acknowledging its source.[1]

There are three different conventions in writing in which you must provide reference.

- When you use someone else's ideas, such as the above definitions of plagiarism
- When the way in which you are using a source is unclear to the reader, make it clear.
- Acknowledge any help you receive from someone on writing the paper.

Citing your sources is easy; do it and save yourself from getting in a lot of trouble.

65.2 Examples of Plagiarism

The following is adapted from Diana Hacker's *A Pocket Style Manual*.[2]

Your research paper is a collaboration between you and your sources. To be fair and ethical, you must acknowledge your debt to the writers of those sources. If you don't, you are guilty of plagiarism, a serious academic offense. Three different acts are considered plagiarism:

- *failing to cite quotations and borrowed ideas,*
- *failing to enclose borrowed language in quotation marks, and*
- *failing to put summaries and paraphrases in your own words.*

If you wrote something in your paper such as this:

When writing a research paper it is important to acknowledge your debt to the writers of those sources. It is a collaboration between you and your sources. Failure to not acknowledge your sources is an act of plagiarism.

and did not put any reference to Hacker, it would be plagiarism. A proper way to use the work would be this:

---

1   Johnson-Sheehan, Richard and Charles Paine. Writing Today. Custom Edition for St. Cloud State University. Boston: Pearson Education, 2013.

2   Hacker, Diana. *A Pocket Style Manual*. New York: Bedford/St. Martin's, 2004. 115.

Diana Hacker stresses how important it is "to acknowledge your debt to the writers" of sources you use in your writing. She states that your paper "is a collaboration between you and your sources". "failure to not acknowledge your sources is an act of plagiarism" (Hacker 115).

It is also important to not only cite your sources in your work but also include a detailed reference to the work at the end of your paper on the works cited page. An example for the previous source is below:

Hacker, Diana. A Pocket Style Manual. New York: Bedford/St. Martin's, 2004.

65.3 Rules to Help You Avoid Plagiarism

The following rules are taken from Rosen, Leonard. *The Academic Writer's Handbook: Instructor's Copy.* 2006, pages 122–124.

- When quoting another writer, use quotation marks and give credit.
- When restating the ideas of others in your words, give credit.
- Avoid using words, phrases, or sentence structures from the original source.

Category:Rhetoric and Composition[3]

65.4 Patchwriting

[4]

Patchwriting means taking another person's words and sentences and reworking them, changing words or phrases here and there, to make it appear that the writing is your own. Patchwriting is academically dishonest and should not be done. Sometimes, students patchwrite even if they don't mean to. But whether it was intentional or not, the offense is still an offense. It's important to summarize and paraphrase carefully to avoid patchwriting and plagiarism.

65.5 References

---

3   http://en.wikibooks.org/wiki/Category%3ARhetoric%20and%20Composition
4   Johnson-Sheehan, Richard and Charles Paine. Custom Ediction for St. Cloud State University. Boston: Pearson Education, 2013.

66 Glossary

This is a glossary of the book. Also see the index[1].

66.1 A

allegory

Narrative where the characters, action and generally also the setting work on two levels. It appears superficially to be a straightforward story, but also conveys deeper meanings. Some examples are:

Absalom and Achitophel by John Dryden tells the story of Absalom's rebellion against King David but also refers to the Duke of Monmouth's rebellion against James II.

Animal Farm by George Orwell tells a fantasy story of animals taking over a farm but is also a thinly disguised history of the USSR.

Note that allegory is not metaphor[2]; it never states that something is something else that it is not.

alliteration

Having several words that are consecutive or close together and begin with similar sounds. In spoken poetry, this can produce an effective sound pattern. A famous example is in Tennyson's "Morte D'Arthur" where there are five l sounds (l being the second letter of "glories"):

lo! the level lake,

And the long glories of the winter moon.

Compare to assonance[3].

ambiguity

The deliberate use of a word that can be taken to have two or more meanings, with the intention of enriching the text by allowing the reader to accept both meanings simultaneously.

allusion

---

1   http://en.wikibooks.org/wiki/Rhetoric%20and%20Composition%2FIndex
2   Chapter 66.19 on page 318
3   Chapter 66.19 on page 318

A reference to a person, place, event or another literary work that the reader is expected to recognise. An allusion may be used to expand upon or enhance a subject, or to undercut it by drawing an ironic contrast between the allusion and the current subject.

anachronism

Making a reference that is clearly out of place in a work set in a particular time. A famous example is Shakespeare's reference in *Julius Caesar* to a clock striking.

anacoluthon

The change to a new grammatical construction before the first one is finished, causing an odd sequence of words.

anaphora

The repetition of an opening word or phrase, often for emphasis; compare epiphora[4], symploce[5].

antiphrasis

The sarcastic use of a word to mean its exact opposite.

antistasis

This means using a word twice in a passage, with two different meanings.

As God in His wisdom ordained, the world would not find him by its wisdom. (I Corinthians 1:21)

antithesis

This means placing two phrases or sentences, of similar structure but opposite or sharply different meaning, in juxtaposition.

APA style

A writing style and formatting standard widely used in the social sciences, and published by the American Psychological Association, a professional organization representing psychologists in the U.S.A.

aposiopesis

A form of ellipsis[6] where an argument is presented and the conclusion is deliberately omitted, to be supplied by the reader or listener.

apostrophe

In rhetoric, this does not mean a punctuation symbol. It is a direct address to someone or something which cannot answer, either because he/she is not there or because it is an inanimate object. The verb is "to apostrophise". Thus in "Ode to a Grecian Urn", Keats apostrophises the urn.

appositive

---

4   Chapter 66.19 on page 318
5   Chapter 66.19 on page 318
6   Chapter 66.19 on page 318

A word or phrase that is in apposition.

apposition

A construction in which one noun or noun phrase is placed with another as an explanatory equivalent, both having the same syntactic function in the sentence, such as:

Rudolph, the red-nosed reindeer, had a very shiny nose.

archaism

The deliberate use of obsolete words, grammar or expressions. This may be done because of the nature of the subject matter, to create a particular mood (for example, solemnity) or simply to help a poem rhyme or scan.

assonance

The recurrence of a similar sound in several words close together. Unlike alliteration[7], this sound need not be the initial letter of a word. A famous example is the opening of Keats' "Ode on a Grecian Urn", with five long "i" sounds:

Thou still unravished bride of quietness,

Thou foster child of silence and slow time.

asyndeton

When consecutive phrases are not connected by a conjunction when one would be expected, e.g. "I came, I saw, I conquered".

66.2 B

bathos

(from the Greek for *depth*) Means that you seem to be saying something very profound but then proceed to a ludicrous anticlimax[8]. it may be intentional, for comic effect, or unintentional. Alexander Pope coined the term in *On Bathos: Of the Art of Sinking in Poetry* (1727), where he gives the example

Ye Gods! annihilate but Space and Time,

And make two lovers happy.

bombast

Bombast is an inflated, extremely verbose style of writing that is wholly inappropriate to the subject matter. bad writers may use bombast unintentionally, but it is often used for deliberate satirical or comic effect.

brainstorming[9]

---

7   Chapter 66.19 on page 318
8   Chapter 66.19 on page 318
9   Chapter 6.1 on page 17

A method of problem solving in which members of a group contribute ideas spontaneously, by first coming up with a long list of even poor ideas and criticizing them later.

66.3 C

cacophony

Writing designed to be very harsh and unpleasant. It is designed to heighten the effect of unpleasant emotions in a passage. Contrast euphony[10].

capitalization[11]

The use of lowercase or uppercase characters in sentences, common and proper names, and titles.

chiasmus

A pair of clauses or phrases where the second has the same syntax as the first except that the ordering is reversed. The two phrases can be very similar, as in Yeats' "An Irish Airman Foresees His Death":

The years to come seemed waste of breath,

A waste of breath the years behind

or rather different, as in Pope's Essay on Criticism:

Works without Show, and without Pomp presides.

circumlocution

Saying things in a very roundabout way, using many words when saying things directly would use far fewer words. It is also called *periphrasis*. For example, Lewis Carroll's description of fixing a photographic negative with sodium hyposulphite:

Finally, he fixed each picture

With a saturate solution

Which was made of hyposulphite

Which, again, was made of soda.

(Very difficult the name is

For a metre like the present

But periphrasis has done it.)

clustering[12]

---

10   Chapter 66.19 on page 318
11   Chapter 50 on page 259
12   Chapter 6.1 on page 17

A prewriting technique consisting of writing ideas down on a sheet of paper around a central idea within a circle, with the related ideas radially joined to the circle using rays.

comic relief

The use of comedy, especially low comedy such as slapstick, to ease the tension of a particularly dramatic or melodramatic passage. This is often achieved by the use of a different character or characters, specifically to be clowns.

comma splice[13]

An error consisting of joining two independent clauses with a comma.

conceit

This has a specific meaning in composition, namely a figure of speech that establishes an elaborate and striking parallel between two situations or objects that are at first sight completely different.

conclusion

copy editing

The correction of spelling, grammar, formatting, etc. of printed material and preparing it for typesetting, printing, or online publishing.

cosmic irony

A literary work in which God, "the gods" or Fate deliberately manipulates events so as to give one or more characters false hopes, only to mock and frustrate them.

cumulative clause

66.4 D

dangling modifier[14]

A word or clause that modifies another word or clause ambiguously, possibly causing confusion with regard to the speaker's intended meaning, such as "Trekking across the desert, fierce winds swirled around the riders": it was not the winds that were trekking across the desert.

dash[15]

The symbol "–" (en-dash) or "—" (em-dash), used to mark an interruption in a sentence.

dead metaphor

---

13   http://en.wikibooks.org/wiki/..%2FComma_Splice
14   Chapter 48 on page 255
15   Chapter 48 on page 255

A metaphor[16] that is so familiar that people have generally forgotten that it is a metaphor, such as "the heart of the matter". It is possible that an apparently dead metaphor may come back to life in the right context, often with humorous results, for example "I worked hard clearing up the garden; it was no bed of roses".

deductive reasoning[17]

"Top-down" reasoning in which one begins with a major premise and a minor premise and from these draws a conclusion.

> **major premise** - applies to all things within a particular category.

> **minor premise** - applies to a particular case, not a general category.

> Men are tall.

> John is a man.

> Therefore, John is tall.

dependent clause

A group of words that contains a subject and a verb but does not express a complete thought. *Compare to independent clause[18].*

deus ex machina

Literally "god from a machine", this originally referred to the classical Greek practice of resolving all the difficulties in a play by having a god descend on the stage via a mechanical apparatus. It now, metaphorically[19], refers to a sudden and arbitrary plot twist to solve a problem.

diction

The style of a work, as manifested by the choice of vocabulary, phrasing and figures of speech. It is often used in the phrase "poetic diction".

doggerel

Poorly-written poetry. While it usually rhymes and scans fairly well, often the rhymes are poor and the rhythm is jerky. Generally it is written by inferior poets, but it may be used for comic effect.

dramatic irony

A form of irony[20] in which the readers of a book, or the audience at a play, know things that a character does not, and can therefore be amused when things are said or done that have a different meaning from what that character imagines.

---

16 Chapter 66.19 on page 318
17 http://en.wikibooks.org/wiki/..%2FRhetorical_Analysis%23Deductive_Logic
18 Chapter 66.19 on page 318
19 Chapter 66.19 on page 318
20 Chapter 66.19 on page 318

66.5 E

ellipsis

The omission of words that are essential in the grammatical construction, but where the context makes it clear what the sense of the missing words is.

enallage

The deliberate use of a part of speech or a tense, when another would be grammatically correct. this is common in poetry for the sake of meter or rhyme.

"Nor dim, nor red, like God's own head,

The glorious Sun uprist"

Coleridge, "The Rhyme of the Ancient Mariner", using "uprist" for "uprose" or "rose up", to rhyme with "mist".

enjambment

In poetry, the placement of words in the next line to complete the sense of a phrase, rather than having each line as a self-contained phrase.

epic simile

A kind of simile[21] invented by Homer and copied by Vergil, Milton and other writers of epics. The secondary subject is not only compared with the first subject, but is developed at considerable length.

epigram

A very short poem that ends with a witty or surprising turn of thought.

epiphora

The repetition of an opening word or phrase, often for emphasis; compare anaphora[22], symploce[23].

epithet

An adjective or adjectival phrase that is used to describe the special quality of a thing or person.

epithalamion

A poem in celebration of a wedding. The Latin spelling "epithalamium" is used occasionally.

equivoque

A play on words where a word or phrase with two different meanings is used in a context where both meanings are appropriate.

essay

---

21   Chapter 66.19 on page 318
22   Chapter 66.19 on page 318
23   Chapter 66.19 on page 318

A short piece of non-narrative writing, often written from an author's personal point of view; including literary criticism, political manifestos, learned arguments, observations of daily life, recollections, and reflections of the author.

euphemism

Replacing an unpleasant word or expression with a more pleasant one. Typically, it is used most often in connection with death, sex and bodily functions.

euphony

Writing designed to be very smooth and pleasant, often almost musical in effect. It is designed to heighten the effect of pleasant emotions in a passage. A good example is in Tennyson's **The Lotos Eaters**:

Music that gentlier on the spirit lies,

Than tir'd eyelids upon tir'd eyes;

Music that brings sweet sleep down from the blissful skies.

Here are cool mosses deep,

And thro' the moss the ivies creep,

And in the stream the long-leav'd flowers weep,

And from the craggy ledge the poppy hangs in sleep.

Contrast cacophony[24].

euphuism

A prose style that is extremely, even ridiculously, elaborate and formal. It was most popular in the 1580s and was parodied by Shakespeare in several of his plays.

exposition

The writing that mainly explains and instructs, assuming no prior knowledge of the reader, contrasted to narration or reference manual.

eye-rhyme

In poetry, rhyming two words that are spelt the same (hence seem to rhyme to the eye) but are pronounced differently (so would not rhyme to the ear), e.g. through/trough or machine/fine.

66.6 F

figurative language

---

24   Chapter 66.19 on page 318

Writing where the intended meaning is not what would be implied by the literal meaning of the words and the standard rules of syntax. See dead metaphor[25], epic simile[26], metaphor[27], metonymy[28], mixed metaphor[29], personification[30], simile[31] and synecdoche[32].

figure of speech

Any word, phrase or sentence where a special use of words conveys a meaning other than the meanings ordinarily assifned to the words.

66.7 H

heroic couplet

Style of poetry consisting of iambic pentameters rhyming in pairs "aa bb cc ..." It was used extensively by Chaucer and many subsequent poets.

homeoteleuton

In poetry, similarity of line-endings. This may be a rhyme, or more generally assonance[33].

hyperbation

The re-ordering of words, for poetical or rhetorical effect, beyond what might seem reasonable.

hyperbole

(From the Greek for "overshooting") Extreme exaggeration or overstatement, for either serious or (more usually) comic effect.

hyphen[34]

Symbol "-", typically used to join two related words to form a compound noun, or to indicate that a word has been split at the end of a line, approximately half the length of a dash.

66.8 I

independent clause

---

25   Chapter 66.19 on page 318
26   Chapter 66.19 on page 318
27   Chapter 66.19 on page 318
28   Chapter 66.19 on page 318
29   Chapter 66.19 on page 318
30   Chapter 66.19 on page 318
31   Chapter 66.19 on page 318
32   Chapter 66.19 on page 318
33   Chapter 66.19 on page 318
34   Chapter 48 on page 255

A group of words that contains a subject and a verb and which express a complete thought. *Compare to dependent clause*[35].

inductive reasoning[36]

"Bottom-up" reasoning in which one begins by examining a number of individual cases and from these draws a conclusion that can be applies to similar cases.

invective

Denunciation of someone or something by a series of derogatory epithets.

inversion

The reversal of the natural order of two words for rhetorical or poetic effect.

invocation

A request by an author for a muse or other divinity to assist him.

irony

A statement where the superficial assertion is not what the author really means. For example, he may say about something, "Oh, wonderful, marvellous, excellent" but mean that it is really very bad.

66.9 L

litotes

The positive assertion of something by stating its contrary mildly, e.g. "He's not the tallest boy in the school" to suggest that he's the shortest or among the shortest.

logos[37]

A rhetorical technique that appeals to logic or reason.

Types of logical arguments, see deductive[38] and inductive reasoning[39].

66.10 M

manuscript

A text that has been written by hand, not printed or published in any form.

mechanics[40]

---

35   Chapter 66.19 on page 318
36   http://en.wikibooks.org/wiki/..%2FRhetorical_Analysis%23Inductive_Logic
37   http://en.wikibooks.org/wiki/..%2FRhetorical_Analysis%23Logos
38   Chapter 66.19 on page 318
39   Chapter 66.19 on page 318
40   http://en.wikibooks.org/wiki/..%2FWriter%27s_Handbook%23Understanding_Mechanics

Spelling and punctuation; aspects of writing that are not shared by speaking.

meiosis

(Greek for "lessening") Synonymm for understatement[41].

melodrama

A form of writing (a book, play or film) marked by very exaggerated characterisation. The "good guys", nmale and female, are paragons of virtue, while the villains are unredeemable monsters. There willl be much violent action, with credibility of plot often sacrificed to thrills and sensation.

metaphor

A figure of speech in which someone or something is said to be something else which it clearly is not, in order to emphasise a characteristic that the writer wishes to describe.

"You are my sunshine, my only sunshine" - popular song.

metonymy

A figure of speech (from the Greek "change of name") in which the term for someone or something is replaced by a term for something closely associated, as "the crown" for "the king".

mixed metaphor

The use of two metaphors in the same passage, with ludicrous results if the literal meaning is considered.

"A torrent of brimstone descended on him, and he was frozen out of the discussion." - Stephen Leacock.

MLA style

The style of writing and citing for scholars of language and literature, published in *MLA Style Manual* by the Modern Language Association, the principal professional association in the United States for scholars of language and literature.

66.11 N

narration[42]

The writing that relates a story or a series of events, with emphasis on events and people.

66.12 O

onomatopoeia

---

41   Chapter 66.19 on page 318
42   Chapter 24 on page 117

The use of a word or words that just by their sound suggest what is happening. Simple examples include "hiss" and "buzz". A more elaborate example occurs in Tennyson's "Morte d'Arthur", where a series of hard sounds, indicating the clattering sound made by Sir Bedivere, suddenly changes into smooth liquid sounds when he reaches the calm lake.

> Dry clash'd his harness in the icy caves
>
> And barren chasms, and all to left and right
>
> The bare black cliff clang'd round him, as he based
>
> His feet on juts of slippery crag that rang
>
> Sharp-smitten with the dint of armed heels--
>
> And on a sudden, lo! the level lake,
>
> And the long glories of the winter moon.

oxymoron

(From the Greek *oxus*, sharp + *moros*, foolish) A figure of speech where two contradictory words are juxtaposed, e.g. "hor ice" or 9it is often joked) "military intelligence".

66.13 P

paradox

A statement that on first reading or hearing seems absurd, but on closer examination is found to be true.

paragoge

The addition of an extra syllable at the end of a word; this is sometimes done in poetry for metrical reasons.

> The Earl of Fife, without**en** strife
>
> "The Battle of Otterburn"

parallelism

The use of consecutive or nearly consecutive phrases of similar meaning and structure. It is common in Biblical poetry and song lyrics.

parody

An imitation of a poem or prose that apparently resembles the original fairly closely in style and seriousness, but is designed by its subject or method of treatment to make the original look ridiculous.

paronomasia

A play on words, like a pun, but intended for dramatic effect rather than as a joke.

pathetic fallacy

The fallacy of attributing human feelings and abilities to plants and inanimate objects. The term was coined by John Ruskin[43].

pathos[44]

An attempt to persuade an audience by evoking feeings of pity, sympathetic sorrow or tenerness.

personification

A figure of speech where an abstract concept or an inanimate object is portrayed as a person, or something endowed with life and feelings. The Greek term is *prosopopeia.*

pleonasm

The use of more words than necessary; superfluous or redundant expression.

plurisignation

A word to describe deliberate **ambiguity** as a rhetorical device, to avoid the pejorative associations of ambiguity in its everyday sense.

poetic licence

The liberties that a poet may take in the name of poetry. These may be grammatical or factual. Supposedly, prose writers should not take such liberties, but they do.

portmanteau word

A new word that is created by a fusion of two existing words and combines their meaning. The term was coined by Lewis Carroll, who gives as an example "slithy" meaning "lithe and slimy"; many examples of such words occur in his books Through the Looking Glass and The Hunting of the Snark.

prewriting[45]

An early stage in the writing process, consisting of loose activities such as brainstorming and outlining; a preparation for writing.

proof copy

In printing and publishing, a version of a manuscript that has been typeset after copy editing.

proofreading

Reading and correction of the final draft, with the focus on spelling, punctuation, formatting, typographical conventions and prevention of textual inconsistencies. See also editing and revising, and copy editing.

prosopopeia

see personification[46].

---

43 http://en.wikipedia.org/wiki/John%20Ruskin
44 http://en.wikibooks.org/wiki/..%2FRhetorical_Analysis%23Pathos
45 Chapter 3 on page 11
46 Chapter 66.19 on page 318

pun

A humorous play on words, using homonyms or similar-sounding words with very different meanings.

When is a door not a door? When it's ajar.

punctuation[47]

Marks to indicate the structure of a sentence and indicate spoken dialogue. They include periods, colons, semi-colons, commas, question marks, exclamation points, apostrophes, hyphens, parentheses, brackets, and dashes.

purple patch

A passage (usually of prose but also of poetry) where the sudden heightening of diction makes the passage stand out from its context. it is now usually used disparagingly of an author who has self-consciously written something he considers especially good.

66.14 R

refrain

This is a passage, typically a line but sometimes a group of lines or even only a part of a line, that recurs at the end of each stanza of a poem. Sometimes it is repeated with slight variations. In some songs, the refrain is an opportunity for others to join in singing, and it is then called a *chorus*.

rhetoric[48]

rhetorical question

This means asking a question, not with the intent of eliciting information, but intending the reader or hearer to know the answer and to achieve an emphasis stronger than a direct statement. Thus in Mark Anthony's speech in *Julius Caesar* he does not say "This was not ambition" but "Was this ambition?"

rough draft

See also early draft[49] and final draft[50].

66.15 S

sarcasm

---

47   Chapter 42 on page 233
48   http://en.wikibooks.org/wiki/..%2FWhat_is_Rhetoric
49   Chapter 66.19 on page 318
50   Chapter 66.19 on page 318

Often used as a synonym for [#irony|irony]], but strictly speaking it refers to dispraising someone by crude and blatant overpraising.

satire

Evoking scorn and derision towards someone or something by making the subject seem ridiculous.

scheme

A figure of speech in which the normal word order or pattern of a sentence is deliberately changed for emphasis. It can also include the omission or repetition of words or phrases.

"The helmsman steered; the ship moved on; yet never a breeze blew up." ~Samuel Taylor Coleridge, *The Rime of the Ancient Mariner*

simile

A figure of speech in which someone or something is claimed to be like something else.

"Nor dim, nor red, like God's own head, the glorious Sun uprist." ~Samuel Taylor Coleridge, *The Rime of the Ancient Mariner*

Socratic irony

A form of irony[51], named after Socrates, in which a questioner pretends to be ignorant, and sympathetic to an assumption or point of view, so that his questions can rubbish the assumption.

soliloquy

The act of talking to oneself, either quietly or aloud. It is mainly used in plays; Shakespeare has several examples, such as Hamlet's "To be or not to be" and Macbeth's "Is this a dagger".

symploce

A combination of anaphora[52] and epiphora[53].

synecdoche

A figure of speech (from the Greek for "taking together") in which the name for someone or something is replaced by the name of part of it, as "hand" for "workman".

66.16 T

thesis

The indicator in an essay, usually one or two sentences, in which the author reveals the main point of the essay; the line of argument that the author is pursuing in his essay; the statement of author's position on an issue, such as:

---

51 Chapter 66.19 on page 318
52 Chapter 66.19 on page 318
53 Chapter 66.19 on page 318

"By granting college students liberal lending arrangements,

credit card companies often hook them on a cycle of spending that can ultimately lead to financial ruin." ˜Matt Watson

Because the internet is filled with tremendous marketing potential,

companies should utilize this resource by creating web pages that offer both advertising and customer support.

tone

The manner in which speech or writing is expressed, such as serious or conversational.

transition

A paragraph or a sentence at the beginning of a paragraph that supports the shift of the reader's attention from the subject treated in the previous paragraph to the new subject.

trope

A literary device that uses words in non-literal ways, changing or modifying the general meaning of a term.

"Life's but a walking shadow; a poor player, that struts and frets his hour upon the stage." ˜William Shakespeare, *Macbeth*

66.17 U

understatement

Implying that something is far less important or significant than it is. This is often done for ironic[54] emphasis, e.g. "i got up at 5am today, just slightly earlier than normal". Compare litotes[55].

66.18 W

writer's anxiety[56]

Anxiety with which writers sometimes have to deal when trying to write, starring in the blank paper, especially in the early phases of the writing process.

66.19 Z

zeugma

---

54 Chapter 66.19 on page 318
55 Chapter 66.19 on page 318
56 Chapter 6.1 on page 17

This comes from the Greek for "yoking". It means having one word in the same grammatical relation to two or more other words in a way that means that the first word has different meanings with respect to each of the others, e.g.

"Or *stain* her honour, or her new brocade" (Alexander Pope).

67 Bibliography

The books on rhetoric, composition, style, grammar and mechanics include the following.

- Strunk & White: The Elements of Style[1] - at Wikisource

Category:Rhetoric and Composition[2]

1   http://en.wikisource.org/wiki/The%20Elements%20of%20Style
2   http://en.wikibooks.org/wiki/Category%3ARhetoric%20and%20Composition

68 Contributors

Edits	User
1	Abigor[1]
1	Adambro[2]
1	Adamwalsh[3]
28	Adrignola[4]
5	AndreaElaine[5]
20	Apickens[6]
90	Arthurvogel[7]
6	Az1568[8]
39	B.Doberstein[9]
55	Baas0804[10]
2	Benilde[11]
7	BethH[12]
2	Bookofchange[13]
1	Briannew220[14]
77	Brittz[15]
6	Brttnyrhea[16]
13	Bscharber[17]
6	Bschauble[18]
1	Buchs[19]
35	Bumpu[20]
1	Bwritings[21]

1   http://en.wikibooks.org/w/index.php?title=User:Abigor
2   http://en.wikibooks.org/w/index.php?title=User:Adambro
3   http://en.wikibooks.org/w/index.php?title=User:Adamwalsh
4   http://en.wikibooks.org/w/index.php?title=User:Adrignola
5   http://en.wikibooks.org/w/index.php?title=User:AndreaElaine
6   http://en.wikibooks.org/w/index.php?title=User:Apickens
7   http://en.wikibooks.org/w/index.php?title=User:Arthurvogel
8   http://en.wikibooks.org/w/index.php?title=User:Az1568
9   http://en.wikibooks.org/w/index.php?title=User:B.Doberstein
10 http://en.wikibooks.org/w/index.php?title=User:Baas0804
11 http://en.wikibooks.org/w/index.php?title=User:Benilde
12 http://en.wikibooks.org/w/index.php?title=User:BethH
13 http://en.wikibooks.org/w/index.php?title=User:Bookofchange
14 http://en.wikibooks.org/w/index.php?title=User:Briannew220
15 http://en.wikibooks.org/w/index.php?title=User:Brittz
16 http://en.wikibooks.org/w/index.php?title=User:Brttnyrhea
17 http://en.wikibooks.org/w/index.php?title=User:Bscharber
18 http://en.wikibooks.org/w/index.php?title=User:Bschauble
19 http://en.wikibooks.org/w/index.php?title=User:Buchs
20 http://en.wikibooks.org/w/index.php?title=User:Bumpu
21 http://en.wikibooks.org/w/index.php?title=User:Bwritings

3	Catoma[22]
24	Ccgemlo[23]
27	Chopin[24]
1	Chuckhoffmann[25]
1	Cjannink[26]
7	Coam0801[27]
2	Cody Reimer[28]
2	CommonsDelinker[29]
3	Cyberman[30]
116	Dan Polansky[31]
1	DavidMeiklejohn[32]
2	Deanhiaz[33]
60	Debkaye[34]
6	Derbeth[35]
5	Detr0301[36]
1	Dirk Hünniger[37]
2	DonnieDD[38]
2	Dr. Davis[39]
2	Edkeer[40]
22	Emily.isackson[41]
46	EmilyGrace[42]
1	ErixTheRed[43]
1	Ervinn[44]
1	Everlong[45]
16	Faithmarie22[46]

22 http://en.wikibooks.org/w/index.php?title=User:Catoma
23 http://en.wikibooks.org/w/index.php?title=User:Ccgemlo
24 http://en.wikibooks.org/w/index.php?title=User:Chopin
25 http://en.wikibooks.org/w/index.php?title=User:Chuckhoffmann
26 http://en.wikibooks.org/w/index.php?title=User:Cjannink
27 http://en.wikibooks.org/w/index.php?title=User:Coam0801
28 http://en.wikibooks.org/w/index.php?title=User:Cody_Reimer
29 http://en.wikibooks.org/w/index.php?title=User:CommonsDelinker
30 http://en.wikibooks.org/w/index.php?title=User:Cyberman
31 http://en.wikibooks.org/w/index.php?title=User:Dan_Polansky
32 http://en.wikibooks.org/w/index.php?title=User:DavidMeiklejohn
33 http://en.wikibooks.org/w/index.php?title=User:Deanhiaz
34 http://en.wikibooks.org/w/index.php?title=User:Debkaye
35 http://en.wikibooks.org/w/index.php?title=User:Derbeth
36 http://en.wikibooks.org/w/index.php?title=User:Detr0301
37 http://en.wikibooks.org/w/index.php?title=User:Dirk_H%C3%BCnniger
38 http://en.wikibooks.org/w/index.php?title=User:DonnieDD
39 http://en.wikibooks.org/w/index.php?title=User:Dr._Davis
40 http://en.wikibooks.org/w/index.php?title=User:Edkeer
41 http://en.wikibooks.org/w/index.php?title=User:Emily.isackson
42 http://en.wikibooks.org/w/index.php?title=User:EmilyGrace
43 http://en.wikibooks.org/w/index.php?title=User:ErixTheRed
44 http://en.wikibooks.org/w/index.php?title=User:Ervinn
45 http://en.wikibooks.org/w/index.php?title=User:Everlong
46 http://en.wikibooks.org/w/index.php?title=User:Faithmarie22

3   FancyPants[47]
1   Ferty[48]
1   Fishpi[49]
2   Furrykef[50]
1   Godsy777[51]
1   Guanaco[52]
2   HEKR0501[53]
64 Hagindaz[54]
32 Hema[55]
12 Hema0302[56]
2   Herbythyme[57]
2   Hesa0501[58]
1   HethrirBot[59]
12 Hodu1201[60]
2   Hoshismom[61]
13 IMFlaherty[62]
1   Iamunknown[63]
19 Ica[64]
1   Jamesparson[65]
65 Jamiejamie[66]
1   Jason Tham[67]
16 Jenne n r[68]
132 Jer54[69]
70 Jess0501[70]
1   Jessicapierce[71]

47   http://en.wikibooks.org/w/index.php?title=User:FancyPants
48   http://en.wikibooks.org/w/index.php?title=User:Ferty
49   http://en.wikibooks.org/w/index.php?title=User:Fishpi
50   http://en.wikibooks.org/w/index.php?title=User:Furrykef
51   http://en.wikibooks.org/w/index.php?title=User:Godsy777
52   http://en.wikibooks.org/w/index.php?title=User:Guanaco
53   http://en.wikibooks.org/w/index.php?title=User:HEKR0501
54   http://en.wikibooks.org/w/index.php?title=User:Hagindaz
55   http://en.wikibooks.org/w/index.php?title=User:Hema
56   http://en.wikibooks.org/w/index.php?title=User:Hema0302
57   http://en.wikibooks.org/w/index.php?title=User:Herbythyme
58   http://en.wikibooks.org/w/index.php?title=User:Hesa0501
59   http://en.wikibooks.org/w/index.php?title=User:HethrirBot
60   http://en.wikibooks.org/w/index.php?title=User:Hodu1201
61   http://en.wikibooks.org/w/index.php?title=User:Hoshismom
62   http://en.wikibooks.org/w/index.php?title=User:IMFlaherty
63   http://en.wikibooks.org/w/index.php?title=User:Iamunknown
64   http://en.wikibooks.org/w/index.php?title=User:Ica
65   http://en.wikibooks.org/w/index.php?title=User:Jamesparson
66   http://en.wikibooks.org/w/index.php?title=User:Jamiejamie
67   http://en.wikibooks.org/w/index.php?title=User:Jason_Tham
68   http://en.wikibooks.org/w/index.php?title=User:Jenne_n_r
69   http://en.wikibooks.org/w/index.php?title=User:Jer54
70   http://en.wikibooks.org/w/index.php?title=User:Jess0501
71   http://en.wikibooks.org/w/index.php?title=User:Jessicapierce

50	Jguk[72]
73	Jodes[73]
3	John Barrett[74]
8	Jomegat[75]
113	JonathanP[76]
4	Josh a brewer[77]
25	Joshboyd[78]
27	KMarie[79]
2	Karl Wick[80]
87	Karmal[81]
10	Kate Moquin[82]
1	Kayau[83]
23	Kellin[84]
140	KellyG[85]
23	Kizzleguy[86]
119	Klka0701[87]
35	Kmmartin[88]
20	Kubbs17[89]
2	Kyoung[90]
2	Larah[91]
1	Lccben[92]
18	Leca0301[93]
48	Lemony[94]
3	Liblamb[95]
2	Llcadle[96]

72 http://en.wikibooks.org/w/index.php?title=User:Jguk
73 http://en.wikibooks.org/w/index.php?title=User:Jodes
74 http://en.wikibooks.org/w/index.php?title=User:John_Barrett
75 http://en.wikibooks.org/w/index.php?title=User:Jomegat
76 http://en.wikibooks.org/w/index.php?title=User:JonathanP
77 http://en.wikibooks.org/w/index.php?title=User:Josh_a_brewer
78 http://en.wikibooks.org/w/index.php?title=User:Joshboyd
79 http://en.wikibooks.org/w/index.php?title=User:KMarie
80 http://en.wikibooks.org/w/index.php?title=User:Karl_Wick
81 http://en.wikibooks.org/w/index.php?title=User:Karmal
82 http://en.wikibooks.org/w/index.php?title=User:Kate_Moquin
83 http://en.wikibooks.org/w/index.php?title=User:Kayau
84 http://en.wikibooks.org/w/index.php?title=User:Kellin
85 http://en.wikibooks.org/w/index.php?title=User:KellyG
86 http://en.wikibooks.org/w/index.php?title=User:Kizzleguy
87 http://en.wikibooks.org/w/index.php?title=User:Klka0701
88 http://en.wikibooks.org/w/index.php?title=User:Kmmartin
89 http://en.wikibooks.org/w/index.php?title=User:Kubbs17
90 http://en.wikibooks.org/w/index.php?title=User:Kyoung
91 http://en.wikibooks.org/w/index.php?title=User:Larah
92 http://en.wikibooks.org/w/index.php?title=User:Lccben
93 http://en.wikibooks.org/w/index.php?title=User:Leca0301
94 http://en.wikibooks.org/w/index.php?title=User:Lemony
95 http://en.wikibooks.org/w/index.php?title=User:Liblamb
96 http://en.wikibooks.org/w/index.php?title=User:Llcadle

1	Lulufp693[97]
1	Magmafox[98]
10	MartinY[99]
95	Matt.helm[100]
1	Mattb112885[101]
218	Mattbarton.exe[102]
16	Mattjp18[103]
72	Melindakay[104]
40	MelissaB[105]
3	Mike.lifeguard[106]
1	Mrbradford[107]
2	Mshonle[108]
44	Mudbat[109]
2	Murray61552[110]
1	Nancyw[111]
4	Nicholsonadam[112]
3	NickC[113]
16	Nymi0501[114]
4	Odjascsu[115]
1	Old Word Wolf[116]
3	Oyvind[117]
9	Panic2k4[118]
61	Parrhesia[119]
9	Paul from Michigan[120]
5	Pcu123456789[121]

97 http://en.wikibooks.org/w/index.php?title=User:Lulufp693
98 http://en.wikibooks.org/w/index.php?title=User:Magmafox
99 http://en.wikibooks.org/w/index.php?title=User:MartinY
100 http://en.wikibooks.org/w/index.php?title=User:Matt.helm
101 http://en.wikibooks.org/w/index.php?title=User:Mattb112885
102 http://en.wikibooks.org/w/index.php?title=User:Mattbarton.exe
103 http://en.wikibooks.org/w/index.php?title=User:Mattjp18
104 http://en.wikibooks.org/w/index.php?title=User:Melindakay
105 http://en.wikibooks.org/w/index.php?title=User:MelissaB
106 http://en.wikibooks.org/w/index.php?title=User:Mike.lifeguard
107 http://en.wikibooks.org/w/index.php?title=User:Mrbradford
108 http://en.wikibooks.org/w/index.php?title=User:Mshonle
109 http://en.wikibooks.org/w/index.php?title=User:Mudbat
110 http://en.wikibooks.org/w/index.php?title=User:Murray61552
111 http://en.wikibooks.org/w/index.php?title=User:Nancyw
112 http://en.wikibooks.org/w/index.php?title=User:Nicholsonadam
113 http://en.wikibooks.org/w/index.php?title=User:NickC
114 http://en.wikibooks.org/w/index.php?title=User:Nymi0501
115 http://en.wikibooks.org/w/index.php?title=User:Odjascsu
116 http://en.wikibooks.org/w/index.php?title=User:Old_Word_Wolf
117 http://en.wikibooks.org/w/index.php?title=User:Oyvind
118 http://en.wikibooks.org/w/index.php?title=User:Panic2k4
119 http://en.wikibooks.org/w/index.php?title=User:Parrhesia
120 http://en.wikibooks.org/w/index.php?title=User:Paul_from_Michigan
121 http://en.wikibooks.org/w/index.php?title=User:Pcu123456789

63	Peabody33[122]
7	Peja0302[123]
2	Pi zero[124]
1	Polintr[125]
10	QuiteUnusual[126]
1	Rafe[127]
5	Recent Runes[128]
1	Red4tribe[129]
1	Rhetorix[130]
1	RickL[131]
1	Rickace[132]
5	Rlc1engprof[133]
3	Rmarkert[134]
1	RobinH[135]
24	Rustystcloud[136]
1	SB Johnny[137]
8	SFaithL[138]
2	SHJohnson[139]
1	Shadab[140]
1	Shadow Disciple[141]
14	Shawn Blank[142]
115	ShellyT-P[143]
59	Smsa0301[144]
117	Spjohannsen[145]
1	TakuyaMurata[146]

122 http://en.wikibooks.org/w/index.php?title=User:Peabody33
123 http://en.wikibooks.org/w/index.php?title=User:Peja0302
124 http://en.wikibooks.org/w/index.php?title=User:Pi_zero
125 http://en.wikibooks.org/w/index.php?title=User:Polintr
126 http://en.wikibooks.org/w/index.php?title=User:QuiteUnusual
127 http://en.wikibooks.org/w/index.php?title=User:Rafe
128 http://en.wikibooks.org/w/index.php?title=User:Recent_Runes
129 http://en.wikibooks.org/w/index.php?title=User:Red4tribe
130 http://en.wikibooks.org/w/index.php?title=User:Rhetorix
131 http://en.wikibooks.org/w/index.php?title=User:RickL
132 http://en.wikibooks.org/w/index.php?title=User:Rickace
133 http://en.wikibooks.org/w/index.php?title=User:Rlc1engprof
134 http://en.wikibooks.org/w/index.php?title=User:Rmarkert
135 http://en.wikibooks.org/w/index.php?title=User:RobinH
136 http://en.wikibooks.org/w/index.php?title=User:Rustystcloud
137 http://en.wikibooks.org/w/index.php?title=User:SB_Johnny
138 http://en.wikibooks.org/w/index.php?title=User:SFaithL
139 http://en.wikibooks.org/w/index.php?title=User:SHJohnson
140 http://en.wikibooks.org/w/index.php?title=User:Shadab
141 http://en.wikibooks.org/w/index.php?title=User:Shadow_Disciple
142 http://en.wikibooks.org/w/index.php?title=User:Shawn_Blank
143 http://en.wikibooks.org/w/index.php?title=User:ShellyT-P
144 http://en.wikibooks.org/w/index.php?title=User:Smsa0301
145 http://en.wikibooks.org/w/index.php?title=User:Spjohannsen
146 http://en.wikibooks.org/w/index.php?title=User:TakuyaMurata

147 http://en.wikibooks.org/w/index.php?title=User:Tigerrat29
148 http://en.wikibooks.org/w/index.php?title=User:Tshs0501
149 http://en.wikibooks.org/w/index.php?title=User:Tspe0401
150 http://en.wikibooks.org/w/index.php?title=User:Van_der_Hoorn
151 http://en.wikibooks.org/w/index.php?title=User:Vialick
152 http://en.wikibooks.org/w/index.php?title=User:Webaware
153 http://en.wikibooks.org/w/index.php?title=User:Webster100
154 http://en.wikibooks.org/w/index.php?title=User:Weckman87
155 http://en.wikibooks.org/w/index.php?title=User:Wost0201
156 http://en.wikibooks.org/w/index.php?title=User:Xania
157 http://en.wikibooks.org/w/index.php?title=User:Xz64
158 http://en.wikibooks.org/w/index.php?title=User:YMS

List of Figures

- GFDL: Gnu Free Documentation License. `http://www.gnu.org/licenses/fdl.html`

- cc-by-sa-3.0: Creative Commons Attribution ShareAlike 3.0 License. `http://creativecommons.org/licenses/by-sa/3.0/`

- cc-by-sa-2.5: Creative Commons Attribution ShareAlike 2.5 License. `http://creativecommons.org/licenses/by-sa/2.5/`

- cc-by-sa-2.0: Creative Commons Attribution ShareAlike 2.0 License. `http://creativecommons.org/licenses/by-sa/2.0/`

- cc-by-sa-1.0: Creative Commons Attribution ShareAlike 1.0 License. `http://creativecommons.org/licenses/by-sa/1.0/`

- cc-by-2.0: Creative Commons Attribution 2.0 License. `http://creativecommons.org/licenses/by/2.0/`

- cc-by-2.0: Creative Commons Attribution 2.0 License. `http://creativecommons.org/licenses/by/2.0/deed.en`

- cc-by-2.5: Creative Commons Attribution 2.5 License. `http://creativecommons.org/licenses/by/2.5/deed.en`

- cc-by-3.0: Creative Commons Attribution 3.0 License. `http://creativecommons.org/licenses/by/3.0/deed.en`

- GPL: GNU General Public License. `http://www.gnu.org/licenses/gpl-2.0.txt`

- LGPL: GNU Lesser General Public License. `http://www.gnu.org/licenses/lgpl.html`

- PD: This image is in the public domain.

- ATTR: The copyright holder of this file allows anyone to use it for any purpose, provided that the copyright holder is properly attributed. Redistribution, derivative work, commercial use, and all other use is permitted.

- EURO: This is the common (reverse) face of a euro coin. The copyright on the design of the common face of the euro coins belongs to the European Commission. Authorised is reproduction in a format without relief (drawings, paintings, films) provided they are not detrimental to the image of the euro.

- LFK: Lizenz Freie Kunst. `http://artlibre.org/licence/lal/de`

- CFR: Copyright free use.

- EPL: Eclipse Public License. `http://www.eclipse.org/org/documents/epl-v10.php`

Copies of the GPL, the LGPL as well as a GFDL are included in chapter Licenses[159]. Please note that images in the public domain do not require attribution. You may click on the image numbers in the following table to open the webpage of the images in your webbrower.

---

159 Chapter 69 on page 335

1		GFDL
2	• Wikinews_collaboration_logo_2.svg[160]: Masur[161] • derivative work: Al Maghi[162] (talk[163])	
3	CEJISS[164]	PD
4	Jamal al-faris	GFDL
5	Stuart Seeger[165] from San Antonio, Texas, USA	cc-by-2.0
6		GFDL
7	Original uploader was Terra Green[166] at en.wikipedia[167]. Later version(s) were uploaded by Noir[168], DanielPharos[169] at en.wikipedia[170].	LGPL
8	Scanned by user:Van Nuytts	PD
9	Bain News Service, publisher	PD
10	White house photo by Eric Draper.	PD
11	Mostafa Azizi	PD
12	Mark Coggins[171] from San Francisco	cc-by-2.0
13	IMFlaherty[172]	cc-by-sa-3.0
14	Jillian Schoenfeld	PD
15		GFDL
16		GFDL

160 http://en.wikibooks.org/wiki/%3AFile%3AWikinews_collaboration_logo_2.svg

161 http://en.wikibooks.org/wiki/User%3AMasur

162 http://en.wikibooks.org/wiki/User%3AAl%20Maghi

163 http://en.wikibooks.org/wiki/User%20talk%3AAl%20Maghi

164 http://en.wikibooks.org/wiki/User%3ACEJISS

165 http://www.flickr.com/people/50203533@N00

166 http://en.wikibooks.org/wiki/%3Aen%3AUser%3ATerra%20Green

167 http://en.wikipedia.org

168 http://en.wikibooks.org/wiki/%3Aen%3AUser%3ANoir

169 http://en.wikibooks.org/wiki/%3Aen%3AUser%3ADanielPharos

170 http://en.wikipedia.org

171 http://www.flickr.com/people/15566770@N00

172 http://en.wikibooks.org/wiki/User%3AIMFlaherty